Anne Bradstreet Revisited

Twayne's United States Authors Series

Pattie Cowell, Editor

Colorado State University

TUSAS 580

That sentence, vanity of vanityes
vanity of vanityes, all is vanity

5.3

He that is to saile into a farre
country, although the ship, cabi-
bin and provision, be all convenient and comfortable for him
yet he hath no desire to make y
his place of residence, but longs
to put in store at that port where
his bussines lyes, a christian is
sailing through this world unto
his heavenly country, and heere
he hath many conveniences and
comforts, but he must beware
of desiring to make this the place
of his aboode, lest he meet with such
tossings that may cause him to
long for shore, before he sees land
we must therfore be heer, as strangers
and pilgrims, that we may plainly
declare that we seek a citty above
and wait all the dayes of our ap-
pointed time till our chaung shall
come.

The frontispiece is taken from a facsimile reproduction of Bradstreet's "Meditations Diuine and morall," published with *The Tenth Muse* in 1965 by Scholars' Facsimiles & Reprints.

Anne Bradstreet Revisited

Rosamond Rosenmeier

University of Massachusetts at Boston

1991

NOV

Twayne Publishers
A Division of G. K. Hall & Co. • *Boston*

Anne Bradstreet Revisited
Rosamond Rosenmeier

Copyright 1991 by G. K. Hall & Co.
All rights reserved.
Published by Twayne Publishers
A division of G. K. Hall & Co.
70 Lincoln Street
Boston, Massachusetts 02111

Copyediting supervised by Barbara Sutton
Book production by Gabrielle B. McDonald
Book design by Barbara Anderson
Typeset in Garamond by Huron Valley Graphics, Inc., Ann Arbor, Michigan.

10 9 8 7 6 5 4 3 2 1

Library of Congress Cataloging-in-Publication Data

Rosenmeier, Rosamond, 1928–
    Anne Bradstreet revisited / Rosamond Rosenmeier.
        p.   cm.—(Twayne's United States author series ; TUSAS 580)
    Includes bibliographical references (p.   ) and index.
    ISBN 0-8057-7625-7
    1. Bradstreet, Anne, 1612?–1672—Criticism and interpretation.
    I. Title. II. Series.
    PS712.R6 1991
    811'.1—dc20   91-7835
                                                                           CIP

In memory of

Floss King Rauch
Ada Whitney Goodsell
Harriet Goodsell Rauch

and for

Evelyn Rauch
Twyla Elisabeth Ramos
Rachel Elisabeth Ramos
Leah Rosenmeier

The Lord by wisdom founded the earth;
by understanding he established the heavens;
by his knowledge the deeps broke forth,
and the clouds drop down the dew.

(Prov. 3:19–20)

Contents

Publisher's Note   ix
Preface   xi
Chronology   xv

Chapter One
Introduction: The Critical Sources   1

Chapter Two
Daughter-Child: Actualities and Poetic Personas   14

Chapter Three
Sister-Wife: Conflict and Redefinitions   71

Chapter Four
Mother-Artist: A Typology of the Creative   129

Notes and References   157
Selected Bibliography   167
Index   171

Publisher's Note

Anne Bradstreet Revisited by Rosamond Rosenmeier draws on a wealth of new perspectives in social history and gender studies—made available since the 1965 publication of Anne Bradstreet by Josephine K. Piercy—to present a timely reevaluation of Bradstreet's literary achievement. We are pleased to offer this new study of Bradstreet's life and works.

Preface

Since the publication of Josephine Piercy's *Anne Bradstreet* in 1965 (the earlier volume on Bradstreet in Twayne's United States Authors series), important developments in literary, biblical, historical, and gender studies have taken place. In this revisit to Bradstreet's life and work, I have attempted to bring some of these new developments to bear on a life about which we have only scant facts and on a body of writing for which we have no widely accepted method of interpretation. Literary analysis, following diverse critical approaches, continues to produce widely divergent readings of individual Bradstreet poems. Although the consensus seems to be that Bradstreet's later work is her better work, there continue to be many different portraits of the person "Anne Bradstreet."

Such diversity can of course be seen not only as inevitable but as desirable. Perhaps more than any other indicator, diversity of interpretation can suggest that a work is rich with possibilities. In Bradstreet's case, each age has discovered its own Anne Bradstreet, and doubtless will continue to do so. There are indeed many and varied reasons to be interested in Bradstreet's work. In her example we find a seventeenth-century woman writing about her life—a comparative rarity even during a period when elite European women were beginning to defy tradition and put pen to paper. Or we can find glimpses of the experience of settling the Massachusetts Bay Colony in the 1630s. Bradstreet, as the daughter and wife of governors, was intimately involved in New World history. Recent interpretations have focused on Bradstreet's feminism, and although, once again, a single portrait does not emerge from these assessments, we can find in Bradstreet a seventeenth-century feminist. I have tried to provide a life of Bradstreet that will be usable to readers who bring a variety of interests to the reading of Bradstreet's accounts of herself and her world.

One large (if not the largest) problem that we students of Bradstreet's life and work face, however, continues to plague us. The problem is not the existence of a diversity of points of view about Bradstreet but an inadequacy in the means available to us for connecting Bradstreet's life with her art. Over the years, religious belief has seemed to provide that connection. Generally, critics have found the key to understanding Bradstreet has been her Puritanism. Puritanism has been said to animate her work—either because she espoused its tenets or because she rebelled against them. Increasingly, as studies of Puritanism proliferate, we become less and less sure what that term means. Puritanism has emerged from half a century of scholarly probing resembling not a monolithic belief system as much as a loose association of threads in a fabric that continues to unravel before our eyes. The work of the social historians has shown us that what was considered to be true of Puritans in one region of England was quite different in its culture and social organization from what was considered Puritan in another and that when Puritans from these regions were transplanted to the New World, the regional differences came with them.

I have thus taken it as my task in this study to try to bring together the life and the poetry into a suggestive, yet firmly grounded relationship, and I have not conceived of this relationship as rooted in Puritan creedal or doctrinal statements. Rather, I have used issues of role and identity as the organizing principles in this study and have depended on Bradstreet's own writing and on her life's history for my definitions of these issues. The historical sources I have used have brought me closer to an understanding of the daily life of women in Bradstreet's time and place than I had been before and have directed my thinking away from assumptions of a unitary Puritanism. The literary sources I have used brought me closer to biblical and scientific writings and to women's writing, which, although commonplace in certain Puritan circles, were neither exclusively nor typically Puritan.

I began this study by asking questions about what it was like to grow up as the oldest daughter in a gentry family in County Lincolnshire in the second two decades of the seventeenth century. I asked what it was like to be schooled at home with three younger sisters, when home was the earl of Lincoln's castle at Sempringham. I thought about what it meant to be married as a girl of 16 (below the usual age for marriage at that time). I considered the curious phenomenon of a young mother, new to outlying Ipswich, Massachusetts, giving birth to a child every other year, and writing long medieval-sounding descriptions of cosmic history and nature. Led on by such questions as these, I found that both the biographical and the literary sides of the picture began to take shape.

Bradstreet turned to the Bible for help with answering her own questions about her life's journey and for a literary paradigm for that journey's expression. The development from child to adult was a subject she returned to repeatedly. From the date of her first poem in 1632 to her last in 1669, Bradstreet alluded to the Bible to interpret and clarify how one stage progressed to the next. Not only do the overtones of biblical lore support, reiterate, and sometimes disrupt a Bradstreet passage about, say, the true nature of childhood, sisterhood, wifehood, motherhood, but the relationship between stages——and the very process of growth and change—is given a distinctive narrative design by the presence of biblical references. Bradstreet's work is nothing if not dynamic, and her preoccupations with movement and change, with transmutation, are underscored by her use of biblical discourse. Bradstreet's portrayals of the staged development of the individual and of the world suggests an approach based on sources and subjects that, throughout, she said were of the deepest significance.

Thus I chose a developmental structure for this revisit to Bradstreet's life and work because I was seeking a means of both analyzing important Bradstreet poems and representing the major periods in her life. I begin chapter 2 by tracing Bradstreet's growing-up years in England, paying particular attention to the Lincolnshire context. Following this biographical section, I turn to the interpretation of a selection of Bradstreet poems that use the persona of the child or daughter. Chapter 3 covers the years of Bradstreet's young wifehood (in Cambridge and Ipswich, Massachusetts). Similarly, then, the interpretation of selected poems follows—poems in which sister or wife is used as the poetic speaker. In chapter 4, devoted to mother-artist, I discuss Bradstreet's later years (in Andover), when her last children and her first grandchildren were born. The poems discussed are those in which Bradstreet employs the persona of mother as her speaker. In these poems Bradstreet's conception of the artist is modeled after biblical mothers who personify change, creation, and re-creation.

Except in a few instances where such applications seem particularly appropriate, I have not treated the poems as if they were direct statements of Bradstreet's responses to immediate experience. Rather, I argue that she was more of an artist than that—weaving and reweaving a fictive design out of the materials she early chose to focus on. I have therefore left open the connections in each chapter between the poetry and the life. Where background material seemed to me to cast light on the text, I have used it, but I have not assumed that what is said in the poems necessarily conveys information about, say, Bradstreet's actual sisters, contemporary political events, or what we imagine to be the circumstances of Massachusetts frontier life.

I am aware, of course, that Bradstreet was a child during the same years that she was a wife and a mother while she was a wife and sister. But I am less concerned with a clinical definition of these roles than I am with using these as points of reference that are featured in Bradstreet's work from beginning to end. The events of the biographical sections of each chapter do follow each other chronologically, while the poems in the persona sections do so, if at all, only in a very general way. It is my hope that this organization echoes themes found from first to last in Bradstreet's work. The result of this approach has been to reveal in the Bradstreet canon more internal consistency than her twentieth-century critics have generally found to be the case.

Because the research for this new look at what I have come to see as Bradstreet's unusual contribution to our literature and history has acquainted me with intellectual fields and research materials that Bradstreet critics have not used before, it seemed desirable to describe the path my research has taken in an introductory chapter designed to introduce the reader to some of my sources.

I owe a very great debt to my husband, Jesper Rosenmeier, whose work on the early life of the Puritan minister John Cotton and on his career in Boston, England, has helped me to see how specific to place Puritanism could be. Of course, I am indebted to Jesper beyond the confines of scholarship for his encouragement and support throughout the whole process of reading for and writing this book. I am grateful, too, to Pattie Cowell, who, in her role as Twayne editor, suggested ways to get into and out of this manuscript, and to my friend and student, Anne Smith, who read this manuscript first as she typed it and who said she discovered that Anne Bradstreet was "quite a person."

Chronology

1612   Anne Dudley born to Dorothy and Thomas Dudley in Northampton, England.

1619   Moves with family to Sempringham in Lincolnshire where Thomas Dudley is steward to the earl of Lincoln.

1624   Moves with family to Boston, Lincolnshire.

1628   Marries Simon Bradstreet, perhaps in Lincolnshire or perhaps in Essex County at Leighs Priory, home of the countess of Warwick, whom Simon Bradstreet serves as steward.

1630   Bradstreet and Dudley families emigrate to New England with other members of the Massachusetts Bay Company. Land in Salem; winter in Charlestown.

1631   Bradstreets and Dudleys move to Newtown (Cambridge).

1632   Date of the first extant Bradstreet poem, "Upon a Fit of Sickness, Anno. 1632."

1633   Bears first child, Samuel.

1635?   Bradstreets and Dudleys move to Agawam (Ipswich).

1638   Date of the elegy to Sir Philip Sidney.

1641   Date of the tribute to Du Bartas.

1642   Date of "A Dialog between Old *England* and New."

1643   Date appended to the elegy to Queen Elizabeth.

1647   Her poems taken to England by Mercy (Dudley) Woodbridge and her husband Rev. John Woodbridge.

1650   *The Tenth Muse Lately Sprung Up in America* published in London.

1652   Bears her last child, John.

1669   Date of the last extant poem "[As weary pilgrim, now at rest]."

1672   Dies.

1678   *Several Poems* edition published posthumously, containing 18 previously unpublished poems.

1867   John Harvard Ellis's *The Works of Anne Bradstreet in Prose and Verse* published containing the prose and poetry from a small manuscript book owned by the Stevens Memorial Library of North Andover, Massachusetts.

Chapter One
Introduction: The Critical Sources

For now, in this study, Bradstreet's critical reputation will rest where it seems presently lodged. No one today, I think, would write a blurb for the back cover of her collected works that suggests (as her seventeenth-century contemporary N.H. did) that Bradstreet was a poet of the power and magnitude of the western star, brighter than the sun. We would not expect the "divine, and lucid light" of her verse to enable us to see "Natures darke secret Mysteries" revealed.[1]

Clearly time itself has invalidated the distinctly opposite assessment made by one of Bradstreet's nineteenth-century editors, Charles Eliot Norton, that Bradstreet's work "hardly stands the test of time." Few readers today would agree with him that "it is not their poetic merit which will lead anyone . . . to read her verse."[2] Bradstreet's other nineteenth-century editor, John Harvard Ellis, was similarly disparaging. He found her work imitative (in his view, a negative quality), but he saved Bradstreet's reputation by explaining that the reader should consider "the peculiarly unpropitious circumstances under which [the poems] were written." The reader who makes allowances for circumstances, Ellis says, will find "a singular and valuable relic of the earliest literature of the country."[3] Sixty years later, Samuel Eliot Morison argued that Bradstreet's work is "good poetry," albeit "minor." For Morison too its chief value lies in the fact that it expresses something he calls "the strength of the puritan woman . . . whose soul was made strong by faith."[4] Most critics no longer find the lot of the frontier Puritan woman who bore eight children to be a principal reason for reading Bradstreet's poetry, even though as late as 1959 John Berryman's long poem *Homage to Mistress Bradstreet* was built from a romantic imagining of that life.[5]

Since the 1940s and 1950s—when George Whicher reintroduced Bradstreet to modern readers in his *Alas, All's Vanity* and Bradstreet's work found its way into *The Oxford Anthology of American Verse*—critics have shown increasing interest in aspects of the work itself. Today no comprehensive study of American poetry would omit Bradstreet's work from consideration. Such studies, beginning with Roy Harvey Pearce's *The Continuity of American Poetry* (1961) and continuing with Hyatt Waggoner's *American Poets: From the Puritans to the Present* and Albert Gelpi's *The Tenth Muse: The Psyche of the American Poet* (1975), tend to locate Bradstreet's significance in the fact of her being first in a succession of poets generally described as American. More recent studies have emphasized her significance in terms of a lineage of gender: Emily Stipes Watts's *The Poetry of American Women from 1632 to 1945* (1977), Wendy Martin's *An American Triptych* (1984), and Alicia Ostriker's *Stealing the Language: The Emergence of Women's Poetry in America* (1986) all link Bradstreet to a variously defined continuity among American women poets. Among such studies, Pattie Cowell's *Women Poets in Pre-Revolutionary America* (1981) and Cheryl Walker's *The Nightingale's Burden: Women Poets and American Culture before 1900* (1982) bite off a smaller chunk of history to reconsider. Although both studies give evidence (in Walker's words) that in America "the act of writing poetry has been a fundamentally different experience for women than for men,"[6] both find in Bradstreet's work a somewhat "perplexing" (Walker, 7) example. Walker writes that "we do not know how to 'read' Bradstreet's Puritan sentiments" (Walker, 17); particularly problematic for Walker are the lines in which Bradstreet appears to speak with a patriarchal voice. Crowell reminds us that Bradstreet belonged to a group of writers who had unusual educational advantages, given their sex, and who, in this regard, were unrepresentative of colonial women generally. Within this select group, as Cowell writes, Bradstreet was a "professional";[7] she had a public reputation both here and abroad. Although Bradstreet studies have gained from placing her work alongside poetry by women who lived before and after she did, I suggest in this study that before we conclude what makes for continuity or even that continuity exists, we should dare to read Bradstreet's work more questioningly than we have so far. Cheryl Walker leads the way, I believe, simply by suggesting that "far too much has been made of Bradstreet's rebellion against the Puritan God" (Walker, 14), and Pattie Cowell invites us to question the exact nature of the relationship to society of "such a diverse group of poets" (Cowell, 3) as are included in her anthology, Bradstreet among them.

In this revisit to Bradstreet's work, then, I attempt mainly to read the poetry and raise questions about what the poetry says and means. I do not attempt to go beyond to find continuities, except in a case or two where similarities seem to throw particular light on Bradstreet's method or her poetic construction. Here too I am content, for now, to join the current consensus about which poems are Bradstreet's finest. Critics may disagree about how to read the poetry, but they generally agree that Bradstreet's finest poetry is to be found in the late poem "Contemplations," in the group of poems known as the marriage poems, in her elegies (both the formal and the occasional elegies), in the poem that begins "I had eight birds hatcht in one nest," and in the poem on the occasion of the burning of her house. I recommend that consensus to my readers.

With this rereading of selected Bradstreet texts, I also suggest that it is time to revisit her life, a life that has been carefully documented by her twentieth-century biographer, Elizabeth Wade White, in *Anne Bradstreet: The Tenth Muse* (1971). Although we still have only the few facts about Bradstreet's life that both White and Ann Stanford report,[8] we now have available the work of more recent historians who present the history of women's lives in the seventeenth century. This work in women's history helps us to conceptualize more richly and fully than we did even a decade ago the cultural context in both old and New England within which Bradstreet's life played itself out.[9]

My methodological problem in attempting to reread both text and life has been to present the two as connected while, at the same time, preserving the greatest degree of flexibility in the interpretation of the relationship between them. We do not know, as Cheryl Walker keeps reminding us in just these words, what Bradstreet meant by what she said. We do not know what in Bradstreet's experience prompted her to write—not just individual poems but what prompted her to turn to poetry at all.

The bringing to bear of new discoveries on such questions is only one part of the task. Another part is the deconstruction of certain persistent assumptions about Bradstreet's intentions. With the publication in 1978 of Robert Daly's *God's Altar*, we began to see that in Bradstreet's use of nature we do not find what we had come to expect of Puritanism.[10] In fact, we observe how un-Puritan Bradstreet can be. Nowhere do we meet that presumably Puritan hallmark, vivid depictions of hell and damnation. The "afflictions" so often referred to in Bradstreet's writings belong to this world—illnesses, losses, the pain of childbirth, or the absence or death of a loved one. Nowhere do we meet a Jeremiad; nowhere does Bradstreet rail at her readers, even when her readers are family members to whom she is writing instructions about how to live their lives. Josephine Piercy observes that, unlike other Puritan writers, "never once, in all her poetry, does Bradstreet turn to the reader and preach a sermon."[11] Nowhere to be found is a mention of witches or of witchcraft, even though by the time of Bradstreet's death in 1672 witchcraft was of considerable public concern in the communities of the Massachusetts North Shore. We notice, too, that Bradstreet's discussion of body parts is both frank and positive. The subject of nursing and weaning babies is graphically, familiarly, put: "Some children are hardly weaned although the teat be rub'd wth wormwood or mustard, they wil either wipe it off, or else suck down sweet and bitter together" (M/R, 200). Elsewhere she dwells at length on the beneficence of the bowels, explaining in a piece of arch self-parody, that the intestinal process is really "transmutation . . . , but not excretion" (M/R, 31). What we have come to expect from Puritans on the subject of the "intestines" is something quite different: graphic and appalled disquisition on the "loathsomeness of the inner man."[12] Nor is Bradstreet much of a moralist. She seems to miss opportunities to score points for morality. In the first two quaternions—both are basically squabbles among siblings—the opening dialogue in each concerns that time-honored childhood issue, who should go first. In each case, the most obstreperous sister goes first, and the others let her—not because she is the most moral, but because she makes the most noise. Although women were exhorted not to speak publicly about church and state matters, Bradstreet's poetry and meditations focus on some of the most important political and ecclesiastical problems of her day.

These apparent anomalies do not, however, make Bradstreet a rebel; she is not necessarily flying in the face of convention when she does not follow our idea of what a Puritan is. She may simply be operating out of another set of cultural norms. David Hall puts the consequences of our misapplications of the term *Puritan* in this way: "we are so accustomed to inflating the significance of Puritanism that we easily forget how much else impinged upon the making of beliefs among the colonists."[13] Anne Bradstreet may not have differed from the norms as defined by her time and place; she may well differ from Puritan norms, as defined by ours.

In addition to "how much else impinged upon the making of beliefs among the colonists," we must recognize too that our conception of Puritanism has been based on the works of Puritan men, almost exclusively so. The works of Anne Bradstreet and Mary Rowlandson, and the recorded words of Anne Hutchinson at her trials, have been used as supporting evidence for points made by and about the predominately male representatives of the age. We have only begun to study the history of colonial women.[14] These and other reconsiderations have led some historians to conclude that the term *Puritan* is a term to despair of, a term "impossible to define with precision, [which] can mean almost anything its users want it to mean."[15] I have thus given myself permission to revisit Bradstreet without attempting to capture the essence of New England Puritanism and wrestle it into the service of my interpretation.

Nevertheless, despite these apparently un-Puritanlike qualities, Bradstreet's work reveals a pervasive biblical intertextuality. Setting aside such questions as how or whether Bradstreet *believed* the Bible or the Geneva Bible commentators (the so-called Geneva Bible was the one she used), we notice simply that in instance after instance Bradstreet echoes biblical voices. She often, to borrow the term Regina Schwartz used of Milton's *De Doctrina Christiana,* engaged in "exercises in ventriloquism."[16] The extent to which these borrowings or echoes shape Bradstreet's poetic statements became clear to me when I began the practice of looking up even rather unbiblical-sounding words and phrases in a biblical concordance—a practice I would recommend to readers of Bradstreet's work. The distinctive shaping of the text then becomes clear as we notice that the borrower has disrupted, switched, reordered, or curiously combined texts in a design that reexpresses and gives new voice to the original. In so doing the original is reaffirmed while the writer claims, possesses, owns it. The material is brought into a life it had not had. It is in this way, I believe, that Bradstreet's work can be seen as an assertion of self of the kind described by the contemporary French critic, Hélène Cixous, who writes: "Woman must write her self: must write about women and bring women to writing, from which they have been driven away as violently as from their bodies—for the same reasons, by the same law, with the same fatal goal. Woman must put herself into the text—as into the world and into history—by her own movement."[17] Certainly one of the most important thngs we can say about the work we are about to consider is that it puts "woman into the world and into history—by her own movement."

The Bradstreet texts accomplish this aim, I suggest, not by renouncing biblical authority but by pulling from the Bible, as Bradstreet herself said, "those places I thought most concerned my Condition"

(M/R, 215). The biblical echoes in Bradstreet's work come primarily from selected texts from the Old Testament books Proverbs, Psalms, Canticles, Ecclesiastes, and Job and the New Testament gospel of John, Paul's letters to the Romans, Galatians, Colossians, and Hebrews and the book of Revelation. Echoes of the Old Testament sources predominate, and these belong to a distinctive group of texts, associated as the Geneva Bible commentators tell us with the wisdom of Solomon. The evidence of Bradstreet's dependence on what was considered to be the works of Solomon led me to explore biblical commentaries on Solomon and on the so-called wisdom tradition.

I have found that by far the most suggestive and the most relevant commentaries for the study of Bradstreet's use of biblical wisdom are those of the minister who married Bradstreet's parents, Dorothy and Thomas Dudley, and who may have baptized the poet herself: John Dod, a Nonconforming member of the group with whom the young Dudleys associated in Northampton and Lincolnshire. By the time of Anne Dudley's birth, Dod had been silenced, and without a pulpit, he turned his energies to the writing of commentaries on the book of Proverbs and manuals on domestic relations. His great subject was the family, especially the family as, in and of itself, a worshipping community. Dod considered himself too old in 1630 to emigrate to New England with the Dudleys and Bradstreets, but he continued to keep in touch with those who did leave. John Cotton was particularly close to Dod in their English years, but later, the Massachusetts settlers provoked Dod and a group of friends in England to criticize the New England "Congregational way." Perhaps here I should add that I and others have emphasized Bradstreet's closeness to John Cotton in her English years.[18] I now believe that greater resonances exist between Dod's and Bradstreet's texts and that these, furthermore, help us to understand the character and meaning of Bradstreet's Solomonic feminism.

In Dod's and others' commentaries, Old Testament wisdom is hypostasized as a female figure, and redemptive power is gendered (in certain contexts) as female. The biblical wisdom tradition valued by both women and men, constitutes an important key to understanding Bradstreet's feminism. Contemporary feminist theologians have helped me to follow the outlines of the wisdom tradition, a tradition that in the Bible itself, and among biblical commentators, modifies, reclaims, and in some ways subverts biblical patriarchy.[19] But in so doing wisdom by no means destroys the gospel; rather, it fills scripture with new and more inclusive meanings, ones that speak of and to women. Cotton

Mather's characterizations of his great aunt Anne Bradstreet direct the reader to indulge in a likeness between Bradstreet's power and the powers of the biblical figure, Wisdom. He places the poet at "the gates of her own city" and "in the high places of the world," which in Proverbs 1:21 and 8:2 are the places where Wisdom is to be found and where she "cries out" to a world that ignores her.[20] In the chapters to come I develop interpretations of Bradstreet poems that have their basis in this likeness.

This exploration of Bradstreet's use of wisdom texts led me to another set of Solomonic sources, to sources in the field of Renaissance science—an important subject for Anne Bradstreet. In the so-called quaternions—the long poems about the structure of human anatomy, psychology, physiology, about the human life stages and about the stages of seasonal nature and of the history of the world—Bradstreet's materials again speak a rich tradition, borrowed, to be sure, but re-shaped and re-presented for a generation of readers that were beginning to move beyond belief in the magical kind of science Bradstreet's texts reflect.[21] Solomon's temple or house was said by Renaissance philosophers to contain wisdom in the sense of scientific knowledge, key to understanding the hermetic or secret foundations of the universe. Sir Francis Bacon, in *The New Atlantis,* depicted an ideal community that he called Solomon's house or "College," in which all of the sciences would flourish with the purpose of bringing about an ideal or utopian society.[22] Renaissance scientists understood the world to be in the process of transformation, and this is the world of Bradstreet's quaternions. In general, Bradstreet critics, caught in the project of evaluating Bradstreet's work, have tended to set aside the quaternions as inferior poetry. Close attention has been reserved for the finer poems published for the first time in Bradstreet's second volume, *Several Poems,* in 1678. Here I offer a reading of Bradstreet's uses of science that relates these ambitious long poems to other parts of the Bradstreet opus.

My explorations of the sources mentioned in Bradstreet's poetry have been informed and enriched by the work of historians Desirée Hirst, Frances A. Yates, and John Debus. These writers have introduced me to the interconnectedness of the occult sciences (including alchemy, white magic, and astronomy) with literature and religion, a view that I offer here as a means to understanding the interconnectedness of Bradstreet's *apparently* diverse interests and poetic subjects. Sir Philip Sidney and his family (related to Anne Bradstreet through her father, Thomas Dudley) stand historically at the center of a literary movement that relied on Renaissance science. Sidney's tutor was the sorcerer-mage John Dee, whose presence is felt in Bradstreet's elegies for Queen Elizabeth and for Sidney, and whose works were generously represented in the science library of the Bradstreets' Ipswich neighbor, John Winthrop, Jr.[23] Quite apart from these demonstrable influences on Anne Bradstreet's understanding of her world, science itself in the Bradstreet texts provided the paradigm for her understanding of the work of the artist who intended, as she says, not "to shew my skill, but to declare ye Truth, not to sett forth myself, by ye Glory of God" (M/R, 215). In the *Divine Weeks,* the work that Bradstreet said set the standard to which she aspired, the sixteenth-century French poet Du Bartas summarized his task as the tracing of the wisdom of the magi down through the ages. In his account of the progress of occult wisdom Du Bartas reminds his readers that wisdom was "first under the Hebrews bred and borne."[24] We are so used to thinking of science as an empirical discipline, a study based on experiment and observation (which indeed it was beginning to be during Bradstreet's lifetime) that we find it hard to imagine something called science that is the revelation of the occult, of "nature's dark mysteries," as N.H. said of Bradstreet's verse. A science that is the fruit of meditation or contemplation seems to modern minds a contradiction in terms. In the Bradstreet texts we discover an overarching interest in the cosmic design, a design based, ultimately, in scripture and in lore that originated in premosaic times. In what sounds like a condensed version of Bradstreet's long poem, "The Foure Monarchies," Du Bartas says that "Wisdom moved from Babylon to Egypt to Arabia to Rome to Germany" (Hirst, 80). Again, set beside Bradstreet's texts, this depiction of the artist as one who is the penman of wisdom's cosmic journey suggests the pattern of the artist that Bradstreet's work reflects.

In essence the task of the artist who follows Du Bartas's example and his advice is to portray a salvific presence, gendered as feminine, or bonded with the feminine, still present in nature and history but now lost from the world's eyes. I argue that the recovery of this healing or revitalizing presence is the project to which the Bradstreet texts set themselves repeatedly. This conception of the poet's task does not follow the Romantic model of self against tradition; Bradstreet selected and used the voices of others within tradition—those that she "thought most concerned [her] condition"—and on these she based her restatements of the workings of the divine presence, in both the macrocosm of history and nature and the microcosm of her own bodily life. It was in this way that "she put herself into the text—as into the world and into history—by her own movement."

Thus Bradstreet's strategies, when viewed as strategies, are highly relational—or in other words, derivative, even imitative, but this tendency, I argue, does not exist in opposition to something else that can be identified as personal or original in her work. Bradstreet critics have (as I do) repeatedly identified tension or conflict at the heart of the poetry, but that conflict has then been formulated in a way that separates out a self—an "essential instinctual emotion," as Kenneth Murdock put it[25]—which is set against constraints seen as Puritan or as simply religious. Ann Stanford characterizes the points of tension not as self and structure but as seen and unseen, as this world and the world beyond (Stanford 1974, i–ii). Wendy Martin writes that Bradstreet's poetry "reflects the tension and conflicts of a person struggling for selfhood in a culture that was outraged by individual autonomy and that valued property to the extent that it praised God."[26] To see the poet as an imitator or ventriloquist, I argue, is not to reduce or eliminate conflict. It is to characterize conflict differently. It is to see it as an inherent aspect of the discourse of which Bradstreet's work is composed.

Bradstreet's reliance on wisdom tradition, in the manner of Du Bartas and Sidney, places her squarely within a transatlantic community of women writers, many of whom were similarly imitative. Bradstreet's membership in that community is attested to in comments by several of her contemporaries. However much Bradstreet may have been an anomaly among colonial Massachusetts women, there is evidence that she belonged to a cadre of well-educated women of the English and European upper classes who had, often by the energetic tutelage of mothers, fathers, and brothers and with great libraries at their disposal, continued to develop their talents and advance their education. A number of England's best-known women writers were within the Bradstreets' family and regional circles, in both old and New England. In Lincolnshire, a century before Anne Hutchinson's ordeal in Massachusetts, Anne Askew's views had been similarly examined; she was then burned at the stake for her stand on the eucharist. Unlike Hutchinson, however, Askew left an "account" of her "sufferings." Anne Bradstreet's childhood friend, Lady Arbella Johnson, was a poet. Lady Arbella accompanied the Bradstreets from Lincolnshire to New England aboard the ship, *The Arbella,* which was named for her. Bradstreet's sister, Mercy (Woodbridge), was a poet. The family of Sir Philip Sidney boasted several published women writers, including Lady Mary Sidney Wroth, who was daughter of Robert Dudley, the earl of Leicester, and Sidney's niece. Her long poem, *Urania*, echoes the title *The Tenth Muse* in that Urania was the heavenly muse who Christian poets said guided their work. Urania was Wisdom's sister, again suggesting feminist Judeo-Christian sources for these seventeenth-century literary women. Lady Mary Wroth was among those women who, like Anne Bradstreet, protested that their work had been published without their knowledge. We have not considered the possibility that John Woodbridge might have been using a conventional disclaimer when he reported that he took Bradstreet's work to London to be published "without [her] knowledge, and contrary to her expectation" (M/R, 526). Sidney's sister, the countess of Pembroke, completed Sidney's translations of the Psalms after his death, and she did several translations of her own. Her "Astrea" in honor of Queen Elizabeth might well have served as a model for Bradstreet's later elegy to the queen.

When Cotton Mather praised Anne Bradstreet's work, he made a point of saying that her work "has been Celebrated in both *Englands*" and he emphasized that "*America* justly admires the learned Women of the other *Hemisphere*."[27] Mather then ran down a list of ancient and modern authoresses that have "come over" to this side of the Atlantic, concluding that Anne Bradstreet's name should find a place on this list. He named the "Tutoresses to the Old Professors of all Philosophy . . . Hippatia, Sarocchia, the three Corinna, the Empress Eudocia," which are the very names, phrased in the same way, that Bathsua Makin cited in her treatise, "An Essay to Revive the Antient Education of Gentlewomen," published in 1673. In this treatise Makin (Bradstreet's exact contemporary) does include Anne Bradstreet as one example of an "excellent Poet . . . (now in *America*)."[28] She is listed (with the countess of Pembroke, Lady Jane Grey, Lady Arbella, and Queen Elizabeth) under the general heading "Women have been good poets." In her argument for the education of women, one of Makin's general points is that the world has been enriched by countless educated women, ancient and modern. Her list, and Mather's citing of it, suggest that Bradstreet was seen as part of that international community. Bradstreet may well have seen herself that way. Certainly her appreciative seventeenth-century blurb writers did.

Makin's treatise contains a wealth of material about the general subject of education for women, with special reference to the radical Moravian educator, John Amos Comenius, who favored education for women. Makin also makes an important statement about what "besides natural Endowments" is required to make a good poet. "A good poet," she writes, "must know things Divine, things Natural, things Moral, things Historical, and things Artificial, together with the several terms belonging to all Faculties, to which they must allude. Good Poets must be universal Scholars, able to use a pleasing Phrase, and to express themselves with moving Eloquence" (Makin, 16). Makin then begins her list of "good poets" with "Minerva, the Goddess of Wisdom," said to be the "first Inventress" of poetry and the other arts. Makin's definition of the good poet is one that the Bradstreet poetry and prose reflect. Even in the later poems, poems that speak rather directly of marriage and children, the poet is, I think, always the "universal Scholar" whose personal world is a synechdoche of cosmic processes.

Seeing Bradstreet named as an example of this kind of poet helps us to understand the complexities that mark her feminism. Makin (and probably most of the other writers Makin names) saw herself as living in a world that no one would deny was androcentric and further, in the reign of James I, increasingly misogynist.[29] The argument about women's education and women's right to speak in public, much less to write and publish, had been raging for decades,[30] and it raged even among those who did not deny that governments and families should be ruled by men. Historian Underdown writes of Bradstreet's century: "Virtually unquestioned and all-pervasive, the notion of patriarchal authority was the ultimate foundation of both domestic and civil order" (Underdown, 10). English women writers (with whom I am suggesting we should place Bradstreet)[31] adopted every device for advancing their claim to the role of writer and thinker without subverting what even the most radical among them saw as the natural order of things. Bathsua Makin writes in her introduction,

Let not your Ladiships be offended, that I do not (as some have wittily done) plead for Female Preeminence. [Cornelius Agrippa's *A Treatise of the Nobilitie and excellence of Womankynde*, published in English in 1542, would be an example of such a tract.] To ask too much is the way to be denied all. God hath made the Man the Head, if you be educated and instructed, as I propose, I am sure you will acknowledge it, and be satisfied that you are helps, that your Husbands do consult and advise with you . . . and that your Husbands have the casting Voice, in whose determinations you will acquiesce. That this may be the effect of this Education in all ladyes that shall attempt it, is [my] desire. (Makin, 4)

Makin's attempts to render benign her feminist advocacy are reinforced by the fact that she writes this thesis using the persona of a man; adopting a male voice would presumably make her advice more palatable and more authoritative. It is in this regard, I think, that Bradstreet differs most noticeably and, I argue, most importantly, from her like-minded contemporary. Bradstreet frequently echoes male voices but in the personas of women: sisters, daughters, wives, mothers.

Thus, there is a dramatic quality to Bradstreet's speakers, a quality that we do not expect to find—perhaps, again, because we do not expect drama to characterize the poetry of a woman whom we think of as Puritan. Attuning our minds and our ears to shifts in the speaker's identity and her tone and diction is necessary if we are to keep from missing the essential drama of the poetry. Although the speakers of Bradstreet's later work are noticeably less parodic and are managed with less self-irony, the relationship of the speaker to the statements the poems make continues to be of the highest significance. A shift in any aspect of her self-presentation signals a shift that we learn to listen and watch for and that frequently tells us something important about the design of the whole.

Mutability in Bradstreet's self-presentation also characterizes certain statements about the poet's personal identity. In a late meditation Bradstreet describes herself as participant in a self-transforming process, and here that process and the phrasing and the figures that describe it are all imitative of biblical tradition. In "Meditations when my Soul hath been refreshed wth the Consolations wch the world knowes not" (M/R, 223), Bradstreet writes of herself as passing through all of the stages of a woman's life and of being finally identified by none of them except insofar as each is a way station in the process of her own self-realization.

One result of the emphasis on transmutation in Bradstreet's work is that all identities, all states and stages (in history, in nature, and in one's personal life), resist definition—definition that is more than momentary. Bradstreet repeatedly makes a point of resisting the world's understanding of the issues that are most important to her. By implication, the effect of Bradstreet's continual replaying of roles is an undermining of the world's definitions of personal identity. On several occasions she states that there is a great deal that "the world knowes not," as she says in this meditation. Elsewhere she characterizes the "earth" as "brittle" (M/R, 159); it counts as fixed and unchanging things whose basic natures actually exist in change. This concern with transmutation marks

Bradstreet's handling of the large subjects, history and nature, as well as the small ones of her own body and her family relationships. Just as I write that word *small,* however, I realize how she would have handled the opposition I have just constructed. Small is only small now, temporarily or from our "brittle" and limited (earthly) perspective. When we realize "how many great things had small beginnings," as Thomas Dudley said about the emigration to Massachusetts, we no longer think of small in quite the same way.

Indeed, for me personally, reading the Bradstreet texts has been a process of repeatedly encountering what I call the resisting "doubleness" with which she treats and invests every significant subject. The texts have a kaleidoscopic quality to them; thus reading Bradstreet requires rereading. Again and again the texts suddenly mean something else or other or in addition to what I thought they did. It seems strange, then, to stop reading and to write a book, thereby freezing certain moments in a process that is in fact ongoing. I find that as I discover more about the Renaissance, the biblical sources, or about colonial New England, I bring new realizations to these texts. I also find that as I discover more about myself and about the multiple roles I play (scholar, poet, mother, wife, child), I bring my own resistance of the world's definitions to the reading of Bradstreet. I find it important, therefore, to reaffirm the contribution to our studies of the reader-response critics and to put forward the possibility that I have found in Bradstreet's work what I in fact have put there. I value the notion of "dialogue as a trope for reading," as Elizabeth Freund puts it, following Geoffrey Hartman.[32] It is such an invitation to join the conversation that I extend to my readers, who I hope will take "responsibility" for their own Bradstreets and will bring her with them when they come to her texts and to mine.

Chapter Two

Daughter-Child: Actualities and Poetic Personas

Anne Bradstreet thought that human life developed through stages, somewhat as modern students of human development do. For Bradstreet, the question of whether that development thrived or failed to thrive was an important one. Perhaps one of the most consistent themes in her work is the significance of early influences. In both human and cosmic history, Bradstreet found one period foreshadowed another; a seed planted in one period ripened in the next. Inheritance—how one generation or one period affects the next—was one of her lifelong concerns.

Childhood

Let us start the story of Bradstreet's childhood and youth (as she called the stages preceding adulthood) with the marriage in Northampton of her parents, Dorothy Yorke and Thomas Dudley, in 1603. Our chief source of information about the Dudleys is Cotton Mather, who a century later described Dorothy Dudley as "a Gentlewoman whose Extract and Estate were considerable" (Mather 1702, 2:16). Six years younger than her husband, she came from a small parish two miles south of Northampton. Her father, Mather writes, was a yeoman, indicating not simply that he was a farmer but that his was a profit-oriented relationship to the land he farmed. At the time of his marriage Thomas Dudley was serving as law clerk to Judge Augustine Nichols. He did not qualify for this position by being trained in the law but came into the post because Judge Nichols was a relative of Thomas's mother. Thomas Dudley had been orphaned when a young boy, and at 14 was apprenticed as a page in the household of a Northampton nobleman. Although he continued to study Latin into his adult years, his highest level of education was grammar school (in Northampton). At that time grammar school education was rigorous: it meant the study of the Greek and Latin masters and of history and rhetoric. Even though Thomas Dudley did not go on to the university, he associated all his life with university men, particularly with men who attended Emmanuel College, Cambridge; this group eventually included the minister John Cotton, as well as the Dudleys' son Samuel and their son-in-law Simon Bradstreet.

The Dudleys were gentry, members of a class that was marked at the beginning of the seventeenth century by mobility and growth and was being transformed by a heady mixture of merchants, successful yeomen, professional men, industrialists, many of whom were nonconforming in their religious views. Thomas Dudley eventually proved himself adept at many callings—financial manager, historian, soldier, poet, husband, father—callings that would equip him to play a major role in the planning and organizing of the Massachusetts Bay Company in the years 1628 and 1629 and in the governing of Massachusetts as secretary, magistrate, and governor.

Those who write of Dorothy Dudley (including her daughter Anne) describe her as adept at one calling: that of wife and mother. As far as we know, Dorothy Dudley played no public role, except as her husband's helpmeet. Bradstreet describes Dorothy Dudley as "obedient wife" (M/R, 167); in exchange for submission to her husband's authority, she could expect protection and support. This was not a bargain typical simply of gentry, or even of Puritan, marriages. Historian Sarah Mendelson writes that in this period "the world view which assigned women a subordinate place was enshrined in institutions from Parliament on down to the humblest family."[1] We can suppose, too, that for the Dudleys such an understanding of their marriage contract was strongly reinforced by the definition of the married couple's roles that the minister John Dod had laid down in his treatise, *A Godlie Forme of Householde Government: For the Ordering of Private Families, according to the direction of God's Word.* For Puritans Dod's was a highly influential tract, and no doubt it was all the more so for the young Dudleys, whose marriage John Dod had presided over. Dod, furthermore, had converted Thomas Dudley in Northampton a few years before the marriage took place. John Dod compared the wife's and husband's roles in the following way:

The Wiues dutie is to keepe the house. The dutie of the Husband is to get money and prouision: and of the Wiues, not vainely to spend it. The dutie of the Husband is to deale with many men: and of the Wiues to talke with few.

The dutie of the Husband is, to be entermedling: and of the wife, to be
solitary and withdrawne. The dutie of the man is to be skilfull in talke: and of
the wife, to be a sauer. . . . The dutie of the Husband is, to bee Lorde of all;
and of the wife, to giue account of all. . . . Now, where the husband and wife
performeth these duties in their house, we may call it a Colledge of quietnes;
the house wherein these are neglected, we may terme it a hell.[2]

Then, in a curious manner of thinking that was also indicative of the
ways husbands should relate to wives, Dod adds that "a Christian
husband must loue his wife, chiefly because she is his sister in the
profession of the sound and Christian religion, and so an inheritor with
him of the Kingdom of heaven" (Dod 1612, 168). Cotton Mather
records that Thomas Dudley's contact with Dod in Northampton re-
sulted in Thomas's growth into what Mather calls "*Real* Christianity"
(Mather 1702, 2:16). That there are different Christianities, indeed
different Puritanisms, was a fact that never ceased to engage Dudley's
intellectual energies. In this regard, I believe, Anne Dudley was her
father's daughter, although there is evidence to suggest that in their
Massachusetts years they may have been on different sides of the question of which one was "real."

In the microcosm of the young Dudleys' life in 1603 we can see
indications of the macrocosm of, if not the whole nation, at least the
section of England in which the Dudleys lived prior to their emigration
in 1630: Northampton, then the Lincolnshire countryside, and finally
the seaport town of Boston. Lincolnshire had extensive fens at this time
and was thus somewhat isolated. Historians observe that the complexity of England's geology reinforced a general tendency to localism.[3]
English life meant country life centered in villages, each of which could
be quite distinct in its culture and history.

Even though the young Dudley's contacts with the world would have
consisted primarily of immediate neighbors, family, and friends, the
remarkable fact is that Thomas Dudley, by the time of his marriage,
had already seen action in Europe as the captain of a small group of local
militiamen who fought on the side of the Protestant king Henry of
Navarre against the Spanish. The explanation of how a troup of Protestant English villagers could be raised to fight for a cause in Europe may,
in Dudley's case, lie in the proximity of the port of Boston, one of
England's principal avenues of international trade since the Middle
Ages. To the inhabitants of that region, Europe seemed close. Indeed

the relationship with the Low Countries was centuries old when the English Puritans needed and found a refuge there during the Catholic Queen Mary's reign. So too, for centuries, had religious and political refugees emigrated from the continent to England through the port of Boston. Thomas Dudley's nineteenth-century biographer observes that the exchange of goods with the Low Countries, through Boston, brought with it the exchange of Nonconformist ideas.[4] News of the more radical Reformation groups—the Anabaptists, the Behemists, the Moravians—mingled with accounts of home-grown separatists such as the Brownists. Boston's harbor and its St. Botolph's Fair (of the kind the poet's "muse" visits in her poem "in honour of Du Bartas") assured the region of a contact with Europe and the world, even when Boston's status as a port had declined dramatically. It is thus not surprising to find in Thomas Dudley's library at the time of his death a potpourri of works reflecting a heterodox and international religious nonconformity.[5]

The center of the young Dudleys' life in Northampton would have been the St. Edmund parish church, which at the same time would have been a major, if not the major, means of access to news of the world. Christopher Hill writes, "The parish church was . . . a social centre for those nine out of ten English men and women who lived in villages and small towns. It was the place where elections were held, poor relief distributed, public and private announcements made; it could be an amusement hall, a school, a library, a storehouse."[6] St. Edmunds might well have been where Thomas and Dorothy Dudley first heard that James VI of Scotland had left Edinburgh and was on his way to be crowned king of England. Certainly they would have heard sermons and discussions about the monarchy and the succession. Hill writes that "In a society without radio, television and daily press, still largely illiterate and with a strict censorship, the pulpit was almost the sole source of ideas on economics and politics. Popular opposition ideas tended to take a religious form" (Hill, 109).

Although historians generally agree that the first decades of the seventeenth century in England were a relatively stable period socially and politically, one locale could differ from another in these respects. Wars in Europe, periods of local economic depression, even (depending on the crops) of starvation, as well as epidemics could make for a life that day to day felt anything but stable. The year 1602, for example, saw a drought in Lincolnshire, followed by an outbreak of bubonic plague, which then hit London in 1603. With the ascension of King James I, nonconforming ministers like John Dod would soon be dismissed from pulpits in many regions.

The climate for women could differ from the climate for men. In the wake of the reign of Elizabeth, known as the female prince, came a king whose self-characterization as father, as historian Lawrence Stone points out, was used to assert masculine hegemony and to "legitimize his assumption of absolutist monarchical prerogatives."[7] This reinforcement of patriarchy under James I took place in a world already intensely anxious about the proper place and role of women. Historian Underdown reports, as have others, the misogynist tradition in Elizabethan and Jacobean literature and the "eternal popularity" of the theme of the "battle of the sexes" (Underdown, 38). The necessity for women to submit to husbands was a frequent sermon subject, a subject that no doubt the Dudleys heard preached about frequently.

Concern about "unruly women" and harsh measures taken to curb religious nonconformity occurred as revolutionary developments in literacy and in education were taking place, with immense consequences for family (perhaps especially for women) and for parish life. In 1560 the Geneva Bible had appeared and with it the possibility that the individual believer could read for him- or herself in English. When Anne Bradstreet recalls for her children that early in childhood she "fovnd much comfort in reading ye Scriptures" (M/R, 215), she is speaking as one who has benefitted from the effects of the revolution in literacy. Thus, when John Dod and others were denied a pulpit, increasing numbers of listeners already had become readers. Mothers in greater numbers could catechize their children and take notes on sermons and review sermons with their children and servants. Anne Bradstreet's poem to Dorothy Dudley suggests these activities were part of Dorothy Dudley's life. Educational reformers in England and on the continent (foremost among these were the Moravian John Amos Comenius and in England Roger Ascham, tutor to Queen Elizabeth and Lady Jane Grey) advocated education in reading and writing for both boys and girls. Clearly Dorothy Dudley had been taught to read; how or when we do not know.

Such developments as these gave the family a degree of independence it had not had before. Ironically, when James I, using the language of the family, legitimized his claims to power, the literal family was, in some instances, moving away from his exercise of that authority. When church services were disrupted or when a village minister was silenced, the family could gather and, in effect, challenge the role of the parish church (Bridenbaugh, 32). "The home could become a cultural and discussion centre as well as a family circle," writes Christopher Hill. He finds "closed parish churches and family worship . . . both characteristic of Protestantism" (Hill, 30). Thus John Dod's exhortation to the wife and husband to turn their house into a "Colledge of quietnes" suggests one of the trends of the times into which Anne Bradstreet was born. That the microcosm of family life might serve not only to reflect the world but to *deflect* it as well would be a theme, indeed would become a strategy, in Bradstreet's mature work.

Anne Dudley, the Dudleys' second child, was born in Northampton four or five years after her brother Samuel (who was baptized in 1608). No baptismal record of Anne Dudley's birth exists. We know her birthdate only by counting back from a poem dated 1632 in which she refers to herself as "twice ten years old" (M/R, 178). We can only surmise too about the quality of her earliest days and months, but the intensity of the family attachments expressed later in her prose and poetry suggests that what historians have observed as characteristic of Puritan families may well fit both her birth family and later her own family in the New World. Historian Levin Schücking writes that the "faithful" considered children to be the "highest form of good fortune."[8] John Dod wrote feelingly, "Consider how noble a thing a child is, whom God himself hath shaped and formed in his mother's womb" (Dod 1612). Since mortality rates for both mother and infant were high, the birth event was fraught with peril (Stone, 54–65), but so too was it laced with significance. Prayer preceded sexual intercourse and accompanied the newborn into the world. Although Puritans did not understand the processes of conception and gestation the way these are presently understood, their advice about prenatal care was consistent with the advice given to pregnant women today: "a good diet, moderate exercise, and a helpful husband" (Schnucker, 639). The local network of family and friends that was important to Thomas Dudley in securing him employment would have been important to Dorothy Dudley during the birth of her five children. Only women attended births, men were excluded, and all the women in the family were expected to lend a hand—the older women to apply their knowledge and experience, and the younger to assist and learn. Midwives guided the birth process. It was not until the eighteenth century that doctors (who were men) took over in that role.[9]

In effect, the domestic manuals, of which Dod's was only one, carried the work of the Reformation into the personal family lives of all believers. Dod exhorts his householders to begin "reforming their owne houses . . . and so suffer the holy Religion of God, to take place amongst their families at home" (1). In this intense personalizing of religion we can see, as Lawrence Stone points out, the "reinforcement . . . of patriarchy" within one's most intimate relationships (Stone, 145–46), but we see, as well, the advent of modern ideas of child rearing. Puritans, particularly, stressed the importance of the earliest stages of a child's development and of the kinds of learning that take place before actual schooling begins.

John Dod, among others, stressed the importance of breast feeding. In wealthier families the practice of hiring wet nurses had been in wide use. William Gouge, Dod's friend who wrote his own manual on domestic duties, estimated (regretfully) that fewer than one woman in 20 nursed her own children (Schnucker, 644). The Puritans felt strongly about the necessity of the mother's nursing her own babies, and this experience made its way into the rhetoric of ministers who saw the church as mother and the milk of her breast as the words that nourished the congregation. Mother's milk was seen as God's provision for the health and spiritual needs of the baby. Cow's milk was rarely used, and the breast milk of an outsider to the family would not do. Nursing was seen, as it is today, as an occasion for what we now call bonding between mother and child. Puritans of Dod's persuasion further believed that through the mother's milk "certain qualities that shaped the infant's future character and behavior" were passed on to the child. They also believed that by nursing children would more surely grow to love their mothers (Schnucker, 645).

Because of the roles that John Dod played in the young Dudleys' lives, there is every reason to believe that they followed his counsel in family matters and, too, that Dorothy was among the group that Lawrence Stone calls "the more puritanically inclined mothers who were the first from well-to-do families to try to nurse their own children" (Stone, 270–71). Nursing was to be an occasion for prayer and instruction.[10] All of the child's very first exchanges with parents should be understood as having religious implications. Bradstreet later put this idea about the children's early training in one of her meditations: "Let the seed of good instruction and exhortation be sown, in the spring of their youth, and a plentiful crop may be expected in the harvest of their years" (M/R, 205).

Anne Bradstreet's epitaph to her mother, written on the occasion of her mother's death in 1643, makes important points about Dorothy Dudley, despite its "formulaic" and "abstract" qualities, as Laura Ulrich points out (3). For one, Dorothy Dudley was a "true Instructer of her family" (M/R, 167), a phrase that suggests that Anne Bradstreet's earliest education came from her mother. Puritans were said to feel that children's "first words should be religious words" and that children should be catechised as soon as they began to use language (Schücking, 69). This earliest stage of a child's education was considered by Dod and Gouge to be primarily the mother's responsibility. She should "order the household so that no exercise of religion be hindered." She is to act in her husband's absence, and it is she, especially, who plants seeds to be nurtured later. This understanding of the mother's role in the family household provided a governing metaphor in Bradstreet's later work.

It is hard to imagine that Bradstreet's lifelong love of learning did not begin early, with warm and familiar encouragement. As Elizabeth Wade White points out, Puritan educator John Brinsley argued that children should begin school at age five "at the uttermost,"[11] but he preferred that they begin sooner. Children should be accustomed "even from their tender years," to know their letters, to spell, and to read (10), but he accompanied this advocacy of early childhood education with the equally important exhortation that school be "a place of play." If learning is fun, Brinsley argued, then "it can no more hinder their growth than their play doth" (12). In this treatise Brinsley is speaking primarily of school curricula, but he does have a word for parents: "Also the Parents who have any learning may enter their little ones playing with them, at dinner and suppers, or as they sit by the fire, and find it very pleasant delight" (20). Thus while Thomas Dudley may have been Bradstreet's "magazine of history" (M/R, 166), Dorothy Dudley would have been her daughter's source of everything that was most fundamental to her learning. Playing games, telling stories, repeating scripture, pronouncing difficult and important words, and perhaps just listening, as the Muse's mother does in "In Honour of Du Bartas." There he [the Muse] "At night turnes to his Mothers cot againe,/ And tells her tales; (his full heart over-glad)/ Of all the glorious sights his eyes have had (M/R, 153).

A second and telling point made about Dorothy Dudley in Bradstreet's tribute to her is that she "ever did frequent . . . publicke meetings." It was the custom for women, who were not to speak in church, to review the sermon at family meetings following services. Women trained themselves (and were encouraged) to be careful listeners and rememberers of what they heard. Children, of course, accompanied their mothers to church and were encouraged to do likewise. Lucy Hutchinson, whose education is often compared to Anne Dudley's, recalls that

by the time I was foure years old I read English perfectly, and having a great memory, I was carried to sermons, and while I was very young could remember and repeat them exactly and being caress'd, the love of praise tickled me, and made me attend more heedfully.[12]

Hutchinson, reflecting on the consequences of this experience, writes that "It pleas'd God that thro' the good instructions of my mother, and the sermons she carried me to, I was convinc'd that the knowledge of God was the most excellent study, and accordingly applied myself to it."

The one place that women gathered in significant numbers was the church, and since the church was such a vital center, the women would have much to report and discuss. Anne Hutchinson had performed this role in nearby Aylford, Lincolnshire, before she came to Boston in New England, where she continued to do likewise until her trials for heresy and banishment to Rhode Island. Likewise did Anne Dudley's younger sister Sarah, who would later be accused of "irregular prophesying" (also by the Boston, Massachusetts, church). Her vocation, too, might well have begun under her mother's tutelage. In this respect, the point made that Dorothy Dudley was a "loving and obedient wife" takes on special significance. Although she took charge of ordering and teaching her household, she did so as Thomas Dudley's "deputy." Thus, as a small child Anne Dudley would have seen the limits placed on her mother's authority as an interpreter, teacher, and prophesier. Historian Levin Schücking writes,

Certainly the performance of such duties [as catechizing her children] did not suffice to get [the mother's] wishes respected in any matter of principle, if they conflicted with those of her husband. The image which was so frequently used, which compared husband and wife to sun and moon, is very illuminating and shows clearly what position the mother really occupied within the family. As the moon obtains its light from the sun, so the mother receives her authority from the father. (88–89)

Thus we see that putting another's words into their own was what women were trained to do—both by their mothers' examples and by their fathers' praise. When Bradstreet's work reflects, echoes, recalls the voices of others (ministers, historians, scientists, biblical "penmen") it evidences a strategy that belonged to all women, one considered not just permissible but desirable as well. The complex hallmark of Bradstreet's mature work is the designation of poetic speakers who are female but who echo the words of voices that are male. In his dedicatory verse, C.B. uses the moon and sun metaphor when he credits Bradstreet with outdoing "mankind." In her work, he writes, "The Moone hath totally ecclips'd the Sun" (M/R, 529). Given the social and cultural context, this is strong praise indeed.

When it came time to learn grammar school subjects, Anne Dudley, being a girl, did not do so in school. Her brother, Samuel, four or five years her elder, was no doubt bringing home schoolwork in Northampton as his little sister was being taught at home. Both children would have been drilled at home in their numbers and letters by their mother and father. Some time prior to 1620 John Dod introduced Thomas Dudley to William Fiennes, who then suggested Dudley for the post of steward when William's young cousin Theophilus, the third earl of Lincoln, inherited a large estate and a large burden of debt. When the Dudley family moved to the earl's estate in Lincolnshire, they moved into a situation where the Dudley children would have shared the services of tutors hired for the earl's children and, as Harrison Meserole suggests, would have had the use of the earl's considerable library.[13] Although Bradstreet does not mention the fact, she occupied what has been called the "privileged position" of the oldest daughter (Schücking, 89). Historian Lawrence Thompson writes of Anne Bradstreet's situation when he observes that "the luckiest girl of the wealthier classes was she who was educated at home, under the supervision of an educated mother, alongside her brothers, at the feet of their tutors. When the boys had gone off to school, she might continue her studies with her father's domestic chaplain or a local clergyman"[14]. In addition, being the oldest daughter, Anne Dudley would have assumed it to be her duty to help educate and guide her three younger sisters. When the family moved to the earl of Lincoln's estate at Sempringham, Anne would have been about seven years old; her sister Patience four or five; her second sister, Sarah, who was baptized in 1620, must have been on the way. The youngest sister, Mercy, would be born a year later. It often happens that teaching someone else what one has learned solidifies that education. It is not too much to suppose that to have been true in Anne Dudley's case.

Bradstreet's letter "To My dear children" provides a glimpse of her early education and of the life context in which these occurred. She writes,

In my yovng years about 6. or 7. as I take it I began to make cons^c. of my wayes, & what I knew was sinfull as lying, disobed^c. to parents, et^c. I avoided it. If at any time I was overtaken wth ye evills, it was a great Trouble, & I could not be at rest 'till by prayer I had confest it vnto God. I was also troubled at ye neglect of private Dutyes tho: too often tardy y^t way. I also fovnd much comfort in reading ye Scriptures, espec: those places I though most concerned my Condition, and as I grew to haue more vnderstanding, so ye more solace I took in them. (M/R, 215)

Although a young reader, she apparently did not simply know how to read (pronunciation, word recognition, and the other skills stressed both then and now); she was reading in order to inform her own life. As we have seen, she read selectively those passages that "concerned" her "Condition." It is noteworthy that she does not say or imply that she was doing something unusual for her sex. Anne Dudley's education at home thus appears to have followed the principle that education should be applied to one's life, as John Brinsley proposed for his revolutionized classroom. "Schollars," he wrote, "are to be taught to do all things with understanding, and to be able to giue a reason for euery matter which they learned" (41). He emphasized that translations ought to be accurate but students should turn the original into their own words. Poetry had its place in his curriculum because poetry "serueth very much for the sharpening of the wit." He advised "extempore verse on any theme" and that all this should be practiced every day (49).

Not only would Bradstreet have been counseled to make the texts she was memorizing and translating her "own," but she was learning to write at a time when the importance of developing "the growth of our own tongue" (21–22) was being emphasized. Bradstreet may have begun her studies of language and literature with the study of Latin, but as she herself suggests, the goal of her reading was to read the scriptures in English. Brinsley's students were expected to learn Greek and Hebrew, but there again their Hebrew was to serve their "knowledge of the grounds of religion" (53). There is little evidence that

Bradstreet's education went as far as Greek and Hebrew. Elizabeth Wade White writes that Bradstreet probably had an "elementary under-standing" of French and Latin (66), since her father could read both. White concludes that Bradstreet's "discovery and exploration of the masters of antiquity lay somewhere between the popular compilations and the whole galaxy of the great translations" (69).[15]

The evidence of Bradstreet's texts points to her interest (ongoing into her adult life) in poets who were also natural philosophers, scientists, and historians. In the quaternions Bradstreet links the arts and the sciences throughout her descriptions of the composition of the natural world. Although she, in the persona of "Blood," writes "To play Phi-losopher I have no list; / Nor yet Phisitian, nor Anatomist" (M/R, 26), her poem's complex and carefully worked out disquisition on Blood's relationship to the other humors contradicts that assertion. In Lin-colnshire she was probably tutored by Thomas Lodge, tutor to the earl of Lincoln's children. Lodge, a physician and a poet, was no doubt attracted to the post at Sempringham because Lincolnshire was a Renais-sance center of science.

Science, thus, may have been the area where Bradstreet was particu-larly well schooled, but she may well have moved into the study of the sciences as an extension of her study of history and poetry. Her reading of Joshua Sylvester's translation of *La Semaine ou Création du Monde* by Guillaume di Salluste, sieur du Bartas, would have demonstrated the "unity" of science, religion, history and poetry. It is generally assumed that Bradstreet read the Joshua Sylvester translation of the *Divine Weeks* (as the English translation of Du Bartas's poem is called), which ap-peared in 1621 (White 147).[16] Actually there were nine partial or complete editions of Sylvester's translation between 1592 and 1641.[17] As early as 1596 Thomas Lodge, the family tutor and physician to the earl of Lincoln, who probably served the Dudleys in these capacities, had translated Du Bartas on the subject of war in his *Wit's Misery* (Snyder, 61). In 1620, while he was at Sempringham, Lodge's translation of a commentary on the *Semaines* appeared (61). It seems likely that Du Bartas was very much "in the air," so to speak, as the eight-year-old Anne Dudley was learning history, geography, and the physical sciences.

Apparently Thomas Dudley too had composed a poem "on the four parts of the world" to which Bradstreet said her quaternions owed a debt (M/R, 5, 313). Bradstreet's strong sense of inheritance from Du Bartas may well come by way of her father's attempts to put Du Bartas into his own words. By the time of Thomas Dudley's military service in

France in the late 1590s on behalf of the Protestant king Henri de
Navarre, Du Bartas's monumental work had been enthusiastically received throughout Europe, and the second volume had been cut short
by Du Bartas's death in 1590. Du Bartas had served as gentleman-
servant to Henri, and it is unlikely that Dudley had not heard of the
person and the poet. Given their similarities of station, politics, religion, and avocations (that of poet), Dudley may well have admired and
identified with Du Bartas.

The interest of the medical man Lodge in Du Bartas indicates the
importance of Du Bartas's poem as a compendium of the sciences of the
day. Its achievement was the "conscious reconciliation" of sacred and
profane traditions. [18] The "sciences" that inform this highly synchretis-
tic work are alchemy, anatomy, Hermetic theology, white magic, or
magia naturalis (what we might call natural science), and astrology.
This synthesis of art, religion, and science is implied in the epithet "the
French Solomon" bestowed on Du Bartas by Edmund Spenser's friend,
the scientist Gabriel Harvey (White, 56). When Nathaniel Ward,
minister in Ipswich from 1634 to 1646, begins his tribute to Anne
Bradstreet's *The Tenth Muse* with references to Mercury and Minerva, he
points Bradstreet's readers toward hermetic lore. He further suggests
that Bradstreet fell heir to these when she used her father's and Du
Bartas's poems as her models. Ward writes that *"Mercury"* introduced
Du Bartas to the God Apollo, indicating that Du Bartas was the gift of
the discoverer of music and the inventor of mathematics and astronomy.
In Ward's hyperbolic parallel Mercury introduces Du Bartas's book just
as Minerva introduces Anne Bradstreet's volume. Minerva, as we have
seen, is the goddess of wisdom (in the Roman pantheon) and a fitting
patroness for this "Auth'resse" whom Ward calls "a right Du Bartas
Girle" (M/R, 526). By placing her as Du Bartas's equal, as well as his
heir, Ward suggests that Bradstreet's work completes the mission of the
Divine Weeks, which was, as we have seen, to continue to trace "the
descent of ancient wisdom from the East, especially from hidden Hebrew lore" (Hirst, 82).

The poet Du Bartas and his followers, who in more modern times
were to take up the historic task of yoking together all branches of
learning under an essentially evangelical purpose, followed a special
kind of "muse," *La Muse Chretienne,* as Du Bartas called her in a poem of
that name. In Sylvester's adaptation she is (as is Mary Wroth's later
poem) "Urania, or, the Heavenly Muse." [19] She is Mercurial in the sense
of an intermediary between heaven and earth. She is "quintessence of

the Soule," an alchemical phrase that, in its reference to the fifth
essence, describes a spirit that is both heavenly and (within the world
body) generative. As muse, Urania is unlike the other muses who are
mere artists—who "warble fine" and "ravish millions with their *Madri-
gals.*" The work of this tenth muse is, rather, to "draw the deafest by
the ears unto—it; / To quicken stones and stop the Ocean's course."
Her concern is *"Faith's Effects"* (Sylvester, 6). Furthermore, she, unlike
the other nine muses, appears to lack art: "An *Azure Mantle* on her back
she wore, / With art-less Art, in orderly disorder" (3). Despite her lack
of art, she will affect change in human life and in the natural world. She
appears to have the power to inhabit all regions and all times—above
and below the earth, ancient and modern times. She here and now
"conducts" the artist's "pen," and she "soars up to heav'n." The poet is
empowered by her to travel that "Sacred Path / Where none but heav'n-
blest happy spirits can pass," (7) just as Bradstreet's poet will later be
lead down "a path, no vultures eye hath seen" (M/R, 160). Urania is,
indeed, sister to biblical Wisdom, and like Wisdom she appears to
assume different genders as well as different bodies. She appears, too, to
affect the gender identification of those "heav'n-blest" authors who,
although male, act in the role of assistant in the process of her coming
to birth in the world: "So, Bartas was but Mid-wife to the Muse, / With
greater ease to utter her Conceits" (67).

   That the "Du Bartas girle" Anne Bradstreet sprang up as the manifes-
tation of the "tenth muse" in America helps us to understand her poetic
purposes, given the philosophical, cultural, and literary contexts to
which this "muse" belonged. Of particular relevance to that understanding is the trope of poet Du Bartas as midwife to the muse and the
gender shifts that that figure suggests. In this instance Du Bartas
assists at the birth of the muse. Sidney, too, translated Du Bartas's *The
First Week,* and similarly, in the first sonnet of Sidney's "Astrophel and
Stella" the muse assisted the poet who is "great with child to speak and
helpless in my throes." Ann Kibbey has suggested that Bradstreet's
later identification of the poet with the persona of mother of an "ill-
form'd" (M/R, 177) child owes a debt to these famous Sidney lines.
Kibbey further suggests that Sidney was working with the figure of
Athena sprung from the head of Zeus, a representation in which Zeus's
head is the womb from which Athena or Wisdom springs.[20] In all of
these instances, the association of gender mutability with the poetic
process, and particularly with poetry as the birth of Wisdom in the
world, is significant for Bradstreet's mature work.

When we consider these masters or models and the probability that Anne Dudley read them or about them as a school-age child, we realize that these literary exemplars belonged to the Elizabethan age, to a period of time a full generation earlier than her own. I would like to suggest that in Bradstreet's uses of these masters we find evidence not simply of a great library at the disposal of a precocious reader, but the evidence as well of the personal identification of Thomas Dudley with both Du Bartas and Sidney. Sir Philip Sidney's mother was the daughter of John Dudley, the duke of Northumberland, a relationship that the Dudley family in Massachusetts explicitly claimed (White, 11–12). Members of Sidney's mother's family followed an interest in "divine science and philosophy." It was Sidney's grandmother, the duchess of Northumberland, who first gave encouragement to Sidney's tutor, the mage John Dee, as then did her husband, the duke, who was himself known as "the Wizard Earl." Thomas Dudley would have known that John Dudley, the duke of Northumberland, followed "the ancient reverend steps / Of Trismegistus and Pythagorus" (Hirst, 78–79).

But it was John's brother, Robert Dudley, the earl of Leicester, who was the closer, indeed the lifelong, friend of John Dee, and who had been Dee's student. Like his nephew Philip Sidney, Robert used Dee's vast library.[21] Frances Yates describes the library and the ideal of learning that it expressed as the collection "of a man of the Renaissance, bent on assimilating the whole realm of knowledge available in his time."[22] Another modern commentator on the Renaissance ideal of the synchretism among all branches of learning finds that the oneness of all knowledge (in Bradstreet's word, its "unity") was "itself a powerful warrant for truth." He writes of the temper of the times during Thomas Dudley's youth, one that marks Bradstreet's inheritance from her father:

The Renaissance thirst for synthesis, for syncretism was unquenchable. Ficino [whose work was in Harvard's library in the first years[23]] was to assert the compatibility of Platonism (more accurately, Neo-Platonism) with Christianity. Pico della Mirandola was to stir together in one pot not only these two ingredients but also Hermetic doctrines and the cabala, which he thought to preserve an esoteric doctrine entrusted to Moses on Mount Sinai at the same time as the written law. In the *De occulta philosophia* of Cornelis Agrippa all these coexit easily with astrology, numerology, alchemy and much else.[24]

The "hermetic-Cabalist core of this movement" Yates finds formulated particularly in the work of the German physician Cornelius Agrippa, whose *De Occulta philosophia* laid the groundwork for this movement by summarizing all branches of "scientific" knowledge (Yates 1979). Agrippa's work on the four humors and the four elements may well have supplied Bradstreet with the information basic to her first two quaternions. Perhaps more important in Anne Dudley's education would have been the fact that Agrippa argued for the superiority of women over men. His argument gives evidence of the habit of mind of the occult scientist-artist, going all the way back to the dawn of human history to demonstrate God's *original* design for the male and the female. Again, it may not be that Agrippa's three-volume work on occult philosophy was placed in Anne Dudley's hand by John Lodge or Thomas Dudley, but it is surely true that Lodge would have known and based his medical practice on Agrippa's work. Certainly the scholarly community in Lincolnshire would have known and taken a great interest in the writings both of Agrippa and John Dee.

John Dee was not only a mage and a scientist. He developed what Yates calls "a politico-religious programme . . . concerned with the imperial destiny of Queen Elizabeth I." In Dee's program for Queen Elizabeth can be seen an implicit feminism that suggests a model for Bradstreet's in her elegy for Elizabeth. Dee found in Elizabeth "the representative of 'imperial reform' of a purified and reformed religion to be expressed and propagated through a reformed empire" (Yates 1979, 84). Key to Dee's "prophetic interpretation" of history was his idealized figure of Elizabeth whose "supposed Arthurian descent" rendered her an appropriate leader in the coming worldwide reformation. Bradstreet's elegiac treatment of the "Phoenix queen" and "fleshly Deity," Elizabeth, reflects Dee's Elizabeth, the "pilot of all Christendom" (85).

Thus we find in Bradstreet's inheritance from Du Bartas and Sidney, and from the writers with whom they were closely associated, elements of what must have been a welcome affirmation of women's identity and women's capacities for leadership and creative work. But Anne Bradstreet must have been aware, also through these very examples, of the tragic consequences of her Dudley relatives' expansionist enterprises and of misguided enthusiasm for hermetic learning among them and within their intellectual circle. Bradstreet's elegy for Sidney, who was "untimely slaine at the Seige of Zutphon, Anno 1586," would remind her readers that Zutphen was the campaign of Robert Dudley, the earl of Leicester, a campaign that Queen Elizabeth halted. She recalled Leicester abruptly; his fortunes had changed, and he died disgraced in 1588.

The circumstances of the elder Dudley's ill-favor and death would have been well known to the Thomas Dudley family. With these events also came a turn in the intellectual climate, in which reports of Dee's "sorceries" began to circulate. Yates calls these years Dee's period of "disgrace and failure." Thus for Bradstreet to call attention to her relationship to the Sidney of these events is to evoke a context of failure and disappointment. This evocation is made doubly intriguing by the fact that in Bradstreet's 1650 version of the elegy she tells us that she has the "self-same blood" as Sidney's "yet in her veins" (M/R, 149). She appears to boast of her kinship with the great poet. In the 1678 version of the elegy, her blood relationship is not mentioned. I will have more to say about this elegy and these changes in it in chapters 3 and 4, but here I would stress that the elegy looks back to events prior to Bradstreet's own era, events that mark the demise of her father's family's influence and ascendency. The Zutphen battle and its aftermath occurred during a period that at first seemed to promise (for John Dee and his followers) passage "into the spacious pleasant fields / Of divine science and philosophy" but that marked instead a passage into a nightmare of isolation and impoverishment. John Dee, the "characteristic philosopher of the Elizabethan Age," was finally accused of witchcraft. The theme of this little history might well be termed "declension," that proverbial New England preoccupation.

In Frances A. Yates's retelling of these events, the theme marks the fortunes of other literary masters whom Bradstreet emulated. Yates connects Sidney's death with the fate of Spenser's *The Faerie Queen,* which was written during Dee's highest point of influence in the court of Queen Elizabeth but which was published after Sidney's death. As a consequence, "the poem entered a harder world," Yates writes, "and one cautiously and doubtfully disposed towards the enthusiasms of former years." Sir Walter Raleigh, another of the poets whom Bradstreet imitated, introduced Spenser to court, but the reception was disappointing. Spenser, too, Yates reports, died poor and unrecognized (1979, 93).

For the young Anne Dudley these events must have had the quality of legend about them, especially since they occurred not in her youth but in her father's. These elegized events and the anachronistic occult formulas of Bradstreet's quaternions supply the subjects of a poetry written in New England at a very different period in history: in the wake of the Antinomian crisis in New England and on the eve not of reformation but of civil war in old England.

Adolescence

According to her account in the autobiographical letter to her children (written near the end of her life) Anne Dudley apparently grew in a short time from a studious, devoted daughter into a rebellious adolescent. As she tells the story, she suffered a "long fitt of sicknes wch I had on my bed," in which "I often comvned wth my heart, and made my Suplicat^{n}. to the most High who sett me free from that afflict^{n}" (M/R, 215). She thus marks a point in her brief autobiography when affliction and deliverance from it, through prayer, began. We do not know what this sickness was. Malaria was common in the Fens; it has been suggested that John Cotton, a frequent visitor to the earl of Lincoln's castle at Sempringham, spent time there recuperating from a malarial fever. Following her illness, which serves as a preparation for a new stage in life, Bradstreet writes that at "about 14. or 15. I fovnd my heart more carnall, & sitting loose from God, vanity & ye follyes of Youth take hold of me" (M/R, 216). No one doubts that Anne Dudley was sick and that sickness was a threat to children in the seventeenth century, but we should see in Bradstreet's little narrative how carefully staged the process of growth is.

Modern historians record that Puritans were tolerant of what was considered typical adolescent behavior—for what Bradstreet in "The Four Ages of Man" called the "vanity" and "folly" of youth, or of what others termed the "corruptions" of adolescence before the "onset of conviction" (Greven 1980, 55). Adolescents were expected to sow wild oats and then to settle into adulthood, which meant marriage and parenting. This transition, historian Roger Thompson has found, did not, in Puritan Massachusetts, evoke young people's resistance.[25] Anne Bradstreet's own rather toneless account of submitting and joining the church at Boston (in New England) (M/R, 216) may suggest (among other things) an acquiescence that was said to be not atypical of Puritan adolescents taking on the obligations of adulthood.

It was in adolescence that Anne Dudley became one of John Cotton's parishioners. In 1624, when Anne Bradstreet was about 12, the Dudley family moved to Boston, apparently so that Thomas Dudley could be near his friend John Cotton and, as Cotton Mather reports, so that he could live "a more private life" (Mather 1702, 2:16). The Dudleys lived across the street from the Cottons. Bradstreet writes about this period in the following section of her letter to her children:

About 16. The Lord layd his hand sore vpon me & smott me wth ye small pox. When I was in my afflict^n. I besovght the Lord, and confessed my pride and Vanity and he was entreated of me, and again restored me. But I rendered not to him according to ye benefitt rec. (M/R, 216)

In this account Bradstreet writes that she moved from sin into what was a truly life-threatening illness (smallpox) at age 16 and then "after a short time" to confession and restoration. Bradstreet's twentieth-century editors point out that this "experience conformed to a classic pattern of affliction and conversion of the kind one sees in Milton's and George Herbert's poetry, in the prose of John Bunyan and Jonathan Edwards and in popular tract literature" (M/R, xvi). Bradstreet's emphasis on what she calls "affliction" may well be a way of underlining an experience that she knows is central to Christian life and essential to the process of salvation. Although the smallpox did occur, her narration conforms to a conventional pattern. Here Bradstreet tells her children that the central lifelong subject of her poetry was her "pilgrimage," with its pattern of affliction and restoration, a pattern that she elaborates as "times of Darkness when ye Almighty hath hid his face from me" and then that "abundance of Sweetnes and refreshment after affliction."

Bradstreet's reporting of her backslidings with such deliberateness emphasizes that she was a true-to-form adolescent, the idea being that the more willful and corrupt the adolescence, the more remarkable the converted adulthood. John Cotton made this point. In "The Pouring out of the Spirit" (a sermon preached in 1624) Cotton wrote that "there is not more ready way to make you a fruitful Christian, then to have run a lewd course in life, and in the end to have our wills subdued, and brought to the knowledge of Christ: such a soule as hath been fruitful in sin, is afterwards as fruitful in the ways of righteousnesse."[26]

Bradstreet's poem "Youth," in "The Foure Ages of Man," characterizes the adolescent in much the same way as her autobiographical letter to her children does. The process through which the youth develops comes finally to a point described by "Middle Age" as a "harvest," with all the doubleness that that image suggests. Middle Age says that "When my Wilde Oates, were soen, and ripe, & Mown, / I then receiv'd a harvest of mine owne." Prior to the sowing of such oats, "youth" is said to be a delight everywhere, to everyone:

> Though thus in field, at home, to all most kind,
> So affable that I do suit each mind;

> I can insinuate into the brest,
> And by my mirth can raise the heart deprest;
> Sweet Musick rapteth my harmonious Soul.
> And elevates my thoughts above the Pole.
> My wit, my bounty, and my courtesie,
> Makes all to place their future hopes on me. (M/R, 39)

This youth too (perhaps composed in part of a self-portrait of the poet at that age, when her soul was already rapt by "Musick") veers away from that happy and infectious condition into a condition that gives "merriment" a different valence: "My gifts abus'd, my education lost, / My woful Parents longing hopes all crost, / My wit, evaporates in meriment" (M/R, 39). He, like the Bradstreet of the autobiographical letter, also falls prey to the threats of sin, of death and illness: "Sometimes the loathsome Pox my face be-mars, / With ugly marks of his eternal scars." (Critics have cited this line as evidence that Bradstreet's face may have been permanently marked by her smallpox.) Youth, although a warrior and a womanizer, is finally left in a condition in which he "yet beholds the light." Youth has barely escaped death, and in a curiously androgynous summation he concludes: "Of Marrow ful my bones, of Milk my breasts, / Ceas'd by the gripes of Serjeant Death's arrests." His identity is filled with a virile sustaining substance and a motherly nurturing one. He has, in effect, not fled his parents but incorporated them.

In these Bradstreet portraits of adolescence, affliction plays a major role in effecting the life-changing transition to adulthood. Again and again in Bradstreet's work the Lord saves by simply smiting the sinner, very much in the manner of a parent who adopts harsh measures to mold a child's behavior. In her "Meditations Diuine and morall" Bradstreet uses a variety of homey images for the process. She writes, "Diuerse children, haue their different natures, some are like flesh wch nothing but salt will keep from putrefaction, some again like tender fruits that are best preserved wth sugar, those parents are wise that can fit their nurture according to their Nature" (M/R, 196). The process of change is here understood as a chemical one; elsewhere it is understood as alchemical. In her autobiographical letter to her children Bradstreet writes that the Lord ground her to powder. Although she may change form, if He is present she will not be destroyed utterly. In meditation 19, she returns to the figure of grinding: "Corne till it haue past through the Mill and been ground to powder, is not fit for bread, god so deales wth his servants, he grindes them wth greif and pain till they turn to dust, and then are they fine manchet [a fine bread] for his Mansion" (M/R, 197). Elsewhere God changes the form of the "good man" as the blacksmith changes iron. "Iron till it be throughly heat is vncapable to be wrought, so god sees good to cast some men into the furnace of affliction and then beats them on his anuile into what frame he pleases" (M/R, 199). God is a craftsman, miller, sorcerer, cook, and the process of mutation or metamorphosis renders the Christian into a new being through fearful stages of pain and nothingness. Bradstreet finds a deep affinity between everyday actions, natural practices and processes, and the reformations that will lead to the ultimate fulfill-ment of God's prophecies for the world.

The God who wants to see his creation develop and change is like a careful parent; He calculates how much grinding—how much of the powerful ingredient of adversity—ought to be added to the child's regimen. As Bradstreet puts it,

A wise father will not lay a burden on a child of seven yeares old, wch he knows is enough for one of twice his strength, much lesse will our heauenly father (who knowes our mould) lay such afflictions vpon his weak children as would crush them to dust, but according to the strength he will proportion the load, as god hath his little Children so he hath his strong men, such as are come to a full stature in Christ, and many times he imposes weighty burdens on their shoulders, and yet they go vpright vnder them, but it matters not whether the load be more or lesse if god afford his help. (M/R, 200–1)

In fact, Bradstreet expresses concern at one point that she may not have had hardships enough. Throughout life "correction" is a vital necessity. In her words,

I have fovnd by Exper^c. I can no more liue w^thout correction then without food. Lord wth y^y correction giue Instrvction and amendment, and then by stroakes shall bee welcome, I haue not been refined in ye furnace of affliction as some haue been, but haue rather been p^rserved wth sugar then brine, yet will he p^rserve me to his heavenly Kingd. (M/R, 227)

Again using metaphors of preserving and refining, she here stresses the existence of a process that works like alchemy. Here one substance is changed into another, as in alchemy where lead is said to change into gold, or household chemistry, where a natural process like putre-faction is altered by the addition of a curing ingredient. On 28

August 1656 Bradstreet wrote to her children to explain that God does not "afflict willingly"; he does not take delight in punishment, nor does he have any "benefitt by my adversity." She then goes on to stress that "he doth it for my Advantage, and y^t I may bee a Gainer by it—" (M/R, 225).

Bradstreet penned these statements in her adulthood, years after her own adolescence. How her adolescent "carnall heart" and her "sitting loose from God" were dealt with by Dorothy and Thomas Dudley and by her minister in those years, John Cotton, we do not know. What is clear is that these passages about the way God intervenes in the world and how He changes sinners describe a very different process from the one we find in Cotton's theology. Perhaps Bradstreet in her mature years, with children of her own, came to a new understanding of the conversion process. If, as I and others have suggested, the preparation (intellectual, literary, spiritual) for the quaternions took place in childhood, then these passages about growth and change reveal that Bradstreet's interests in natural processes had early origins and developed over a lifetime.

Cotton too emphasized the role of afflictions in the conversion process. He says that "it will be a vaine thing for men to think to escape scott-free from afflictions, and yet live a godly and holy life." But the secret or key, Cotton says, to discerning God's presence in afflictions is to see afflictions as "common to you with the Lord Jesus Christ." According to Cotton, the use of affliction is centered in the believer's experience of Christ on the cross. The Christian then "sees" his or her sins as afflicting, or wounding, Christ. Christ is the one who then suffers, in a reenactment of the crucifixion, and Christ's suffering is the source of the sinner's salvation. Christ is, as Cotton says elsewhere, the "Fountain." From his wounds issue the blood and water that effect the changes in "us." This reenactment of the crucifixion, in which the believer gives his afflictions to Christ, is essential, Cotton says, to salvation, to the ability to "walke at more liberty." It is faith that is crucial in Cotton's understanding of the role of affliction. If the sinner takes afflictions "as desert for my sin, [then] they are salt and unsavoury; but by faith looke at them, as coming out of Gods hand in his special favour, and then they wil breed you much joy & consolation" (Cotton 1644, 480). Bradstreet's figures for this same process suggest that the very structure of the cosmos includes affliction and that affliction operates as the effective agency in the "curing" of souls. Patterns within nature (ones provided by God, of course) assure us of the succession of both afflictions and deliverances. However, in Bradstreet's work, the natural proceses do not always work the way they should. Thus the numerous reminders to her readers not "to forget to giue [God] thankes" when he "shal deliuer you out of distresse" (M/R, 227). There is nothing in Cotton's description that considers the question Bradstreet does: will God "proportion the load" so as not to crush the "weak"? For Bradstreet the answer to that concern suggests a different kind of reliance on Christ, whose strength to endure is the model and measure for "strong men" who are "in" him.

There is much more to be said about Bradstreet's understanding of the cosmos and of the work of affliction in God's design for the world. Here I would like simply to flag a fundamental difference between Bradstreet and Cotton, one that should not be dismissed as simply a point in theology. It is a point that implies much for the poet's sense of self and for the processes of growth and change with which so much of her work concerned. I have argued elsewhere that Cotton was a strong influence on Bradstreet's poetry in her later years (C/S, 190–204). I now see differences between them that cause me at least to question the assumption that I and others have made of Bradstreet's later reliance on Cotton's preaching. I do not think that we have enough evidence to suggest that Bradstreet was at odds with Cotton during her adolescent years, but certainly in her Massachusetts years their relationship evidenced none of the closeness that Anne Hutchinson's and Cotton's did. We know that Anne Bradstreet experienced conversion at 16 (according to her own report), but we do not know more than that about the circumstances. We can assume that she attended services led by Cotton and was catechized and instructed by him. We also can assume that, as at Sempringham, Cotton would have continued to be a frequent visitor to the Dudley household in Boston, England.

By age 14 Anne Dudley was living through political upheavals that had serious and immediate consequences for her family. In Cotton Mather's words, "the times began to look black and cloudy to the full" (Mather 1702, 2:16). Anne Dudley must have been aware that her father was advising the earl of Lincoln about the prospect of going to war in Europe, this time under James I, on behalf of the Elector Palatine of the Rhine. After consulting with John Preston, Dudley's old friend and the master of Emmanuel College, he advised against the earl's involvement in that unfortunate engagement, which James abandoned and which Anne Bradstreet would later say meant that the "poor Palatinate [was] forever lost" (M/R, 45).

Shortly thereafter (in 1625) James I died and Charles I succeeded him. Anne Dudley at that time must have participated in the strenuous weekly schedule of worship at the Boston church. Cotton had thus far avoided being silenced despite the significant changes he introduced into the structure of the worship service. In 1626 Anne's brother entered Emmanuel College to study under Preston. Theophilus Clinton, the earl of Lincoln, had matriculated at Emmanuel, and Simon Bradstreet had just completed his master's degree there. Cotton had earlier served as an Emmanuel fellow, lecturer, and dean. Thus, although not permitted to go to college, Anne Dudley, who grew up among Emmanuel men, must have received partial replication of an Emmanuel education. Anne Dudley was the oldest child at home in this troubled period.

In the spring of 1627 Lord Lincoln was emprisoned in the Tower of London for disobeying King Charles's order to lend the crown money for further military exploits on the continent. Over that summer Thomas Dudley was accused of harboring a fugitive, a member of the earl of Lincoln's household, and Dudley also risked arrest for failure to lend money to the king. They escaped trial chiefly because they were only two among many noblemen to defy the king's order. Elizabeth Wade White observes that "Anne's formal verse reveals an interest in politics, generally of a controversial kind, that is remarkable for a woman of her time. It is reasonable," White continued, "to conclude that this interest sprang from her consciousness, during the first five years of Charles's reign, of being a member of a dissident and threatened minority" (White, 82–83).

Thus Anne Dudley's marriage to Simon Bradstreet took place against a backdrop of near civil war and planning for their escape from persecution, an escape that was formulated as emigration to New England in 1627 and for which a patent was secured in 1628. Simon Bradstreet, 11 years Anne's senior, was part of that planning and those negotiations and may well have been the bearer of messages since he traveled frequently to London and beyond.

Simon Bradstreet also had come from Lincolnshire. He was born in Horbling, the son of a vicar, and was orphaned at 14. The earl of Lincoln's family took him in, and he was in Dudley's charge until Preston, who became Simon's guardian, suggested that Simon go to Emmanuel in the role of governor to Lord Rich, the son of the earl of Warwick. After Emmanuel, Simon became Dudley's assistant at Sempringham, and when the Dudleys moved to Boston, Simon remained behind to assume many of Thomas Dudley's duties as steward. Soon after that, Simon moved to become steward to the dowager countess of Warwick, and Anne and Simon spent the first two years of marriage in that household.

Although virtually nothing is known about the exact circumstances surrounding the Bradstreet marriage, several general points can be made about marriage itself and about events in the lives of the young people. Anne Dudley was on the young side of the normal range for marriage among women of her class.[27] It is not easy to say what this fact means. The bride and groom had known each other since childhood (Anne was nine when they first met), so although there seems to have been no betrothal, perhaps it had been assumed from a very early age that Simon and Anne would marry. That the time came sooner rather than later may be attributable to the fact that Thomas Dudley was in some jeopardy because of his political and religious positions. He was in his early fifties, which was well beyond life expectancy. (The death rate had risen sharply in the early decades of the seventeenth century, and Dudley may have had concerns about the care, particularly of his daughters, should he die.)

On Simon's side, a life-affecting event occurred in the year of his marriage: John Preston, Simon's guardian, died in the summer of 1628. Whether before or after the Bradstreet's marriage we do not know, but the funeral at Fawsley Church in Northampton was a large occasion for the gathering of Preston's friends. "A world of godly people came together" for it, writes Samuel Clarke,[28] where they heard John Dod preach the eulogy. It is likely that Thomas, Dorothy, and Samuel Dudley and Simon Bradstreet attended, and Anne and her sisters, if Anne had recovered sufficiently from her smallpox. John Dod's role in Preston's funeral suggests his continuing importance to the group of Nonconformists who were making final plans for emigration and suggests Dod's importance in the Dudleys' and Bradstreets' lives. John Cotton (writing from New England) later described Dod as "the chief of our people" (White, 46). Thus, the loss of Preston, the prospect of emigration, and the concern of those at risk especially about the support of daughters might have been factors leading the young couple to marriage in 1628.

For the Puritans marriage was not a sacrament and did not take place in the church. White suggests that the Bradstreet wedding took place in the Dudley's house in Boston and was presided over by John Cotton.

It is also possible, since marriages took place usually at the home of the groom, that the Bradstreets were married in Essex in the house of the countess of Warwick, perhaps by Preston who was a regular visitor there—his health permitting, of course. Although we do not have a record of the event or an account of how the marriage was arranged, we can say some general things about how the Dudleys and Bradstreets, again following Dod, may have approached the decision. First, as important as children are said to be in Dod's *A Godlie Forme of Hovseholde Gouernment,* the relationship of husband and wife is more so. Dod writes, "There can be no greater societie or companie, then is betweene a man and his wife; whose House, whose Goods, whose Chamber, &c. is common, their children are common, and they themselves partakers of all good and euill successe, of prosperitie and adversitie" (Dod 1612, 152). The relationship between wife and husband, in Dod's (and others') view is closer than that between fathers and children. Dod continues, "The child is part of the father, and through a natural pitie, they love each other: but yet the wife is more annexed & joyned to her husband (153).

Because of the significance of the state of being so "joyned" and "annexed," the Puritans felt that a great deal of thought should go into the choosing of a mate. Dod emphasizes that the choice (made by the two families as well as by the individuals) must consider all factors. He advises that they take time for deliberation in order to discover potential problems. The families, not simply the parents, should determine that a "meetnesse for marriage" exists between the two partners. Meetness means, Dod says, that the man and woman are of a similar age, class, and disposition. By the same token, Dod advises his readers to be particularly sensitive to the qualities of the young people's feelings for each other (120–30).

We will never know the precise kind or amount of parental and familial arranging that went into the Bradstreets' marriage, but we can be sure that the Dudleys took part in the arranging, with attention to the mutual affections of Simon and Anne. Surely Thomas Dudley would have approved of Simon Bradstreet's nonconforming views, especially as these had been nurtured and refined at Emmanuel College. As Cotton Mather described Dudley, he walked a narrow line between "[hating] fanatics and wild opinionists" and strenuously "[oppugning] conformity & the ceremonies of the Church of England" (Adlard, 8). Simon Bradstreet must have seemed to Dudley one who walked such a line. Simon was, furthermore, almost like a son to the Dudleys; certainly he had served as Thomas's apprentice for enough years to have created strong ties between the two men. Both men were orphans, and that may have made a bond between them.

It is important, I think, not to read into the scant words we have about the Bradstreet's early relationship the existence of a modern romantic attachment that perhaps did not exist. Elizabeth Wade White interprets Anne Bradstreet's description of her heart as "more carnall" (at the time prior to smallpox and conversion) as a reference to "Anne's awakening consciousness of [Simon's] image [that] was beginning to take a place that increased in importance as their separation widened" (77). Similarly White suggests that Simon may have realized "all at once that during their separation Anne had grown from childhood to young womanhood, that she was threatened by death, and that he loved her and wished her for his wife" (90). We do not know what Bradstreet was referring to when she said that at about age 14 or 15 her heart was "more carnall," and she sat "loose" from God and that the "vanity" and "folly" of "youth" took "hold" of her, but it is clear that she meant to describe her actions at that time as diversionary, as a veering away from the eventual path she took and God intended her to take. Her marriage follows a "change" in her "Condition"; the passage conveys the sense of the expression "I finally came to my senses," changed my condition, was married, and came into this country. It is possible that at 14 or 15 she was resisting the idea of marrying or resisting the idea of Simon or both.

I wish to open up the interpretation of these lines from Bradstreet's autobiographical letter to more careful scrutiny, not because I think we should doubt the feelings of Anne for Simon but precisely because the poems written to and about marriage at a later point in Bradstreet's life are so expressive of a complex and extraordinarily strong love between wife and husband. It is possible that that love developed in marriage, following the birth of children and following Anne's slow, and one suspects from the later poems, painful process of separation from Thomas Dudley in the latter years of their lives in New England. There is, as I describe in the next chapter, a gradually widening rift between Simon Bradstreet and Thomas Dudley, in part an aftereffect of the Antinomian controversy. There is evidence that the Bradstreets' and the Dudleys' separation was not only physical (by 1640 the Dudleys and the Bradstreets no longer were neighbors), but political, psychological, and to some extent religious as well.

A Reading of Selected Poems

In this section my focus shifts from Anne Bradstreet's life to her poetry, particularly to a group of poems in which she presents her material in the persona of the child. By child Bradstreet does not necessarily mean little girl. To this role belong those speakers who have not yet come into their powers, who are still apprenticing, who are still in a state of attachment and indebtedness to masters, mothers, teachers, fathers. Included in this group are the daughter of the tribute, "To her Father with some Verses," and the schoolchild speaker of the dedication and "The Prologue" to the quaternions. Here too we find the "faltering," undeveloped poet of Bradstreet's elegy to Queen Elizabeth, and the daughter speaker in "A Dialogue between Old England and New." Finally, the long poem "The Foure Monarchies" (a poem that has not received much critical attention) is narrated in a copybook voice that abruptly changes when the "doubt"-filled apologist takes over what the novice historian did not finish.

In all of these cases, the speakers present themselves as not yet fully developed, and there is, in each case, an implied or stated standard of maturity or fulfillment that is not yet reached but nevertheless seems to be part of the child's destiny. The worlds that these novices inhabit is a world in transition, a world where one thing is in the process of becoming another. Indeed transmutation and transition are frequently the subjects of the poems that the child speaker takes on. The poet's sense that she is in the midst of cosmic change is a constant theme.

We find this theme initially stated in the dedication of the first poem of *The Tenth Muse,* which opens with these words: "From her, that to your selfe more duty owes, / Then waters, in the boundlesse Ocean flowes" (M/R, 6). A typically cryptic and typically complex Bradstreet statement: the "duty" owed by daughter to father appears to be greater than the ocean. In her phrasing of this "debt," however, the daughter suggests that the debt is lost in the "boundless" body of water to which it belongs. After all, how does one separate waters from an ocean? This debt is more like a great source that the father and daughter share than it is like a specific sum to be paid or duty to be performed.

Similarly, the enormity of the child's debt is the theme of the poem, "To her Father with some Verses," a poem included in the second volume, *Several Poems,* posthumously published in 1678. Here is the poem in its entirety:

To her Father with some verses

Most truly honoured, and as truly dear,
If worth in me, or ought I do appear,
Who can of right better demand the same?
Then may your worthy self from whom it came.
The principle might yield a greater sum,
Yet handled ill, amounts but to this crum;
My stocks so small, I know not how to pay,
My Bond remains in force unto this day;
Yet for part payment take this little mite,
Where nothings to be had Kings loose their right
Such is my debt, I may not say forgive,
But as I can, I'le pay it while I live:
Such is my bond, none can discharge but I,
Yet paying is not payd until I dye. (M/R, 183–84)

In this poem the "principle" that the daughter handles was originally invested by the father, yet he is not necessarily the source of this sum of money. He too may have inherited it. He is a "self," endowed somehow with "worth" that he then has passed on. The "bond" (repeated) "remains in force" and is unique: "none can discharge it" but the child. This covenant is not between a father God and a human believer or between a master and a servant. The remarkable thing about this business transaction is that it appears to be between two financiers, both entrusted with an endowment that can be given or sold by one to the other and that they both want to see grow. Only from the title do we know that their relationship is daughter and father, but we do hear that the speaker feels that she has not gotten the large returns on her investment that she should have. Her poems are a "little mite," a "crum." The "small" size of the yield does not, however, affect the basic contract between them, the "paying [of which] is not payd until I dye."

There appears to be something planted in the poet like the "seeds" she said were planted in childhood, on which she draws for her poetry. The metaphor of financial indebtedness is curiously handled, I think, particularly so given the fact that women (except widows) did not have control over their financial or legal lives and that the poet here emphasizes that no one but the daughter can discharge this debt. It would seem that this would be an opportunity to point out the role of women in financial matters or to apologize for assuming that she, being a woman, could handle money or to go beyond the metaphor and address the issue of women's roles as writers. There is nothing of the sort in this poem. Nor is the relationship between the donor and the debtor other-worldly. She is not thinking of a debt to be paid in heaven or in the world to come. She is speaking of paying (that is, of writing) *until* she dies, not afterward.

Because so many have taken Bradstreet's apologies as the strategy of a poet who, because she was a woman, felt unsure about her claim to the role of writer, I wish to begin this consideration of the child persona by pointing out that although apparently convinced of the smallness of her "stock," she is certain of the rightness of her role as manager of the endowment. She is not particularly subordinate; she is next in a line of succession. In fact she is charged with protecting something that if reduced to "nothing" reduces (indeed it can destroy) the right of kings.

There is a seriousness and a directness to this statement that is echoed in Bradstreet's letter to her children, where in the persona of mother she dismisses the usual literary claims for poetry and writes that she hopes that from the work her children will "gain some spirit" and will "Advantage by my exper^c." (M/R, 215). The metaphor of children's "gaining" or increasing from the bequest of a parent is basic to this letter too, where it is the poet who has the principle that she hopes her children will invest and profit from. Her purpose, as we have seen, is "to declare ye Truth, not to sett forth my self, but ye Glory of God." She makes these statements as a woman in old age. No apology accompanies this bold claim that her words will convey the "Truth" (the word as used here can mean Christ). She further amplifies this claim, directly identifying the feminine as the means to power: "As I have brovght yov into ye world, and wth great paines, weaknes, cares + feares brovght yov to this, I now travail in birth again of yov till Christ be formed in yov" (M/R, 216). Here Bradstreet is speaking the words of Paul in Galatians 4:19 as if they were her own words: an important example of her use of "ventriloquism." In this triumphant moment, the speaker revels in her parturient powers, here presented as both physical and spiritual. In this letter, the mother does not wrest power from the biblical speaker; she puts on his power. Here, in effect, Paul's verbal investment is the one she is trying to make yield a "greater sum." Her artistic powers, here and in the tribute to her father, do not come from her originality, her individuality. Her claims to expressive power are rooted in her inheritance, here in the voice of scripture. Her words derive seamlessly (in effect, she plagiarizes them) from Paul's, as if the same blood ran in her veins as in his (to borrow a metaphor from her Sidney elegy). In Bradstreet's universe, the child speaking the tribute to her father and the mother here endowing her children with the power of rebirth are playing their parts in a continuum. The continuum relates members of the literal family as well as members of the spiritual family. Bradstreet here shows herself to be interested in power, particularly in the power of her poetry to speak the Word that has been entrusted to her.

For Bradstreet, both men and women constitute this continuum, but as Wendy Martin has pointed out, in the elegy to Queen Elizabeth, in "A Dialogue between Old England and New," and in the first two quaternions, Bradstreet nevertheless articulates a particularly "gynocratic vision."[29] Bradstreet's speaker in the elegy is a woman who identifies with a feminist view of the wrongs done to women. She writes,

> Nay Masculines, you have thus tax'd us long,
> But she though dead, will vindicate our wrong.
> Let such, as say our sex is void of reason,
> Know 'tis a slander now, but once was treason. (M/R, 157)

This speaker, unlike the endowed daughter, adopts a self-deprecating manner. She is a faithful but unaccomplished follower. Hers is the "tribute of a loyall Braine"; her verse is called "bleating," the cry of sheep, and she places her "acclamations among those of the "poore." The fact that Queen Elizabeth did not "disdain" the poor makes the poet feel that her own "rudeness is no wrong." Some of this is, of course, the conventional apology of the elegist, but Bradstreet's speaker is one who "doth but aspire, / To read what others write, and then admire" (M/R, 157). Like women and children at church, she disclaims the role of speaker. She is content to be an amanuensis and to let the "living vertues" of this "unparralell'd Prince," Elizabeth, speak. The poetic speaker, in being characterized as a sheep of the queenly shepherd, as poor, bears the faint outline of the traditional faithful Christian, with Elizabeth as her deity—indeed, as Bradstreet puts it, as God made flesh, "a fleshly Deity" (M/R, 155).

Neither Bradstreet's feminism nor her "revolution" means what it does today. In this elegy, Bradstreet anticipates a "revolution," but not the kind we generally have in mind when we use that term. She foresees a worldwide natural and societal change but one that depends on the reemergence of "old form":

> Then wonder not, *Eliza* moves not here.
> Full fraught with honour, riches, and with dayes:
> She set, she set, like *Titan* in his rayes,
> No more shall rise or set such glorious Sun,
> Untill the heavens great revolution:
> If then new things, their old form must retain,
> *Eliza* shall rule *Albian* once again. (M/R, 157–58)

Elizabeth is here remembered as "the pride of Queens," and she still lives as the "pattern of Kings." She belongs to a palimpsest of queens (from Semiramis to Zenobia) who have reigned in various places and at various times throughout history. Eliza, Bradstreet says, is the original, and like the phoenix she has the power to surface repeatedly throughout history, not only in outstanding women leaders but as the form to which kings should be molded. Eliza periodically sets, like the sun, and then (when the heavens go through the "great revolution"), she, Bradstreet predicts, will reappear. She is figured here as the sun, not the moon, as though some transformation has taken place in which the time-honored equivalence of women to the moon, the lesser deity, has been permanently altered. The quality the queen possesses is said to be wisdom, the quality Bradstreet calls essential to any monarch. Bradstreet writes, "She hath wip'd off th' aspersion of her Sex, / That women wisdome lack to play the Rex" (M/R, 156).

It is in her ascribing of wisdom to Eliza that we see not only the shape of Bradstreet's political statement, but the full Christ-likeness of this portrait. In the larger commonwealth as well as in the "little commonwealth" of the family, the "reform," to use John Dod's word, will come by means of wisdom. What Dod calls "good government" is not, he writes, "a thing men can stumble on by chance, but *Wisedom* must lead us unto it (Dod 1612, 13). Wisdom is the quality that Solomon had in such abundance and that is expressed in what the Puritans thought of as the Solomonic books of the bible. Dod writes that "through wisdom (saith Solomon) is an house builded, and with understanding it is established: and by knowledge shall the Chambers thereof be filled with all precious pleasant riches." Dod explains that he does not mean "natural wisedom" but what is "fetched from the fountaine of all wisedom, God himself: who by his Word giueth unto us pure light to walke by, not in the Church alone, nor in publicke societie of men onely, but even within the secret of our owne walls" (14). Wisdom is Solomon's in the Old Testament and Christ's in the new.

Paul refers to Christ as "the Wisdom of God" in 1 Corinthians 24, "in whom are all the treasures of wisdom and knowledge hidden" (1 Col. 2:37).

Christ as Wisdom is Christ in his earthly, immanent presence. Wisdom traditionally affects everyday life. "Wisdom," Dod writes, "is that by which we observe comelinesse in euery action; that is to say, by which wee obserue what wee doe, how, in what place, at what time, before whome: that all things may be done in a convenient place, time and manner" (53). It is the wisdom of Eliza that enables her to teach the "Hoast" of the Armada "better manners to their cost." Apocryphal wisdom appears as guide, protector, providential pathfinder to the tribe of Israel in the wilderness, as the Elizabeth of Bradstreet's portrait does for her English subjects. The queen is termed "our *Pallas* Queen," a reference to Athena, the Greek equivalent of Wisdom. Indeed, wisdom in the Old Testament is often hypostasized as female. Her appearance is rather mysterious: she comes and goes, in the manner Bradstreet attributes to Queen Elizabeth as the Christlike Phoenix of this portrait.

The pattern of the ideal monarch here, thus, depends throughout on scripture and on a well-worn biblical-literary Renaissance tradition that figures Queen Elizabeth as a woman who is both a mighty warrior-amazon and a deity. In Bradstreet's palimpsest the presence of Wisdom-Athena undergirds the portrait and serves to frame the elegy. Gender, in the divine and female presence of Wisdom, is used here to convey the unique kinds of power that Elizabeth is said to have exerted, the power of self-re-creation and of reoccurrence. It is not too much to suggest that in the prospect of Eliza's return lies the implicit promise that this poor, loyal, simple speaker will be restored to wholeness and power.

Bradstreet's method in the Elizabeth elegy is similar in major ways to that of H.D., the modern American poet, whose creation of a gendered universe similarly depends on the life-giving recurrence throughout history of "Athene," in ongoing cycles of what H.D., too, called "revolution."[30] In H.D.'s epic poem, *Trilogy,* it is the power (in Bradstreet's words) of "new things" to "retain" "old form" that revitalizes the universe. There, too, "*living vertues speak (though dead long since)*" (M/R, 158). Neither H.D. nor Bradstreet is content with a generalized, abstract notion of just power relations. Both poets attempt to recreate a female figure who represents, throughout time, just and righteous uses of power. And they both go a step further, asserting that a dead feminine presence still "speaks." The voice of a grandmother speaks through the poet-child in H.D.'s *The Gift* just as ancestral voices speak too through

Bradstreet's personae. One of biblical Wisdom's likenesses is that of the smith or potter or artist who continues to make and remake and unmake the creation. For H.D. and for Bradstreet the feminine aspect of divinity (at work in society and in nature) is just such a patterning, forming, and reforming presence whose work of transmutation will eventually bring about what both poets call a "new day."

In this elegy and in "A Dialogue between Old England and New," Bradstreet anticipates what Ivy Schweitzer has called "a glorious gynocentrism," one that, in Schweitzer's words, is "indefinitely deferred."[31] In Bradstreet's dialogue, the principal speaker is the "daughter" New England, and the implied theme of the poem is the necessity and power of the continuum between mother (England) and daughter (New England). The identification of the poetic speaker with "poverty" suggests a likeness to the speaker of the Elizabeth elegy. Dated 1642, a year earlier than the elegy, the daughter-child identifies herself in the following lines:

> Your humble Childe intreats you, shew your grief,
> Though Armes, nor Purse she hath, for your releif;
> Such is her poverty, yet shall be found
> A supplyant for your help, as she is bound. (M/R, 142)

In this allegory it is the mother rather than the child who is filled with "woes"; she says her "tatter'd state" is the wonder of all Christendome"; she is furthermore ill with some malady beyond the ability of ordinary "medicine" to cure. The relationship of mother to daughter is initially presented as extremely close—*symbiotic* might describe it. The mother says,

> And thou a childe, a Limbe, and dost not feele
> My weakened fainting body now to reele?
> This Phisick-purging-potion I have taken.
> Will bring Consumption, or an Ague quaking.
> Unlesse some Cordial thou fetch from high,
> Which present help may ease this malady.
> If I decease, dost think thou shalt survive?
> Or by my wasting state, dost think to thrive? (M/R, 141)

As her mother's diagnostician, the daughter-doctor "guesses" that the mother's woes come from internal and external political and military attacks to the body commonwealth, but Old England explains that as damaging as these have been, it is rather "Sins, the breach of sacred Lawes" that are the true causes of her ill health. Old England reviews the terrible recent era of persecutions, particularly of the Nonconformists ("Some lost their livings, some in prison pent, / Some grossely fin'd, from friends to exile went") (M/R, 144). What she calls the "bottom dregs" of the whole history of corruption and abuse she fears "reserved are for me." In response to her daughter's request of her to speak "in plain termes" about the exact nature of her "present grief," Old England cries out that "I that no warres, so many yeares have known, / Am now destroy'd, and slaughtered by mine own." The Civil War in England is the cause of the mother's grief, particularly because she knows that war cannot decide "this cause." In the mother's voice Bradstreet writes concisely and powerfully of the effects of war, which here center on the tearing of the fabric of everyday life:

> My plundered Townes, my houses devastation,
> My ravisht virgins, and my young men slain,
> My wealthy trading faln, my dearth of grain,
> The seed time's come, but Ploughman hath no hope,
> Because he knows not, who shall inn his crop:
> The poore they want their pay, their children bread,
> Their woefull mother's tears unpitied. (M/R, 146)

The potion that the mother earlier thought would be "fetch[ed] from high" is here said to come from within the daughter's heart:

> If any pity in thy heart remain,
> Or any child-like love thou dost retain,
> For my relief now use thy utmost skill,
> And recompence me good, for all my ill. (M/R, 146)

Daughter New England has not only the curing power (or a remnant of it), she also has the last word. She does not accept the mother's sense of the process of cure as "recompence"; she rejects the idea that her skill (even an "utmost" skill) could bring Old England "relief." She speaks out of what her mother calls "child-like love," but it is the perspective she brings to the situation that proves curative. She explains that Old England is in the throes of a necessary and painful transition. These afflictions, the daughter says, precede a better time to come—in effect,

a millennial day. She counsels her mother to "cheer up" and cast her
eyes on the future:

> Shake off your dust, cheer up, and now arise.
> You are my mother, nurse, I once your flesh,
> Your sunken bowels gladly would refresh:
> Your griefs I pity much, but should do wrong,
> To weep for that we both have pray'd for long,
> To see these latter dayes of hop'd for good,
> That Right may have its right, though't be with blood; (M/R, 146)

New England then lapses into a passage of visionary, martial rhetoric
of the kind familiar during the American Revolution, when such were
used *against* old England. Here the rhetoric is aimed at "dark Popery"
and the "Churches foes." The promise, as in the book of Revelation
and in Bradstreet's Elizabethan elegy is that "now the Sun in's bright-
nesse shall appear." New England celebrates all parts of English life
and castigates her enemies. Bradstreet pulls no punches as she has
New England advocate execution "toth' full the vengeance threatened." Toward the Antichrist she has no childlike or tender "wom-
anly" feelings:

> Bring forth the beast that rul'd the world with's beck,
> And tear his flesh, and set your feet on's neck,
> And make his filthy den so desolate,
> To th'stonishment of all that knew his state. (M/R, 148)

This warrior-daughter New England seems to have emerged somehow
from the "humble Childe," the "supplyant" for her mother's help of the
earlier part of the poem. The tone, the posture, the elements of the
verse lines—here percussive, emphatic—sound like the Psalmist's exhortation to God to inveigh against Israel's foes. Bradstreet's speaker
here cries out with the sanctioned brutality of the Psalmist when he
calls down God's wrath on the enemy.

Bradstreet concludes this dialogue with New England's apostrophe,
not only to Old England but to all English descendants of Abraham.
Her tone sounds like that of magisterial, if not ministerial, New England. Both this dialogue and the elegy to Elizabeth conclude with
predictions (laced with images of the resurrection); a "time" is approaching when the millennial sun will shine:

> Oh Abrahams seed lift up your heads on high.
> For sure the day of your redemption's nigh;
> The scales shall fall from your long blinded eyes,
> And him you shall adore, who now despise,
> Then fulness of the Nations in shall flow.
> And Jew and Gentile, to one worship go,
> Then follows dayes of happiness and rest,
> Whose lot doth fall to live therein is blest:
> No Canaanite shall then be found ith' land,
> And holinesse, on horses bells shall stand.
> If this make way thereto, then sigh no more,
> But if at all, thou didst not see't before.
> Farewell dear mother, Parliament, prevail,
> And in a while you'l tell another tale. (M/R, 148)

Mother here is said to have the capacity to change: in time her story of affliction will shift. She will "tell another tale." Somehow the daughter's message to look up, look beyond, has served as the *medicine* that the mother needs. It seems not to come from above but from within the conversing daughter. The daughter's ability to "simpathize" (M/R, 141) with her mother's condition and her ability to stay mindful of her mother's state (M/R, 147) seem to be important. In the end, however, even though she once shared her mother's body and as much as she now pities her woes, she pulls away from empathy and makes clear that what both of them have long prayed for is now happening, however painful that happening may be. All along the two women have shared in the anticipation of the resurrection, hard as that is for the mother to realize. There is a kind of solidarity being etched here between women of the kind we saw at work in the Elizabeth poem. There the return of Elizabeth is associated with the vindication of the female sex: "Let such, as say our sex is void of reason, / Know 'tis a slander now, but once was treason." This observation directly precedes the exclamation "O happy, happy, had those dayes still been, / But happiness, lies in a higher sphere" (M/R, 157). In effect, Eliza has not died; she has retired for the present, but she will return. Presumably when she does, such calumnies about women's powers will again no longer be allowed.

In both poems the roles Bradstreet assigns to the poet and the ways she treats women's lives suggest that *at present* all is not well, but these poems also suggest that at Christ's Second Coming (at a time that is future) women's lives will be restored to health and wholeness. The millennial vision in these early poems is one of equity and power for women, not (explicitly, at least) a vision of marriage to Christ. Other points are being made about women's lives. Here women do have sources from which to draw to imagine a full life for themselves and for their society. For Bradstreet the example of Queen Elizabeth is one such source, but with her and behind her example Bradstreet places the figure of biblical wisdom, who when restored to the world will guide the nations to righteous and just governments. Further, Bradstreet throughout both poems seems to be distinguishing the "Masculines" of the elegy who have "taxed" women for "so long," from the biblical patriarchs, like Solomon, who were spokesmen of the Holy Spirit. Similarly, Bradstreet seems to be distinguishing between the claims made on the basis of the natural bond between mother and daughter, and those made on the basis of their shared faith in the dream of the millennium. The fact that Bradstreet casts her poem in the form of a dialogue suggests that their natural bond is somehow necessary, per- haps as a precondition for their spiritual one. The daughter who finally emerges with the solution to the mother's problems had first to ask questions. She seems not to have known how the conversation would turn out. She did not have the answers in advance, any more than her mother did. The daughter's answers, in effect, put matters into perspec- tive; they come as the result of a process, and they suggest that if the mother continues to "sigh," she should "sigh" over the fact that she did not see the way providence works—that is, that her present afflictions are a prelude to "dayes of happiness and rest."

In the quaternions another kind of perfection is sketched out. Brad- street there aims to demonstrate "how divers natures, make one unity" (M/R, 6). She seems sometimes to be referring to an eventual, future unity, as she does in "The Foure Ages," but in the first three poems an essential, though hidden or unrealized, unity already exists, particu- larly in natural and earthly things. As she explains in her dedication, the elements and the humours make up everything that is here and now:

> These same are they, of whom we being have,
> These are of all, the life, the nurse, the grave,
> These are, the hot, the cold, the moist, the dry,
> That sinke, that swim, that fill, that upwards flye,
> Of these consists, our bodyes, cloathes, and food,
> The world, the usefull, hurtfull, and the good: (M/R, 5)

The quaternions map the true four-part character of what we might call the natural world and the world of human everyday experience. In the first four quaternions the principal subjects speak their own parts; in the last, "The Foure Monarchies," the narrator is a historian who is inexperienced and loses confidence. The first four quaternions (the poems themselves), Bradstreet tells us, are the direct descendants of Thomas Dudley's poem on the four parts of the world, a poem that has been lost. The "four times foure" are "bounden handmaids," and like Dudley's four "Dames" and "sister" of the lost poem all are female figures. They are said to bear us, nurse us, and be with us in the grave. Their sweet harmony is like that of the heavenly spheres, except that they are earthly and can therefore lapse into discord, anger, fault-finding. To know them is to understand the hidden patterns that shape the mysteries of the human sciences, physiology and psychology, and the other natural sciences and of history. Bradstreet's use of these figures is highly traditional and derives from a knowledge of the occult sciences, principally alchemy.

Alchemy was a respected part of the traditions from which Bradstreet drew, especially in the quaternions but in other poems too. Because it is easy as modern readers to trivialize the role and importance of alchemy, perhaps we should review a few central points about the practice of alchemy in the Middle Ages and the Renaissance in order to understand the design of Bradstreet's quaternions. Galmini Salgado writes about the four elements in a way that helps us to picture the kind of "unity" that Bradstreet said "divers natures make":

The four elements earth, air, water and fire, of which all substances were supposed to be constituted, were . . . to be found in their perfect proportions in gold, which was, therefore, eternal and indestructible ("whatever dies was not mixt equally" wrote John Donne). Thus the true alchemical inquirer was not led on by a sordid desire for wealth but by an urge to bring metals to their highest state, part of the greater urge to clothe the creation in the habit of perfection—as the search for the elixir of life, the other great alchemical quest was promoted by the desire to banish the body's imperfections and bring it to a condition of perfect harmony.[32]

Alchemists referred to the process of bringing things to perfection or harmony as "affliction." Christian alchemists saw the life of Christ as characterized by just such affliction; he, after having undergone God's grinding of him, achieved restoration to oneness with God. One medi-

eval treatise explains the process this way: " 'As our chemical com-
pound . . . is subjected to the action of fire, and is decomposed,
dissolved and well digested, and as this process, before its consummation, exhibits various chromatic changes, so this Divine Man, and
Human God, Jesus Christ, had, by the will of His heavenly Father, to
pass through the furnace of affliction . . . in the course of which His
outward aspect was grievously changed' " (Shumaker, 188).

"The equating of transmutation to redemption" (189) appears in the
same text, and thus, in addition, Christ becomes the Stone, the means,
as he will in Bradstreet's adaptation of the prophet Daniel in "The
Foure Monarchies" and in her reference in "Contemplations" to "the
White Stone" (M/R, 174).

Bradstreet's uses of alchemy suggest a deep interest in the processes
of transmutation, which she, too, following Du Bartas and other Christian alchemists, attributed to Christ—to Christ's presence and power
in the creation (where He takes the form of Wisdom). In Bradstreet's
dialogue and her portrait of the "Foure Monarchies," she depicts the
last days as days of devastation and cosmic upheaval, or to use the
alchemist's term, affliction. Thus history, too, undergoes a process of
distillation, a dissolution, and emerges (as the prophets all tell us) into
a period that will be a "consummation." The Judeo-Christian union of
God with His people is mirrored in the alchemists' vision of the eventual cosmic marriage of mercury and sulphur.

In Bradstreet's work the broadest possible applications of alchemy
are made. There alchemy is not seen as a set of sorceries or magic tricks.
It follows, rather, the original understanding of alchemy as a natural
science and philosophy.

The original alchemists did not think of themselves as magicians, but almost
as scientists, attempting to achieve certain results by exploiting what they
believed to be laws of nature. All *matter,* they believed, was one, and it was
form that gave it variety; not only were metals, animals, and vegetables forms
of the primitive elements of earth, air, fire and water, but these latter were
themselves the basic forms of inchoate matter. Since we see all about us the
forms of matter changing (seed into plant, egg into bird, wood into ash, and
so on) there was nothing inherently impossible or absurd in the notion that any
form or matter could be changed into any other. These changes were thought
of as part of the general pattern of life and growth, as the whole universe was a
living process. Thus when a substance changed its form and took another (as
when a heated metal changed its appearance and texture and lost its solidity)
the process was conceived of in terms of death and resurrection, and the union

of different substances as a marriage. These were not mere metaphors, or colourful descriptions of processes that could be more accurately defined in other terms. They correspond exactly to the categories of medieval and Elizabethan thought. Thus the process of transmutation and multiplication was a life-creating process, the "generation" of new forms through the "corruption" of the old. (Salgado, 110)

Alchemical processes constitute the essential subject matter of the quaternions, and alchemy—as "transmutation and multiplication," as characterizing all "life-creating" processes—can be found at the heart of every aspect of these ambitious works, not least of all in the identities of their speakers. Even the dedication of the poems, which precedes their "Prologue," shows us the persona of the child as alive with potential change. In the dedication she presents herself as honoring Du Bartas but also as one who "dare[s] not wear his wealth." That expression, "wearing another's wealth," is a way of signaling to us to look for borrowings from other writers. It connotes, too, "dress-up," or dissembling, as actors do and as children do, who are rehearsing to be grown-us. Bradstreet dedicates these poems to her father, but here her indebtedness takes an interestingly devious expression. How complex, how cryptic the statement of dedication is, in comparison with the poem to the poet's father we reviewed earlier. Indeed it smacks of the metaphysical quirkiness, the puns, the "painful ingenuities"[33] of which Moses Tyler complained in his discussion of Bradstreet's work. Just as our ears are beginning to pick up a doubleness in the poetic statement, the poet assures us of her innocence:

> My goods are true (though poor) I love no stealth,
> But if I did, I durst not send them you;
> Who must reward a theife, but with his due.
> I shall not need my innocence to clear,
> These ragged lines, will do't, when they appear. (M/R, 6)

The poet, again "poor," does not (for some reason) fear the judgment of her father. He will *try* her verses. If they prove to be stolen goods, he will apparently punish her accordingly, but she is sure that when judgment comes her "lines" will "clear" her "innocence"—these lines "when they appear," that is. Here is a little last judgment scene, with her father dealing out the rewards. She respects his ability to see through appearances. In fact, anything that was not "true," she would not dare to bring before him. She asks that he shed "his mild aspect" on her work and then "accept my best, my worst vouchsafe a grave." Her father (who is given a god-like presence here) will try (in the sense of process, melt, refine) her verse, and in that process the kernel will separate from the husk. That generative process will prove and save her work.

A process that looked like death is life. That kind of doubleness is ascribed to the poet and her poetry. Each of the key signifiers here (goods, true, poor, thief, innocence) and the actions of rewarding, clearing, and appearing belong to Christ in the Bible, where to be poor is to be chosen, to be blessed. It is the rich in Revelation who are actually poor. The figure of the thief has a similarly two-faced use in scripture; after maligning thieves throughout both Testaments, the Bible writers promise that Christ will come "on thee as a thief" (Rev. 3:3), meaning as a surprise. Similarly all things will be clear and whole in the last days. At that time all things that were partial or broken will be done away. When Christ appears, all things will appear as they really are. The sense of the well-known lines from 1 Corinthians 13 is echoed in this Bradstreet dedication: "When I was a child, I spoke as a child, I reasoned like a child; when I became a man I gave up childish ways. For now we see in a mirror dimly, but then face to face. Now I know in part; then I shall understand fully, even as I have been fully understood." So, to speak as a child or as an imperfect or apprentice poet is, in one reading, to be blessed or if not presently blessed to await blessedness. These lines will undergo a process that will clarify them. Stealing other people's words is a crime (then, as now) but is seen here as a stage that the poet's work presently reflects but will finally pass through and beyond. Perfection and vitality are future states in this dedication, as they were in the dialogue and the elegy, but this future is already visible in the child-novice-thief-imitator. She needs only to be tried, proved, tested in order for the promised transmutation to occur.

Thus the reader approaches the well-known "Prologue" anticipating a doubleness in the verbal manner of its speaker.[34] In the "Prologue" the poet sets herself forth again as lesser. Hers is a "mean pen," not capable of singing of "superior things" like "Wars, Captaines, Kings," "Cities founded, Common-wealths begun." In this poem the poet is situated not in heaven with other poets (where the "high flown quils . . . soare the skies") but on earth where imperfection mars her poetic efforts. Although she is willing to consign history to other poets, she is nevertheless grudging and envious when she considers Du

Bartas's work. As the Du Bartas elegy makes clear, the poet wishes for his kind of art. Du Bartas's verses shine like the sun and have the life-enhancing effects of spring sunshine. The speaker of Bradstreet's "Pro-logue" says she must settle for being a *lesser* power: "A *Bartas* can, doe what a *Bartas* wil, / But simple I, according to my skill" (M/R, 6). Here her speaker consigns herself to a level of mere skill. *Simple* means, of course, without guile; the line reinforces the point made in the dedication: "My goods are true (though poor) I love no stealth."

The poet, apparently, is not only poor, simple, artless, and obscure, but she is likened to a schoolboy. She is not yet adult, not yet fully developed.

> From School-boyes tongue, no Rhethorick we expect,
> Nor yet a sweet Consort, from broken strings,
> Nor perfect beauty, where's a maine defect,
> My foolish, broken, blemish'd Muse so sings:
> And this to mend, alas, no Art is able,
> 'Cause Nature made it so irreparable. (M/R, 6–7)

In this prologue it is not "Art" but "Nature" that causes the speaker's deficiencies and makes her condition resistant to cure. She is at that life stage, the schoolboy stage, where, as she says, one would expect to see the preparatory work of the novice[35] and not the great flourishes of a fully formed stylist. It would appear that nothing more should be expected of her half-grown "foolish, broken, blemish'd Muse," yet implied throughout is the idea of a staged growth and natural process—in short, mutability.

When the speaker turns to the rancorous, broken, blemished relation between the sexes, a similar doubleness characterizes her message. Her natural and artistic powers are deficient, and on top of that, she was created a woman. Her relations with the world, because she is a woman, are damaged seemingly beyond repair. She is caught in a double bind: "If what I doe prove well, it wo'nt advance, / They'll say its stolne, or else, it was by chance." The discord here between the sexes mirrors the discord among the elements, humours, and stages, which is a main theme of the quaternions. In her dedication Bradstreet prepared us for this theme: "Sweet harmony they keep, yet jar oft times, / Their discord may appear, by these harsh rimes" (M/R, 5). Thus the "harsh," elsewhere "ragged," "unrefined" qualities that Bradstreet attributes to her verse are further evidence of the contentiousness in the present nature of things—and of the underlying certainty that contentiousness and imperfection will change.

Her contemporaries who "cast" "despight" on "female wits" appear to be of a harsher temperament than the "more milde" "antick *Greeks*" who "feigned" the nine muses out of, or based on, "our Sex." The Greeks' mistake seems to have been that they placed the "divine" arts among the muses, a link or "knot" that Bradstreet predicts will not hold. In the line, "The *Greeks* did nought, but play the foole and lye," the poet appears to dismiss an entire civilization, perhaps masking her positions so that they not be understood as Greek, Platonic, or worse, Neoplatonic.

By stanza 7 the speaker appears to come to some resolution (though by what means is not clear) of the conflicts between women and men and between Greeks and her contemporaries. There she simply declares for the status quo: "Let *Greeks* be *Greeks,* and Women what they are, / Men have precedency, and still excell." She gives up on this "unjust" warfare: "Men can doe best, and Women know it well." Similarly, in "The Foure Elements" the question who should go first was decided by acquiescence. After a cataclysmic argument that "looked like Chaos, or new birth," the elements stopped contending and decided "That Fire should first begin, . . . / Being the most impatient Element." In "The Prologue" who should go first is put as the issue between the sexes and one that the speaker of the prologue is willing to concede without a struggle. "Preheminence," or rank, belongs to men, and the bargain appears to be a weak one on women's side: the speaker asks merely that men "Yet grant some small acknowledgement of ours."

The closing apostrophe is addressed to the great poets, prophets, and rhetoricians (the "high flown quils, that soare the skies") and suggests that here again the speaker is content to occupy the role of lesser stature; she asks only that the great (male) poets merely "deign these lowly lines." The poet asks for the homely herb parsley instead of the traditional laurel of the Greek athlete or poet, and she returns to the theme of her lesser art, which will nevertheless affect (if only by contrast) the great poet's value or reputation: "This meane and unrefined stuffe of mine, / Will make your glistering gold but more to shine" (M/R, 8).

Having given what I hope is a reasonable paraphrase of "The Prologue," let me now proceed to argue that the poem (in the way that the dedication did) may not mean what it says or rather that there may be more than one way to read this speaker's words. It has often been argued that Bradstreet's use of subservient postures constituted a self-protecting strategy, a means of getting past or around those who thought her "hand a needle better fits" than a "Poets Pen." But timid subterfuge has not been Bradstreet's stance elsewhere, and as Jane Eberwein argues (C/S, 220), fear of reprisals by her readers seems an unlikely state of mind for a poet who was so extravagantly praised by the important friends who wrote dedicatory verses for *The Tenth Muse.* These men seem to exaggerate her powers in the opposite direction, overstating rather than understating them. To such readers, Bradstreet's professed schoolboy ineptitude may have seemed affectation, if not parody.

One of the curious features of Bradstreet's self-presentation in "The Prologue" is her use of declarative present-tense sentences when she speaks of her inadequacies. The subjects of war and politics "*are* too superiour things for her 'mean Pen.' " "I *doe grudge*" is the form of her complaint when she says she envies Du Bartas. Similarly she writes, "I *am* obnoxious to each carping tongue," and "Women *know* it well" (that "Men *can do* best") and "I *ask* no Bayes." (All these italics are mine.) Read against the background of the rest of the poem, which is elaborately tensed, past, future, and subjective, these sentences appear to lay stress on the fact that these conditions prevail at the present time. The line that marks the poem's turning point—"Let Greeks be Greeks, and Women what they are"—not only appears to ordain a present nature to women but does so in a strangely godlike form of address. There the verb *are* is utterly ambiguous. What *are* women, anyway? The line almost dissolves into absurdity. At the very least, it suggests that women and Greeks are whatever the world says they are, but the godlike "Let . . . be" undermines that apparent celebration of the status quo. The echo takes us back to Agrippa's thesis that in the original creation women were created to be something other than the world has made of them. We are reminded of the moment when God set a highly mutable creation spinning on its way. The effect is to imply a status quo that is merely temporary and one that is not necessarily in harmony with the creation.

This theme is struck in the elegy to Queen Elizabeth where "women's worth" is said to be vulnerable to eclipse in the line: "Now say, have women worth, or have they none? / Or had they some, but with our Queen ist gone?" Bradstreet answers her own questions qualifiedly. Elizabeth is the true measure of women's worth, and her "absence" from present time makes it impossible to believe that what women (or rulers, or life itself) presently *are* is an indication of their true natures. The fact that Elizabeth, though gone, is still a potentiality within the creation means that the answers to these questions cannot be put in the present tense.

At one level, then, the Bradstreet of "The Prologue" declares that women's worth (presently), especially for poets, is the way she has reported it: in the persona she has adopted and in her reports of what people say. The rest of the poem, however—particularly in its brief reference to history, its mention of the Greek muses, and its suggestion of a relationship to the future of the world's great poets—invites us to think that this stage in history and in the immature life of the poetic persona will pass.

There is yet another way that the Elizabeth elegy makes this point: there Bradstreet writes, "The World's the Theatre where she did act," and the image reinforces the sense of Elizabeth's having come to earth and played her part and then returned to the "higher sphere." The image of the world as a stage in which players play their parts (as Shakespeare's Jacques observed) serves to diminish the ultimate reality of that stage. It is possible in "The Prologue" to find a similar undercutting of the importance of rank and position, and so when the speaker gives way on the matter of who goes first, she is giving up nothing of very real importance. "Men can doe best" can be understood to imply that *doing* (even "best") is not all that the world accounts it to be.

That Bradstreet may be deliberately, even facetiously, taking the role of one who only appears to care about men's "preheminence" and "Precedencie" is reinforced by an interesting gloss on the often-quoted lines, "I am obnoxious to each carping tongue, / Who sayes, my hand a needle better fits." In Cornelius Agrippa's treatise "Of the Nobilitie and Excellencie of vvomankynde," he argued that "man is the work of nature and woman the worke of God." Agrippa's treatise belongs to that long-lived Renaissance debate about the superiority of the sexes. Nathaniel Ward may have been referring to this tradition when in his dedication to *The Tenth Muse* he suggests that Bradstreet's book provides evidence for settling the question "Sex weigh'd, which best, the Woman, or the Man?" (M/R, 526). Agrippa argues that women were given liberty and responsibility in ancient cultures but that in modern times such practices are "forbydden by lawes, abolished by custome, extincted by education." It is not God's law, in Agrippa's view, that silenced women but men's laws and customs. He deplores the "modern" domestication of women and describes women's unnatural present-

day condition in these terms: "For anon as a woman is home, euen from
her enfancy, she is kept at home in ydelnes, as thoughe she was unmete
for any hygher busynesse, she is permitted to know no father than her
nedle and her threede. And than whan she cometh to age, able to be
married, she is delyuered to the rule and gouernance of a aielous
husband."[36] If Bradstreet's readers, especially an inner circle of readers
who shared, say, Ward's education, interests, and wit, heard the echo
of Agrippa's treatise here, they would have understood the doubleness:
those "carping tongues" represent the force of a recent tradition that
Agrippa pointed out has not always existed, is not God's law, and since
its sanctions are mere custom, law, and education, can change. Bradstreet's critics frequently assume that the phrase "carping tongues"
refers to Puritan society generally, dominated as it was by androcentric
values; critics then equate Bradstreet's own attitudes with those expressed by her poetic speaker: acquiescent, defensive, deviously subversive.[37] I think it possible that the "carping tongues" represent an
indeed prevalent, but in some circles, much discredited view of
women's lives. Thus while appearing to give ominous weight to a
publicly antifeminist position, Bradstreet's line, in its citation of
Agrippa, would signal to her readers that she expects them to cry
"slander" here, as she assumed they would in the elegy to Queen
Elizabeth (M/R, 157).

Finally, seen from the obverse side—for the other, even opposite,
meanings the poetic statements can be said to convey—the last stanza
casts yet another light on the role of the poetic speaker. The mention of
the great poets' "gold" alongside the speaker's "mean and unrefined
stuffe" brings alchemical process to mind. Although transmutation is
being suggested here—schoolboys do grow up to be great poets, and
metals do, the alchemists promise, turn into gold—the lowly speaker
is not suggesting that she will achieve the preeminence of the great
poets. They "soare the skies," but her lines are earthly ("lowly" and
"meane"). Her path does run parallel to the path of the great ones; she
too recevies a garland, but hers is the "wholsome parsley" not the laurel
wreath of male poets and athletes. Yet the fact that she calls her poetry
"unrefined stuffe" suggests that she expects her work too to change: it
too is perfectible, but not in the world's terms. In the "small acknowledgement" she seeks can be found a promise of a large acknowledg-
ment, one perhaps more blessed finally than the "prey" and "praise"
that the "high flown quils" catch.

The poem's argument comes to rest in the implicit comparison between the world's gold and the child's "unrefined stuffe," between the world's laurels and the speaker's "wholsome parsley." The word "wholsome" is important. The speaker expects a reward that unlike the world's gold is truly health giving and that, in its anagram, suggests "wholeness" or in Bradstreet's word, "unity." Thus, at its most basic level, the poem is an argument for art and life as dynamic, as opposed to the static terms set for and by a man's world. The poem underscores the role of women as novices, whose "day" is presently in eclipse but who see, because they have experienced it, the underside (the invisible past and future) of things as they only presently *are*. The poem turns away from the value (here ascribed to men) of acquisition and the achievement of "precedencie." In the final lines of the poem the gold of the world is made to shine for what it really is, and the novice poet claims the power to reveal the ultimate truth of this apparent "glistering."

If such complexities of meaning—the actual always implying the potential—do mark Bradstreet's work, they tell us something about the character or identity of the readership Bradstreet seems to expect. She is writing for a readership both of men and women who possess the quality of mind and temperament that in her dedication she ascribed to Thomas Dudley—the ability to judge, prove, try, and sort the work and to distinguish chaff from wheat. Bradstreet may have been writing for what, in theological terms, could be called a "sanctified" reader— one who sees this world and uses this world from the perspective of the Resurrection. In more modern terms, her readers would be those who see possibilities in actualities or the spiritual dimension of earthly, everyday phenomena.

When we turn to the ambitious "Foure Monarchies," the longest and least accessible of the quaternions, we find the poet speaking initially as a copyist, but her identity changes as the poem proceeds. Possibilities in the actualities of history are her subject. Here her interest is in providential history—how the world has come to be the way it is—an interest that is consistent with her view of the natural world as dynamic and changing, albeit in ways that are hidden from view. The events of history are not, of course, hidden, but the patterns that inform events are. In "The Foure Monarchies" the narrator persona is not introduced as such until the end of the third, the Grecian monarchy. Wars begin to be omitted from her narrative after the reign of the Ptolemys: then the history of Roman emperors is severely abridged and finally not finished. At that point the speaker summarizes her work so far and writes,

> With these three Monarchies, now have I done,
> But How the fourth, their Kingdoms from them won;
> And how from small beginnings it did grow,
> To fill the world with terrour, and with woe:
> My tired braine, leaves to a better pen,
> This taske befits not women, like to men:
> For what is past I blush, excuse to make,
> But humbly stand, some grave reproof to take: (M/R, 135–36)

She writes, again, as in "The Prologue," that "The subject was too high, beyond my straine" and then adds an explanation that provides a clue as to why she feels the need to apologize: "To frame Apologie for some offence, / Converts our boldnesse, into impudence." The unbefitting act of a mature woman ("boldnesse") is transformed, by apology, into the act of a mere child ("impudence"). The poet here suggests that her use of speakers is an intentional strategy. To convert herself into a child is a self-protecting gesture that may "requite" the critics who see her writing as "presumption." Here, again, doubleness masks the apology. Being on the verge of writing about the Roman empire means that the poet is approaching the period of Christ's life and death. She identifies this moment as a moment of "small beginnings" with the same ironic understatement in her use of the word *small* as we have seen before. During the fourth monarchy, the most violent of them all, the power of the "Lambe" will be manifest, and the poet appears to draw back from writing this story. She turns silent and takes on (or reverts behind) the mask of a lesser power—an inept child-woman.

She then goes on to explain that after "some dayes of rest," she set out again "to finish what begun." She gives two excuses for the "confus'd brevity" of the fourth monarchy: "Shortnesse of time, and inability." Then she names the condition or stage to which either she as writer or her history has arrived: "Yet in this Chaos, one shall easily spy, / The vast limbs of a mighty Monarchy." In what "Chaos"? It sounds as if the world is being created once again, anew. The "vast limbs of a mighty Monarchy," one arising out of "small beginnings," sounds rather more like Christ's kingdom than like any of the Roman reigns about which she is (hesitantly) about to write. Of course, it is reasonable to read this passage at face value: it must have taken both ability and time to write this history and shortness of either of these would affect the process. In an important non sequitur, however, Bradstreet's concluding (and emphatic) couplet stresses that the writing of this last monarchy somehow involved the "heart." She writes again of the faults in her work; "What e're is found amisse, take in best part, / As faults proceeding from my head, not heart."

Whatever we make of this "failure" to continue, we must include a recognition that Bradstreet's speaker (in a schoolchild's copybook manner) recounted the first three monarchies without hesitation or apology. As John Harvard Ellis has shown, Sir Walter Raleigh is her ventriloquist here as she lifts large pieces from his history of the world and appropriates them to her own text (Ellis, xlii–l). (The Queen Semiramis portrait, for example, is almost all Raleigh's.) Schoolchildren, as we have seen, were taught to copy and adapt passages of great literature into their own words. For a woman, too, to copy the words of others, especially ministers, was considered both appropriate and desirable. Thus, the poet's earlier protest that "some will say it's stoln" has a perhaps even comic doubleness to it because in part her materials were stolen—that being what children and women were supposed to do. Her readers would have understood all this and deemed the thievery appropriate.

In "The Foure Monarchies," then, the speaker moves into uncertainty after more than 80 pages of unfalteringly tracing the march of empire. In this respect, she moves oppositely from the New England daughter of "A Dialogue between Old *England* and New . . ." in which the daughter confidently concludes by sketching a prophesy for her mother and where her empathetic tracing of recent English history is elaborated with echoes of the war of Gog and Magog from the book of Revelation. Posing the question of why Bradstreet brought the narrator of "The Foure Monarchies" to a point of self-doubt and silence leads us to consider the larger question of what this ambitious poem is about. Is it simply a schoolchild's copybook exercise? If so, why does the schoolchild not conclude? Apology is a conventional gesture, of course, and one of Bradstreet's stock-in-trade features, but here the apology purports to explain, and its intrusion into the text has impact.

In an effort to suggest ways of reading the entire poem, let us consider first its overall design. Again the intertextuality of biblical predecessors enables us to see what the poet changed, emphasized, and reproduced. As large a debt as Bradstreet owed to Du Bartas, she did not here copy

from his text. In fact, his "Second Week" ended at the point where "The
Foure Monarchies" begins—with the Assyrian Monarchies, the Babylonian captivity, and the reign of Nebuchadnezzar. Du Bartas's story is
here taken up where his death ended it. Bradstreet, instead, copies from
the book of Daniel, presenting Nebuchadnezzar as the pinnacle, the
"best" of kings, as the Geneva Bible says, despite his self-indulgent
destructiveness ("This was that King of Kings, did what he pleas'd, /
Kild, sav'd, pull'd down, set up, or pain'd, or eas'd") (M/R, 64). "This
was of Monarchies that head of gold [Dan. 11:32] / The richest, and the
dreadfull'st to behold" (M/R, 135). From this first and yet ultimate
stage in history, the progression, Bradstreet closely following Daniel
tells us, is downhill. Bradstreet retells Daniel's interpretation of Nebuchadnezzar's dream, characterizing each monarchy by drawing a likeness
to a body part, a metal, and an animal, and each monarchy in order is
presented as lesser in value and nobility than the one that preceded it.
Finally all that is left at the end of this downward evolution is "chaff"
and "residue," the result of the grinding of the "stone out of the mountaine." Here is the way Bradstreet summarizes her strongly alchemical
conclusion of history in "The Foure Monarchies":

> The *Assyrian* Monarchy long time did stand,
> But yet the *Persian* got the upper hand;
> The *Grecian,* them did utterly subdue,
> And Millions were subjected unto few:
> The *Grecian* longer then the *Persian* stood,
> Then came the *Romane,* like a raging flood,
> And with the torrent of his rapid course,
> Their Crownes, their Titles, riches beares by force.
> The first, was likened to a head of gold,
> Next, armes and breast, of silver to behold;
> The third, belly and thighs of brasse in sight,
> The last was Iron, which breaketh all with might.
> The Stone out of the Mountaine then did rise,
> And smote those feet, those legs, those arms and thighs;
> Then gold, silver, brasse, iron, and all that store,
> Became like chaffe upon the threshing-floor;
> The first a Lion, second was a Beare,
> The third a Leopard, which four wings did rear;
> The last more strong, and dreadful, then the rest,
> Whose Iron teeth devoured every beast;
> And when he had no appetite to eate,
> The residue he stamped under's feet: (M/R, 135)

The history of each monarchy is marked (in both Bradstreet's and Daniel's interpretations) by increasing degrees of brutality, until the Roman period whose "Iron teeth" destroys its predecessors and achieves a kind of perverse or inverse preeminence. Clearly the destruction of the world is at hand (as Daniel prophesied and Bradstreet recollects) in this most degraded period of human history. Daniel's imagery is recalled in the book of Revelation (the stone, the beasts, the metals), and its effects are further intensified by echoes found in the book of Jeremiah in the figure of the "Threshing floor." Jeremiah tells Israel that the Lord likened the "daughter of Babylon" to a "threshing floor / at the time when it is trodden; yet a little while / and the time of her harvest will come" (Jer. 51:33). Thus the poet, by use of biblical allusions, is painting a picture of the end of human history.

In this portrayal of the evolution of the monarchies, history grows and changes alchemically in the way that base metals are transformed into gold. Here, however, the reverse of alchemical change seems to be happening. Gold (the period of Nebuchadnezzar) is transformed into lesser metals (the periods of the Persians, Greeks, and Romans), and these lesser metals are finally reduced to or left as "chaff." In Bradstreet's poem the actions of the "Stone" work on the monarchies, just as the philosopher's stone was said to work—with transforming consequences. The monarchies are changed backward—toward lesser and lesser states until they are like the "residue" left in the bottom of the alchemist's cauldron. In the book of Daniel from which this section of Bradstreet's history is taken, Nebuchadnezzar's dream is more emphatic about the kingdom's utter destruction and less designedly alchemical. In the Geneva Bible, Bradstreet would have read this wording of the king's dream: "Then was the yron, the clay and the brasse, the siluer & the golde broken all together, and became like the chaffe of the sommer floores, and the winde caryed them away, that no place was founde for them: and the stone that smote the image, became a great mountaine, and filled the whole earth" (Dan. 2:35).

Thus we see that Bradstreet's references to gold in "The Foure Monarchies" and in "The Prologue" are consistent in their double valence. Nebuchadnezzar's "gold," the Geneva Bible editors point out, is a qualified "best": "[Daniel] calleth the Babylonia kingdome the golden head, because in respect of the other three, it was the best, and yet was of it self wicked and cruel." The "gold" of Bradstreet's portrait of Nebuchadnezzar is similarly qualified. In "The Prologue" Bradstreet's attribution of gold to the great poets and prophets is also undercut, as

we have seen. There is, however, an important reason for beginning
with the Babylonian kingdom, as the Geneva commentators explain—
not because it was gold but because "it wolde declare the things, y^t
were to come, to the coming of Christ for the cōfort of the elect among
these wonderful alterations." So, too, Bradstreet's interests are focused
on the "wonderful alterations" that history undergoes. There is another
gold, in effect, a hidden gold (like the "hidden manna" of "The Flesh
and the Spirit") that is at work in the progressive historical stages she
traces. The power is not called gold in Bradstreet's poetry but is called
"the stone" or "the white stone." She seems to leave the epithet
"golden" for the world to seek and admire in the same way she left
"preheminence" to men. Bradstreet's use of these alchemical figures
follows tradition: "As the Philosopher's Stone, which is the Chemical
King, has virtue by means of its tincture and its developed perfection to
change other imperfect and base metals into pure gold, so our heavenly
King and fundamental Corner Stone, Jesus Christ, can alone purify us
sinners and imperfect men with His Blessed ruby-coloured Tincture,
that is to say, His Blood" (Salgado, 111).

Thus it is against a background of biblical prophecy and scientific and
philosophical lore that the meaning of "The Foure Monarchies" emerges.
Again, let us imagine what I have called a sanctified reader of this text,
one who could sort out the attributions to gold made in the quaternions.
This reader would search the visible in Bradstreet's history for signs of
the invisible. He or she would, as the commentators to the Geneva Bible
said Daniel did, read history for indications of "things . . . to come."
He or she would consider the events of ancient history, in and of themselves, not of much value (these were chaff), but if these shadowed forth
evidences of Christ's kingdom, then they would be worth the telling.
One thing our hypothetical reader might observe is that as corrupt and
un-Christlike these rulers were, there were moments when they inti-
mated, to a slight degree, Christ's life: Darius's death is one example as
are his prayers of forgiveness and thanksgiving. The miraculous recovery
of Nebudchadnezzar from a seven-year severe emotional depression
would be another. There are occasional evidences of Wisdom and the
edifices and artifices that Wisdom can inspire: Queen Semiramis's temple and the tower she ordered to be built from which astrologers could
view the stars, and Alexander's great library where the Bible was translated into Greek. Mothers, sisters, and wives do not distinguish their sex
in any of the monarchies, but Bradstreet mentions them throughout,
and occasionally we see acts of kindness, bravery, and loyalty similar to

those of the women in Christ's life. Suggestions of spirituality are indirectly put, as when the "Poets feign [Semiramis] turn'd into a Dove, / Leaving the world, to *Venus* soar'd above" (M/R, 56).

Not only would our sanctified reader see portents in the life stories of the monarchs of ancient times, he or she would look to see the direction history seemed to be taking. This downward movement of the monarchies, in terms of the humane and spiritual qualities of life, would not have surprised our hypothetical reader. This was the movement that Daniel's interpretation predicted. What might have been disconcerting would have been the discovery of increasing degradation as a pattern in history, one that might apply as well in modern times. We have seen several portrayals of the darkness and violence (of the "afflictions") that would precede a not-too-distant millennium. Those readers (of whom there were many in the Massachusetts Bay Colony and in Old England, as well) who took Bradstreet's view that the Civil War was the last act in the drama of history before the second coming of Christ, would have read the lines "Yet in this Chaos, one shall easily spy, / The vast limbs of a mighty Monarchy," not only as a description of the onset of the Roman monarchy but also as the description of their own times, which they saw, above all, as a time of transition.

I would like to suggest that for the reader who looks to history for a confirmation of hope (of the kind we saw at the end of "The Four Ages"), Bradstreet's failure to conclude might indeed signal alarm. If we read these words as the words of a modern spokesperson for Daniel, we are jolted by the absence of a triumphantly spoken vision of the millennium. Thus it is quite possible to read "The Foure Monarchies" as a warning to modern-day "Israel": this poet felt herself and her "nation" to be in the midst of "Chaos," a reference that she did not borrow from Daniel. That appears to have been her idea.

When Bradstreet later explains that she did try to finish her history in subsequent years but that "All thoughts of further progress laid aside, / Though oft perswaded, I as oft deny'd" (M/R, 139), she is not speaking as the immature poet who cannot handle subjects too big for her "mean Pen." This note was added to the 1678 version of the poem, and there the poet speaks as someone who, fully adult, has lost her way or who is depressed about the impossibility of finding that way. She blames the loss of the last pages of her history on her house fire in 1666 (about that I have more to say later). Her monarchies, she writes, lack "their legs," like mannikins or dolls that are half built. Even so, their imperfect structure does not seem to matter a great deal since "the

world now sees" that this last monarchy "Hath many Ages been upon
his knees" (M/R, 140). The expectant seventeenth-century reader who
wants to see how the story of universal history is going to turn out is
told that it has been a depressingly long wait for this infant to stop
crawling and to walk. The earlier disclaimer (published in the 1650
edition) has the impact both of a frightening blow in the word "Chaos"
and then of an even more terrifying dropping off of expectation, as the
poet calls a sudden halt to her project. Her readers may well have
registered a sense of profound unease at this conclusion in doubt, a
sense reinforced by the description of the present time as developmen-
tally delayed.

Whether the unfinished history is evidence that Bradstreet herself
lost faith in the millennium is not possible to say on the basis of this
poem alone. In the other quaternions, Bradstreet works with God's
promises in a variety of ways that suggest her delight (not to say faith)
both in nature's unified construction and in its permanent potentiality
for change.

Up to the moment called "chaos" in the 1650 edition, the history—
the infant who has not learned to walk—has been the expression of a
novice-apprentice who knows how to recite what he has been taught
but who does not know how to move beyond that rote exercise. Modern
readers find the history bookish and wooden as, at least at one level,
seventeenth-century readers would have. The history does not mature;
it does not undergo adolescence. Unlike the "youth" of Bradstreet's
"The Foure Ages," it does not survive the affliction of its own dark and
sinful ways. The intervention of silence, which the voice of the woman
marks, concludes a seemingly endless series of increasingly grim
events. Perhaps silence is thus a salvific gesture on the poet's part,
signaling at least change, perhaps suggesting that the time of "Masculines, [who] have thus tax'd us long" (M/R, 157) is over.

"The Foure Monarchies" is thus unusual among the quaternions in
the stiffness and tonelessness of its voice. The universe of history lacks
the playfulness and the mutability that characterize the worlds of the
other quaternions. The four elements act on each other; they change
and even exchange shapes and appearance. Yet each has her own Christlike quality or substance to contribute to the cosmos: Fire enables
"transmutation" to occur; Earth contributes her "dust" to "mould" all
her sons, including Christ; Water contributes blood, and Aire provides
the "breath of every living soul." As mothers of the Humours, the
Elements interact with their daughters too: It is only after each Hu-

mour "makes obeysance to each Mother," that she "has leave to speake" (M/R, 20). Although there is nothing to suggest that the "day" of Christ's coming is imminent, all the Humours aspire to stop fighting and to end the "spight" (M/R, 34) and to be joined in a "golden ring, the Posey, Unity" (M/R, 35). The Element "Aire" describes the kind of oneness that change can bring about in the natural world:

> My moist hot nature, is so purely thinne,
> No place so subtilly made, but I get in.
> I grow more pure and pure, as I mount higher,
> And when I'm thoroughly rarifi'd, turn fire.
> So when I am condens'd, I turne to water;
> Which may be done, by holding down my vapour.
> Thus I another body can assume,
> And in a trice, my own nature resume. (M/R, 18)

Aire is the last of the elements to speak, but she presents herself as first in importance to human and natural life. Aire is essential to music making and to the poet's words. She sustains the birds, and among these the phoenix and the eagle, the prophetic birds. The "mighty Monarchs fear their Fates, / By death, or great mutations of their States" when they see "Portentous signes, of Famines, Plagues and Wars," which appear in the air as "strange flaming swords, and blazing stars." Thus, prophecy is not absent from the natural world; it simply manifests itself differently. Aire suggests that the world's leaders fear "mutations," and thus the portents of change that Aire produces and supports in the forms of comets, birds, and stars.

Just as the identity of the elements is marked by mutability, so too is the poet's identity. In "Meditations when my Soul hath been refreshed wth the Consolations wch the world knowes not" (M/R, 223), Bradstreet speaks of her identity, as we have seen, as caught up in a transforming process. She turns to servant, child, sister, wife, and finally into a part of God, in the same way that Aire turned into the other elements, fire and water. The implication is that the potentiality for all these roles is present and active. When she has undergone change—or as the alchemists would say, the "grinding" of the soul that is necessary to her "refinement"—something quintessential survives or is born again. When the poet imagines herself as arriving at an ultimate condition or identity, that condition is not gold, but, in effect, gold's opposite: dissolution. At the same time, she has a selfhood that persists through dissolution and that allows her to join (as herself) the Almighty. Thus, she, like Aire, has a "nature" that she is able to "resume," even though she has assumed several identities throughout her life. Such was the alchemists' notion of the way forms change: each living creature had what the alchemists called its own "signature," its self-identifying pattern that would allow it to go through changes, even death, and to come alive again as itself in the spring season or in the next generation.

Thus to be a novice speaker, a schoolboy reciting his notes, a poet whose "stuffe" has not as yet been "refined" places one in a condition of blessedness in that it places one at the point of change. Growth is what is anticipated when one is at these stages, when one is experiencing even a "small beginning." This meditation and the speech by Aire to her sisters should serve as a caution to Bradstreet readers to listen for the voice that is speaking and to expect it to be any one of a variety of selves. As I think these poems show, Anne Bradstreet had a highly malleable sense of reality—her own and the world's.

Chapter Three
Sister-Wife: Conflict and Redefinitions

Emigration

In 1630 when the Bradstreets embarked from Southampton, England, for Massachusetts, they surely did so sharing the assumption that they played a special role as originators of the venture. They were aboard the flagship, *Arbella,* named for the daughter of the countess of Lincoln, who, with her husband, Sir Isaac Johnson, was among the emigrees. As Thomas Dudley the following year would make clear in a famous letter to the countess of Lincoln, Lincolnshire men claimed for themselves the original idea of "planting the gospel" in New England, which they then "imparted," as Dudley says, to "some in London and the West Country." Only later, according to Dudley, did others who were not from Lincolnshire join in, others including such important planters as John Winthrop, Sir Richard Saltonstall, and John Endecott, all of whom were aboard the *Arbella,* all of whom would prove to be difficult companions in Christ for Thomas Dudley almost from the start.[1]

Could eventual enmities have been imagined as Anne Bradstreet, her husband of about two years, her parents (then in their late middle age), her three younger sisters, and her older brother gathered on deck to hear their father's old friend John Cotton preach a sermon of farewell? With Cotton's remarkable faculty for making theological ideas seem like nature's own creations, he vividly sanctioned a people's right to remove from places overspread with evil or where "men be overburdened with debts and miseries."[2] Cotton cited biblical precedent for a wide spectrum of reasons for leaving—for the sake of knowledge, for business advantage, to set up a colony, to employ one's talents, to practice one's own religion free from persecution. Understood abstractly, such a list translates into an expression of God's desire for richness and complexity in His Plantations. Translated into a set of personal goals from which the company members might select their individual reasons for embarking, the list allows for (perhaps it reflects) real differences among them. As if in anticipation of the divisions, indeed the factionalism, that would beset this group, Cotton throughout the sermon invokes the image of the single "house" of David. God promises, Cotton says, "to give his people a place wherein they should abide forever as in a house of rest" (12). A faithful people, however marked by diversity, will grow as one: as an oak tree or a "noble Vine" or a "right seede" (13). If the planting should not take, the failure is laid at the feet of the plants themselves and is attributable to their rebellion against God.

Anne Bradstreet also would have seen strangers on the deck and heard speech accents unlike her own from people whose manners were foreign to those of her family circle in Boston, Lincolnshire. When Cotton exhorted the assembled not to forget the "*Ierusalem* at home," did he recognize the many different pictures that the group brought in their minds of that place? Perhaps so, since he reserves the most powerful metaphorical language for the image not of a place but of the nurturing presence to which the voyagers are to remain faithful: "Forget not the wombe that bare you and the brest that gave you suck." Cotton acknowledges differences among his listeners then with his use of the image of ducklings: "ducklings hatched under an henne, though they take the water, yet will still have recourse to the wing that hatched them." He then asks, perhaps as a prod more than as a statement of faith, "how much more should chickens of the same feather, and yolke?" (14). Bradstreet's dialogue between Old and New England reflects a similar sense of the "feather and yolke" shared between the two English commonwealths. Whether or not she felt she was out of the same egg as her fellow voyagers, with whom she was about to undergo what John Winthrop described in a letter to his wife as "a long and troublesome passage" (Emerson, 400), is another question.

Bradstreet, in fact, later wrote that she "came into this Covntry, where I fovnd a new World and new manners at wch my heart rose"(M/R, 216). In this now famous sentence Bradstreet does not accuse the new country of "bad" manners but of "new" ones. The word "manners" should not be understood to mean superficial politenesses; it probably means something closer to what we might call cultural norms, but of a malleable kind, susceptible in Bradstreet's other uses of the term to change. In her dedication of "Meditations Divine and morall" to her son Simon, she observes that "parents perpetuate" both their "lives" and their "mañers" in their posterity, but that children tend "natureally, rather [to] follow the failings then the vertues of their predecessors" (M/R, 195). In other words, manners are part of the generational continuum, almost like a genetic endowment, and yet manners (quite "naturally") may be resisted by children. The great Alexander, in Bradstreet's portrayal, underwent a "change of manners, and of minde" that "griev'd" his "vertuously enclin'd" captains (M/R, 106). Bradstreet's Queen Elizabeth has the power to teach the Spanish at the Armada "better manners to their cost" (M/R, 156). Her lesson's success is the consequence of her possession of "wisdom to play the Rex." Manners, in other words, are expressions of habits that dwell in the generational lifestream; they are spiritually and physically vital components of families.

The word "new" in this context means foreign or altered or unfamiliar, and its use is particularly remarkable given the theological and cultural associations with the idea of the "newness" of the "world" to which the young bride was voyaging. There is little doubt that Bradstreet prepared to cross the Atlantic with the attitude of others who thought the voyage would take them into a new stage or place in history, like a "christian [who was] sailing through this world unto [her] heavenly covntry" (M/R, 203) in the words of one of her meditations. Clearly what Bradstreet met was not the kind of newness she had expected. This country was not heavenly; it was filled with manners that she was unaccustomed to and that she resisted. Her "heart rose," but then, by a process that is not described, she was "convinced it was ye way of God, [and] submitted to it & joined to ye chh., at Boston" (M/R, 216). The tone of that statement of conviction and submission for a woman who all her life passionately sought to "go forwards to the Citty of habitation" betrays tension and disappointment.

Bradstreet's distress, then, was not simply at the unspeakably foul living conditions that she experienced for 10 weeks aboard the *Arbella*[3] nor at the harsh first winter in makeshift huts in Charlestown, Massachusetts. "Manners" would include all the ways that people cope with dire circumstances—how people live in tight quarters and how they share the last drops of fresh water weeks before landing. For women "manners" meant housekeeping practices, hygiene, the way care was provided to the sick and dying. The women aboard the *Arbella* would have attended to the young mother who at sea gave birth to a stillborn child, and there too manners and manners in conflict would have been at issue. "New manners" suggests that Bradstreet registered differences with the other settlers at a level of coping with everyday necessities. This group of emigrees, which the leaders believed (or expected) would be of one seed, one vine, Bradstreet knew by their "manners" were not.

The *Arbella* landed in Salem in June, and when the husbands and fathers left to make Charlestown ready for winter settlement, the women remained behind. Historian Edward Johnson reports that "The Lady Arbella and some of the godly Women aboard at Salem, but their Husbands continued at Charles Town, both for the settling of the civill Government, and gathering another Church of Christ."[4] This was the church (later called the Boston church) that Anne Bradstreet joined—probably in early autumn. She was undoubtedly with the other women at Salem, particularly since her older childhood friend Lady Arbella and her husband were among those whose healths had not withstood the voyage well and who fell ill during that first hot summer. Lady Arbella died in Salem about 1 September and her husband a month later. It is easy to imagine how these deaths would have pained Anne Bradstreet. Sickness and mortality were widespread that first year. To Lady Arbella's mother, Thomas Dudley likened the mortality of the settlers to the "Egiptians [at Passover] that there is not an house where there is not one dead, and in some houses many" (Emerson, 76).

All of the Dudleys and Bradstreets, however, survived that first winter and in the spring of 1631 moved up the Charles River to a location in Cambridge (then called Newtowne) now occupied by Harvard University. At first it seemed as if Newtowne might become the capitol of the new settlement, but by the end of the year most of the membership of the Charlestown church had followed John Winthrop to the opposite peninsula, which had been named Boston in anticipation of the settlement of a large influx of people from Lincolnshire. Although the seat of government moved to Cambridge during Dudley's first governorship (1634–35), Boston soon had more of the character of a capitol city.

When they arrived in Cambridge, the Dudleys and Bradstreets together were allotted two acres on which to build their houses, plant their gardens, and raise livestock. The Bradstreets probably were among those in Cambridge and Watertown who felt the need for more land. An acre would not allow for much livestock and so would not enable the apparently business-minded Simon to profit from his animals. However, as Edward Johnson reports, simple survival may have been the important issue. He writes that in their first year the people of Cambridge were "in such straites for food that many of them eate their bread by waight, and had little hopes of the Earths fruitfulnesse" (Johnson, 91). They were apparently saved from starvation only by the arrival of a ship from Ireland with food supplies.

Although Simon Bradstreet throughout his life was active in Massachusetts government (from 1630 on he was an Assistant in the General Court), there is some indication that even Newtowne (named Cambridge in 1638 when Harvard College was founded) was considered a bit isolated from the center of affairs and particularly from the Boston church, to which both Bradstreets belonged. Edward Johnson described Newtowne as "compact closely within it selfe" and formed "like a list cut off from the Broad-cloath of [Charlestown and Watertown]" (Johnson, 90). "Dispersion," as Dudley pointed out in his letter to the countess of Lincoln, was a concern in the first year when settlers quickly chose sites as far afield as Medford, Watertown, and Dorchester. Johnson had harsh things to say about dispersion, especially about "certaine persons, whose greedy desire for land much hindered the worke"—that is, the "wonderwork" of God's providence in the Commonwealth. This hindering was the result, according to Johnson, of families' settling in locations that were out of earshot of "the sweet sound of the silver Trumpets blown by the laborious Ministers of Christ." As sympathetic as Johnson was with the plight of the inhabitants of Newtowne in the bitterly cold winter of 1631–32, he termed them a "Race of Jacobits"—a complex reference that accuses them of fleeing (as the biblical brother Jacob did) to escape the family's wrath but also places them in the company of the elect (Johnson, 77).

North to Ipswich

The Bradstreets and the Dudleys did leave Cambridge for Ipswich in 1635 or 1636, but even before that migration took place, the Bradstreets may have found the church at Boston an inconvenient distance. Perhaps additionally "inconvenient" because Boston was fast becoming John Winthrop's turf, and Winthrop and Dudley were in the midst of a series of personal and political altercations that would take some years to resolve. In her letter to her children Bradstreet reports that in 1632 she suffered a long illness. That illness—along with the "terrible cold . . . , weekly Snowes, and fierce Frosts betweene" (Johnson, 88) of that winter—might well have kept her home. Boston was across the water, and church services took an entire day. Given the precedent in old England of families' gathering in lieu of attending church (if minis-

ters were silenced or services disrupted), it would not be unlikely for
the Bradstreet-Dudley clan to have done likewise in New England, if
travel were difficult. Edward Johnson's distressed observation that "Sab-
bath Assemblies prove very thin if the season favour not" (74) suggests
that it would not be unusual for the Bradstreets to "sit loose" (to use
Bradstreet's phrase) from church during that important first year in
Cambridge. If it seems unlikely that a "good Puritan" would have been
permitted to absent herself from church, consider the example of
Anne's brother Samuel who in 1632 married Mary Winthrop, the
governor's daughter and a Boston church member, but who never did
join the Boston church.

The first Bradstreet poem of which we have a record was written that
winter on the occasion of that illness. Titled "Upon a Fit of Sickness,
Anno 1632. Aetatis suae, 19." it was included in the posthumous 1678
volume of her poetry (M/R, 178–79). Even though that "fit of sickness" may well have interfered with her church going, it was associated,
as the poem itself suggests, with a deepening and livening of her
faith—in much the same way as her small pox had been four years
earlier. The poem records this illness as a turning point, particularly as
a new recognition of the role of poetic expression in her life.

In this poem Bradstreet describes herself as only "twice ten years
old," yet somehow facing death. Echoing Ecclesiastes, she writes, "My
race is run, my thread is spun, / lo here is fatal Death." There are four
kinds of time woven together in the poem: the poet's literal years, the
moment of her "death" as a present moment, the human lifespan ("from
Womb" to "the Tomb"), which appears "small" against the prospect of
the fourth time (eternity), which is not described in terms of time but
in terms of place (a "place of highest bliss"). To each of these stages
belongs a form of verbal expression. The first is the story of her youth,
which is "not fully told / Since nature gave me breath." The second is
the word of God that set death into the universe at the Fall; the third is
a "word that's speaking," which in a delightful quatrain the poet says
bursts like bubbles "that alwayes art a breaking." Finally comes the
"profession pure" that is the means to salvation and the expression of it.
"Profession" of faith was a requirement for church membership, but in
the context of this poem where Bradstreet has been citing kinds of
verbal statements, this profession has overtones of literary expression as
well. As she does in the quaternions, here she celebrates "breath,"
which nature gives at birth and which vanishes as it speaks. It is "no
sooner blown" but is "dead and gone." Yet by implication, breath is

essential to the act of "professing"; despite its transience, "profession" is elevated to the means of confronting "death's arrest." The Solomonic echo is repeated but in an altogether different tone: "the race is run," but this time "the victory's mine I see."

Admittedly death, the unnamed "foe," owns the "soyle," the body's eventual resting place. Yet death here envies the poet's power of speech, breath, profession. In a final statement that turns the poem—subtly and delicately toward life, the word soil is used rather than, say, dust, dirt, or chaff. "Soyle" connotes planting and new growth, and the process hinted at in the final line is the one we have so often seen in Bradstreet's verse: out of apparent ends come new beginnings. The poem does not end on a note of conventional piety. It ends with the use of a figure that renders ambiguous life's apparent finality: it appears to give death the victory, while at the same time suggesting in the implied planting metaphor that "envious" death acts in the service of life. Transience is somehow lifegiving.

The poem is an important one. Perhaps the family knew or felt its importance when the poem was selected for publication. The poem is dated, suggesting that this year marked a moment in Bradstreet's life, which was a moment of crisis, of turning. The poet, at this dark time, turns to the subject of words, and fully (if briefly) spells out the varieties of literary expression with which she is concerned. Finally, it is significant, I think, that her own body (its illness and cure) is the arena where she finds God's dealings with the world being played out. The "little" commonwealth of her physical and psychological being is the focus, reflecting the larger worlds that her young personhood epitomizes. In the paragraph in her autobiographical letter in which this "lingering sickness like a consvmption" is described, Bradstreet then proceeds to recount how God cured another affliction—infertility. In the poem the fact of "pain" marks the "gain" of "profession," just as it marks Bradstreet's description of the arrival of children in her life. She writes, "It pleased God to keep me a long time without a child wch was a great greif to me, and cost me many prayers + tears before I obtained one, and after him gave me many more, of whom I now take ye care" (M/R, 216).

The year 1633, then, saw the birth of the Bradstreets' first child, Samuel, and the arrival in Cambridge of Thomas Hooker, the charismatic minister from Chelmsford, Essex County. That year Cambridge gathered its own church, of which Thomas Shepherd, also from Essex, became minister when Thomas Hooker and a loyal band of followers

left Massachusetts to settle Connecticut in 1635. No doubt the Bradstreets had mutual ties with the new settlers to Cambridge, which
would have dated from the time of the Bradstreets' early married days
in Essex and from Simon Bradstreet's service there in the household of
the countess of Warwick. In 1634–35, the years Thomas Dudley was
governor, Simon Bradstreet was selectman in Cambridge. He thus
presided during the time when the burning issue appears to have been
the need for more land. In 1633 John Winthrop, Jr., who had arrived
in Boston with his mother, new wife, and sisters in 1631, had been
permitted to settle Agawam (Ipswich), and although for a while it
looked as though Thomas Hooker and his congregation might be persuaded to follow Winthrop to Agawam, they chose instead to move to
an even more distant outpost in Connecticut.

Cotton Mather cites "straightness for want of land especially meadow"
as the reason for settling Agawam, explaining (in more even tones than
Edward Johnson did) that "those in Newtown . . . desire leave of the
court to look out either for enlargement or removal, which was granted;
whereupon they sent men to see Agawam and Merimack, and gave out
they would remove" (1702, 1:24).[5] By 1636 the Dudleys had moved to
Ipswich, followed or accompanied by the Bradstreets, Samuel and Mary
Dudley, and the Dennisons (Patience Dudley had married Captain John
Dennison). It was in Ipswich that Bradstreet's literary production, begun apparently in Cambridge in 1632, came into full flower.

The Bradstreets' acquaintance with John Winthrop, Jr., began in
their Cambridge days. Simon Bradstreet and the younger Winthrop
served together as Assistants to the General Court, and they were in-laws
through the marriage of Samuel Dudley and John's sister Mary. In the
words of one biographer, John Winthrop, Jr. was "totally unlike his
father, who immediately imposed a disciplined social system on New
England and spent the rest of his life defending it."[6] The son, however, is
said to have had a "frank exploratory attitude toward the wilderness"—
and, one might add, toward the world. John Winthrop, Jr. was not an
Emmanuel man; he had gone to Trinity College, Dublin, and studied
law but did not practice it. He turned his energies instead to science and
industry (Morison, 269). After graduation he spent a year traveling
throughout the Mediterranean and the Middle East.

When John Winthrop, Jr. arrived in Boston, he brought with him
"several hogsheads of bookes, a large supply of chemical glassware and
seeds for a herbal and medicinal garden" (Dunn, 33). He was, in short,

as Cotton Mather said, an "Eminent Philosopher" with a particular "genius and faculty for Experimental Philosophy" or, in modern terms, natural science. He applied his knowledge of science as a physician. Cotton Mather wrote that he was "furnished with *Noble* Medecines, which he most Charitably and Generously gave away upon all Occasions; insomuch that where-ever he came, still the Diseased flocked about him, as if the Healing Angel of *Bethesda* had appeared in the place" (Mather 1702, 2:31). Those hogsheads of books went with John Winthrop to Ipswich in 1633, and when he returned to England in 1634 (following the death of his wife and infant daughter), that library remained in Ipswich, as part of the house and household that Winthrop let to the new minister, Nathaniel Ward. It is not too much to suppose that Simon Bradstreet consulted John Winthrop during Anne Bradstreet's "consumption" of 1632, and it is highly likely that she had the use of Winthrop's library during her first years in Ipswich. That library has been called "the most significant and extensive alchemical library in colonial America" (Wilkinson, 33). Cotton Mather dubbed Winthrop *Hermes Christianus*, suggesting that he was an adept in hermetic lore who used his knowledge for Christian purposes (Mather 1702, 2:31).

When we imagine what Anne Bradstreet's daily life was like in Ipswich, we thus should not obscure the fact that she was a literate woman with libraries available to her. At the end of her life, the Bradstreets' library (by their son Simon's count) contained over 800 books (White, 347). Thomas and Dorothy Dudley's library also was thought to have been considerable, and, again, in Ipswich the Dudleys and the Bradstreets were given adjoining house lots so that Anne Bradstreet would have had her parents' books for her use. After the birth of Samuel seven more children were born to the Bradstreets in the years 1635 to 1652. The births of the children occurred during the very years that Bradstreet's major poems were written. Although much has been made of John Woodbridge's assurance to Bradstreet's readers that her poetry was the "fruit but of some few houres, curtailed from her sleep, and other refreshment" (M/R, 526), she seems to suggest that reading and writing, and the activities of meditation and contemplation of which literary work was the "fruit," were part of the whole mosaic of her life.

The interconnectedness of the spheres and activities of her life is emphasized in the first of Bradstreet's meditations. She writes that "There is no object that we see. No action that we doe, no good that we inioy, no evill that we feele, or fear, but we may make some spiritull aduantage of all and he that makes such improvment is wise as well as pious" (M/R, 195). So it is that even the work of the housewife can serve as a basic metaphor. In Bradstreet's prose and poetry there is abundant evidence of "women's work": nursing and weaning infants, caring for the sick, clothing children, keeping daily accounts, pickling and preserving foods for the winter, making sure the grain is ground for meal. Reference is made to the husband's absence on "public business" and to the traditional role of the wife as her husband's deputy. In all these instances the work of the housewife is realized and expressed in the work of the poet.

Laura Thatcher Ulrich's portrait of the northern New England "goodwife" of the years 1650–1750 emphasizes that the role of wife was a many-faceted one, based ultimately on the good woman of Proverbs 31. To the wifely self-portrait implied in Bradstreet's meditations, we can add a role that Ulrich describes as "heroine"—women, like Mary Rowlandson, who were public examples of Christianity tested or "private virtues [thrust] into the public sphere" (10). John Woodbridge indicates this public-private role for the Bradstreet of his introduction to *The Tenth Muse*. The poet is a "Woman, honoured, and esteemed where she lives, for her gracious demeanor, her eminent parts, her pious conversation, her courteous disposition, her exact diligence in her place, and discreet managing of her family occasions" (M/R, 526). Here a design is being given to the life as well as to the work. Indeed, this portrait of Bradstreet's personality and experience is as formulaic as her tribute to Dorothy Dudley was, but in it is evidence of what Bradstreet called the effort to make "spirituall aduantage of all." Here Bradstreet's life functions as a public example of both wisdom and piety. With help from family and supporters, a wifely "heroine" (in Ulrich's sense) is being created who, like the good wife of Proverbs 31:26, "openeth her mouth with wisdom." In the creation of that public image, the same spiritual source—namely, Wisdom—fills the works of the good wife as is on the tongue of the poet. In Bradstreet's self-creation the roles of poet and wife share a dependence on biblical Wisdom and are profoundly joined.

Simon Bradstreet was among the first group of Ipswich selectmen in 1636–37, which suggests that the Bradstreets already had become people of wealth and property. In Ipswich, although a town composed of a diverse population of artisans, farmers, and businessmen, the social structure was highly stratified, with leadership tied directly to wealth.[7] Selectmen took their charge from Acts 6:3: "Therefore brethren, pick out from among you seven good men of good repute, full of the Spirit and of wisdom, whom we may appoint to this duty." However restrictive their measures to control production, to regulate manufacture and agriculture, Ipswich selectmen were to act out of the fullness of the Holy Spirit and divine wisdom, the divine attributes that Anne Bradstreet described as essential to good government.

Undoubtedly the families who settled Ipswich had met together and found themselves to be like-minded about the need for large-scale agricultural holdings and commercial trading. They sought and found an area ideally suited for agriculture and cattle, and they were soon selling their surplusses. Since no roads had been built, travel from Boston to Ipswich was problemmatic. It is possible that when the Bradstreets moved, they traveled part of the way by water. Secured, in a sense, by a difficult distance from Boston, the town of Ipswich in 1635 then declared against dispersion: no house was to be built more than half a mile from the meeting house. In Ipswich then, the Bradstreets were close to the meeting house, and they had the use of land outside the town center for their grain and animals. They soon prospered. Cotton Mather refers to Simon Bradstreet as the "venerable Mordecai of his country" (1702, 2:18): this little legend for Simon Bradstreet's life expresses the mutability of fortune. Like Mordecai, Bradstreet in his Charlestown and Cambridge years may have felt himself an impoverished aristocrat in exile in an alien land, but like Mordecai, Bradstreet, too, through his skill, insight, probity, Mather's likeness suggests, rose finally to power and riches.

As early as 1638 (the date of Bradstreet's elegy to Sir Philip Sidney, the earliest poem in *The Tenth Muse*), there appears to have been an ever-widening political, economic, and cultural distance between Ipswich and Boston. Ipswich historian Thomas F. Waters is surely correct in pointing out that in her Ipswich years Bradstreet experienced a rich and privileged life, a "fine intellectual atmosphere," and "generous recognition of her talent."[8] Nevertheless, 1638 must have been a tension-filled year for Anne Bradstreet, as it was for others in Massachusetts Bay. It was a year of separations, in every sense of the word. Mercy and Sarah Dudley were both married and were the last of the Dudley children to leave home. The citizens of Ipswich were drawing up a petition to try to keep John Winthrop, Jr. from settling permanently in Connecticut. They argued that "the distance we are sett at" made it difficult to get and keep "the company of able men "[9]—but to no avail. Moreover, in 1638 Simon Bradstreet, with his brothers-in-law, Samuel Dudley, Daniel Dennison, and John Woodbridge (Mercy's husband), was granted the rights to develop Cochichewick, later to be called Andover. Thus in 1638 the Bradstreets had taken the first steps toward another move, indicating (already) restlessness and dissatisfaction. The Dudleys too may already have begun plans for their next and last move (in 1639) to Roxbury, a move that took them back to the center of Massachusetts affairs.

These personal changes were taking place at a time when life in the colony was darkened by the so-called Antinomian controversy—as bitterly divisive an episode in Massachusetts history as the Civil War was to be in American history. The central figure in that controversy was Anne Hutchinson, who went before the Massachusetts court in 1637. In 1638 following her church trial in Boston she was banished to Rhode Island for her "irregular" views. No doubt that Dudley-Bradstreet family separations (to Ipswich, Roxbury, and Andover) in part reflected divisions among them toward public events. Tensions must have escalated, too, when in 1637 a letter to the Massachusetts magistrates arrived from England, signed by none other than John Dod with 13 others. The letter admonished the young colony for allowing individual congregations an ever-tightening control over family life and the religious and political freedoms of its citizens. Underscoring the ties between old England and New, the letter accused the magistrates of breaking with the original spirit of independency and with the international solidarity that English Puritans felt was an essential part of their movement.

The letter could not have arrived at a worse time for the Boston leadership. John Cotton had been installed as teacher in the Boston church since 1633 and in 1634 his former parishioner, Anne Hutchinson, arrived in Boston with her family. She began to hold sermon discussions in her house, attended by mostly women at first and later by men too. Cotton's preaching had kindled a revival in Boston, which not only produced a large influx of new members but also intensified the debate over qualifications for church membership. It is clear from Bradstreet's autobiographical letter to her children that she felt confused and somewhat distant from these issues and this uproar, which nevertheless had an impact on her faith. She writes of "some new Troubles I haue had since ye world has been filled wth Blasphemy, and Sectaries, and some who hauest been acct^d. sincere Xtians have been carryed away wth them, that somt: I haue said, Is there Faith vpon ye Earth & I haue not known what to think, But then I haue remēbred the words of Christ that so it must bee, and that if it were possible ye very elect should be deceived" (M/R, 218).

When Anne Hutchinson was brought to trial before the General Court in November 1637, Simon Bradstreet was in attendance as an assistant, as was Thomas Dudley, who was then deputy governor. Bradstreet's contributions to the dialogue are minimal, yet they show him to be unmoved by the religious implications of the trial and more interested in clarifying the legal issues raised by Hutchinson's actions. He does make a point of saying that he is not opposed to women's meetings and thinks such meetings "lawful."[10] Simon Bradstreet was not in attendance at the church trial in 1638, but he would not be expected to be since he was not a minister and no longer a member of the Boston church. John Winthrop, Jr. stayed away from Anne Hutchinson's trials, the implication being that he did not favor the actions against the Antinomians but did not want to confront his father openly (Dunn, 359). Clearly Simon Bradstreet did not share his father-in-law's vitriolic opposition to Anne Hutchinson, but neither did he oppose Dudley—at least, not publicly. There is no evidence that Simon Bradstreet was sympathetic to the Antinomians; certainly, he was not one of those disarmed in Ipswich when Governor Winthrop, fearing civil war, clamped down on all suspected Antinomians in the commonwealth.

Anne Bradstreet records the path of her spiritual journey in these years as uneven, when she was susceptible to conviction in one period and doubt in the next. She was, as she writes, beset even by "Atheisme how I could know there was a God" (M/R, 218). She confesses that she was drawn in several directions at once and did not know that to think. In the later poem "Contemplations" she reflects on the "sorrow, losses, sickness, pain" to which "man" is subject, giving special emphasis to tensions within families as one of the pains from which "he never finds cessation." She describes these stresses as ongoing: "day or night within, without, vexation," pointing out that these "Troubles" come not only from "foes" but "from friends, dearest, near'st Relation" (M/R, 173–74). Her family was indeed split on the Antinomian controversy: her brother-in-law's father, William Dennison, was one of the Hutchinsonians disarmed in Roxbury, and her older brother Samuel moved first to Salisbury and then followed the Antinomian minister John Wheelwright to Exeter, New Hampshire, in 1650.

Thus, Bradstreet suggests that the macrocosmic events surrounding the Antiomian crisis registered on the microcosm of her personal world but that they did so in a way that did not involve her in directly taking sides on the issues presented at the Hutchinson trials. Bradstreet seems primarily to register the profoundly disturbing impact of multiple (and passionately held) positions, about which she felt in conflict. We might ask how it was that Bradstreet, given her sensitivity to women's roles in the world, apparently did not see the Hutchinson trial as yet another example of men's abuse of their (in her view temporary) "preheminence." Indeed she may have, but judging on the basis of the poetry we have reviewed so far, I think we can see that Bradstreet, however she may have empathized with Hutchinson's ordeal, did not share Anne Hutchinson's sense of nature and history. Unlike Hutchinson, Bradstreet at this time was still working within a New England view of the history of redemption, but as I think is evident in her "failure" to conclude her history, she began—during her Ipswich years—to have second thoughts about the pattern of sacred history that she, following John Cotton and others, assumed to underlie the voyage to the New World. Perhaps more significantly, she was deeply tied to a view of nature that assumed a radically different role for the workings of the Holy Spirit than Hutchinson's did.

If one image illustrates the core of Bradstreet's idea of the way the Holy Spirit works, it is as we have seen, the seed or kernel. For Anne Hutchinson it is the image of light. In Hutchinson's first trial she cited the same passage from Daniel that Bradstreet did in her "Foure Monarchies" to make clear to her accusers the nature of the time she (Hutchinson) felt she was living in prior to her emigration from England. But then Hutchinson chose the story of Daniel in the lion's den (Dan. 6:4–5) to make the point that God's promise to Daniel to deliver him from the lion's den was the same promise He made to Hutchinson and that she sees "this scripture fulfilled this day." She warned them to "look to it" because the revelation of scripture was happening then and there (Hall, 356). She uses the figure of light in three senses: first, in the sense of what was promised has here and now come to light; second, that she herself has seen or "been given" the "light," which the elders are bearing witness against; and third and most significantly, she imagines the "soule to be nothing but Light" (359), and as such it cannot be eternally attached to the body. She links light with redemption, which she feels she has already experienced. When she says, "I thanke *the Lord I have light*," she is referring to all three kinds of "light." The problem for the elders is not only that a woman is saying these things, attempting to admonish and to teach *them* but that they have a different sense of history and of the hereafter than Hutchinson does. Hutchinson appears not only indifferent to their conceptions of power and gender role; she seems indifferent, as well, to death. The ministers want to talk about what happens when the body dies. She understands this conversation to be about what happens when one is redeemed. John Davenport, perhaps the most patient of her interrogators, explains that "the same Body that is sowen the same Body shall rise agayne. It is sowen a naturall Body but it shall rise a spirituall Body." Hutchinson insists that "We all rise in Christ Jesus" and that our union with him cannot have anything to do with the natural body. It is the "spirit that God gives that returns" (361).

Davenport's imaging of death as planting is an important one for our understanding of Hutchinson's conflict with the magistrates and of the contrast between Hutchinson and Bradstreet. Both women came from Lincolnshire, but Hutchinson was 21 years older than Bradstreet. Hutchinson was married the year of Bradstreet's birth. Hutchinson was the wife of an Aylford merchant and made weekly trips (or more often) to Boston to hear her beloved minister, John Cotton. Bradstreet preceded Cotton to Massachusetts and Hutchinson followed him there. Anne Bradstreet, as a privileged child taught by the earl of Lincoln's tutors, brought a breadth and level of Renaissance learning to the new English experience that Hutchinson, the daughter of a clergyman, did not.

The two women had significantly different views of the relationship of the body to the spirit. For Bradstreet the spirit and the body were inextricably bound, and the bond between them was a necessary part of the process of salvation—of the individual and of the world. In Bradstreet's working out of this complicated perception she was less the parishioner of John Cotton than she was the disciple of John Dee, who wrote that " 'as in every kernel is contained a whole good fruit or tree, so likewise is included in the little body of man the whole great world.' "[11] That the human body is a little commonwealth was a Puritan commonplace, but the idea of a whole great "world" developing from the kernel of the human body is distinctive. For alchemists, nature is the birthplace of Christ's future kingdom, the prediction being that "God wil make new Heaven and a new Earth, and bring all things to a christalline cleernes, & wil also make the 4. Elements perfect, simple, & fixed in themselves, that al things may be reduced to a *Quintessence of Eternitie.*"[12] In this reduction (even dissolution) the identity of the body is not lost; it is perfected. Bradstreet's conclusion to "Old Age" describes this process in a way that tells us that on this point at least she was no Hutchinsonian: "when this flesh shal rot, and be consum'd / This body by this soul, shal be assum'd" (M/R, 46). As it was for Hutchinson's accusers, who insisted that Moses, Elijah, and Enoch would rise again as themselves, here too Old Age will not escape from his earthly identity but will "assume" its body and furthermore "shall see, with these same very eyes / My strong Redeemer, comming in the skies" (M/R, 46). Thus, transmutation is the heart of this ultimate process, a process in which Old Age does not try to avoid bodily "corruption" but claims it as his "kindred store," as "Father," "Mother," and "sisters." Death is one stage in the body's perfecting.

We see in this contrast with Hutchinson's insistence on the imperfect-ibility of the natural body how many-faceted the so-called Puritan tradition was. To use Karl Keller's term, the "mythic" in Bradstreet's case and in Hutchinson's case—the "system outside which [her] life would have no meaning"[13]—differed for each woman even though each was a Puritan, each came from the same English locality, and each was for a time parishioner of the same minister. Where Hutchinson read the Bible as supportive of a mystical, even martyring relationship to her redeemer, Bradstreet read it as supportive of a sacramental one in which the body of the world, whatever its damage as the result of the Fall, is yet potentially expressive of the Word. Another way to put the differ-ence would be to notice again how important Christ as Wisdom was to Anne Bradstreet. Bradstreet's emphasis on his immanent presence in nature as well as his expected presence at the second coming made it impossible for her to dismiss the body of the world, even though she expected it to go through a continuing process of death, or planting, and rebirth. We see too in the mythic differences between the two women how one became a prophet and other a poet.

Poetry thus served Bradstreet by being both the expression of and the creation of a source, reservoir, or (in the word Bradstreet used) a "store." To recreate the reality of Queen Elizabeth and Sir Philip Sidney in a world that needed them as "living stones" (Edward Johnson's term) would be to repeople the present with past exemplars of all that the poet considered vital and energizing. Bradstreet's can be seen as a strategy akin to Edward Johnson's[14] and Cotton Mather's in *The Mag-nalia,* both of whom chose poetry as an appropriate vehicle for monu-mentalizing the first generation, thereby addressing the decline of the New English enterprise. We can thus see Bradstreet's elegies, and the poem, "David's Lamentation for Saul and Jonathan" as the first poetic fruits of New England's declension: the poet in these cases acts as the "Necromancer," as Cotton Mather did. She too "unseals our Hero's Tombs, and gives them Air" (Mather 1702 [10]), thus enabling them to rise up, walk, and talk among the present generation. In this penchant for re-creation she differs from Hutchinson, but we see too that Bradstreet's ancestral heroes were significantly different from Mather's and Johnson's.

Bradstreet, on a more personal level, no doubt felt the need for restoration and reconciliation. The indications we have of the growing distances between her older brother and her father, between her husband and her father, may have made her feel it necessary to affirm and perhaps redefine her frayed ties to her father, whatever the differences between them may have been. When critics dismiss the quaternions as imitative of her father's work, they sometimes do not go the next step and inquire into the purpose of that imitation. In their scientific outlook these poems date back to a science that the poet's father was taught as a boy, although made current perhaps by references to more recent names and events. Indeed, for Bradstreet's readers some of their charm may have been the capacity of the quaternions to evoke nostalgia or reminiscence. For her generation these would be comparable to our experience when we see the first silent films of the flight of the *Kitty Hawk* or the sailing of the *Titanic*. Poetry then could offer a perhaps gently persuasive means of staying in touch with her parents even though politics had come between them and generational time and physical distance separated them.

Finally, at a yet more personal level, writing (both her poetry and her prose) may have been a means of self-creation in a world whose "new manners" no doubt still troubled her, a world where she could not find her way through the thicket of conflicting theologies to what she called "ye true God." But, beyond doctrine would be the matter of her identity as a woman. To be sure, the spectacle of Anne Hutchinson's confronting the leadership of the colony seems very far away from the example of Sir Philip Sidney. Bradstreet, however, as a woman, had an anomalous and complicated role to play in the society and may have been brought up short by Hutchinson's *blinding* declarations—not just by their ideologies but by the evidence they presented of another woman's "putting herself into the world and into history," to use Hélène Cixous's phrase. Bradstreet's autobiographical letter records her Christian pilgrimage from youth to age; her poetry records her efforts to work out her self-identity in relationship to this world and the next.

If "The Four Elements" and "Of the four Humours in Mans Constitution" were presented to Thomas Dudley in March 1642, Bradstreet must have been at work on them at the time when the Dudleys moved

back "nearer the Center of the whole" to Roxbury, which Cotton
Mather points out was "two Miles out of *Boston,* where Dudley was
always at Hand upon the Publick Exigencies" (Mather 1702, 2:39).
These poems suggest too the presence of an audience of other *Hermes
Christiani,* who, in addition to being what I have called "sanctified
readers" would also find the scientific reinterpretation of the four elements and four humors important, interesting, and amusing. Ipswich
and vicinity boasted a number of learned men, and several of them, not
just John Winthrop, Jr., had medical backgrounds. Giles Firmin,
Nathaniel Ward's son-in-law, accompanied Ward to Ipswich in 1634
and was a physician. The young John Rogers (the person who may have
edited Bradstreet's works after her death) would later decline the presidency of Harvard College and ordination to the ministry in order to
study medicine. He assisted his father Nathaniel Rogers at the Ipswich
church. John Norton, who was called to be teaching elder in Ipswich in
1637, was learned to the point, Edward Johnson wrote, of arousing
"illettered Men and Women that doe love / Preheminence, [to] con-
demne thy learned skill" (104). Cotton Mather wrote that Nathaniel
Ward was an "exact *Grammarian,* [and] an expert Physician"(1702,
3:167), and Edward Johnson addressed Ward as "an ancient Sage" who
"with [Christ's] helpe" will "refine Gold" from the "drosse" of the
world's errors[97]: he too was, in other words, a curer of souls—by means
of spiritual and intellectual alchemy.

Anne Bradstreet would have been aware of this learned group's
international scholarly contacts. John Winthrop, Jr., in particular,
corresponded throughout his life with scientists in England and on
the continent. By the year 1641 the Antinomian crisis had inflicted
severe damage to the fabric of Massachusetts life. Tensions existed
between the Essex County leadership and Boston,[15] and the learned
men of science that Essex County boasted were not generally ap-
pointed to speak for the colony. In old England, however, at the
meeting of the Long Parliament in 1640, a very different mood was
evident, and a very different role for scientifically minded men pre-
vailed. At that meeting of Parliament, the scientist Samuel Hartlib
(Milton's friend and a long-time correspondent of John Winthrop,
Jr.'s) described a utopian vision reminiscent of John Dee's Elizabethan
millennial evocations. Frances Yates writes that "in this thrilling
hour . . . it seemed that England might be the land chosen by Jeho-
vah to be the scene of the restoration of all things . . . [and that] here

imaginary commonwealths might become real commonwealths, invisible colleges real colleges" (1984,248).

No doubt riding this wave of enthusiasm, Winthrop traveled to England to meet with European and English scholars and educators who were attempting to realize such a vision of world reformation by following the "Baconian programme" as expanded by Hartlib and Comenius. They were seeking a location for a "pansophic" scientific university at which the new and renovated learning would be taught. Bradstreet (whom Makin, as we have seen, cast in the role of "universal scholar") would have been especially interested in the fact that the pansophic group met in Lincolnshire and that the group were the guests of her former bishop, Dr. John Williams, a friend of Sir Francis Bacon. Comenius's educational methods were used by John Eliot to teach Native American students English, and both Massachusetts and Virginia were considered possible sites for the New World college; on this occasion Winthrop may have offered Comenius the presidency of Harvard College. One can only speculate what education in the colony would have been like if Comenius had been persuaded to take up residency there. In the bitter wake of the Antinomian controversy, Comenius would have pressed the magistrates to make education available to girls as well as boys, and learning of a somewhat different stamp might have been the aim of Harvard's curriculum.[16]

Additionally, Winthrop's trip to England in 1641 would prove to be of immediate political significance to Anne and Simon Bradstreet because it was during this visit that John Winthrop apparently persuaded the Presbyterian physician Dr. Robert Child to return to New England. Child had visited New England in 1638 and 1640 and shared with the younger Winthrop an interest in chemistry (like Winthrop, he invested in iron mills in Massachusetts) and in agriculture of rather experimental kinds (he brought wine grapes to New England). As scientist, naturalist, industrialist, Child, like Winthrop, was convinced that the right technology would bring millennial prosperity to New England. He returned in 1645, ever a "generous and hopeful" investor in New England (Morison, 247).

Robert Child is, however, chiefly known in Massachusetts history because his name was attached to what came to be known as "Child's remonstrance." Child and a group of other nonchurch members who wanted the right to vote in the colony petitioned the English Parliament in 1646 in a protest that touched on the issue raised in the letter

that John Dod and his fellow ministers had sent in 1637—the binding
nature of church membership in the colony. Because Child was a Presbyterian, he was not a member of any Massachusetts congregation, and
since suffrage was tied to church membership, he was unable to vote in
Massachusetts. Simon Bradstreet sided with the younger Winthrop
against the magistrates in support of the signers of Child's remonstrance. Bradstreet's fellow selectmen in Ipswich considered this an
"irregular departure" on his part (Waters, 515), and it was at about this
time that the Bradstreets moved to nearby Andover where Simon Bradstreet already owned a sawmill and considerable land. When Simon
broke with the leadership in Boston on this issue, he was breaking with
his father-in-law, Thomas Dudley, an arch foe of toleration. John Winthrop, Jr. had by that time settled permanently in Connecticut, where
distance enabled him, as it did during the Hutchinson trials, to avoid
the business of the magistracy when he found it personally painful. He
was unable to help his friend Child, who was both jailed and fined in
Boston and returned to England with his hopes dashed for a stake in
New England's future.

Anne Bradstreet would have been caught up in these events, even
though as a woman she did not have a public say on the matters to be
decided. Historian Lyle Koehler reports that Child's remonstrance was
"very popular among women who also wished to be included among the
enfranchised" (Koehler, 243). Bradstreet did not directly express such a
wish. We do not know whether she favored woman's suffrage, but we
can say with some certainty that a spirit of egalitarianism and respect
for women existed in this educational and scientific community, one
that did not characterize the dominant culture in Massachusetts at this
time. Bradstreet and others must have read it as significant that when
Robert Child returned to England in 1646 he was presented with a
copy of Agrippa's *Three Books of Occult Philosophy,* newly translated by a
Puritan physician, John French, and dedicated to Robert Child. Bradstreet thus would have associated Child with a feminist world view
characteristic of Agrippa and Comenius.

We do not have direct evidence that the Bradstreet and Dudley
families were split on the subject of feminism (in any of its forms), but
we have evidence that toleration was a question in dispute. Only indi-
rect evidence exists of Thomas Dudley's attitudes towards women: the
tone of his accusations in the Hutchinson trial, for example, was harsh.
It is, however, clear that, from his Cambridge days, Dudley was an
antitolerationist, and from that we can assume that by 1646 his and

Simon Bradstreet's relationship must have been strained. Her autobiographical letter suggests that Bradstreet, like her husband, found toleration to be a reasonable position. She asks, "why may not ye popish Relign. bee ye right, They haue the same God, the same Christ, ye same word, They only enterprett it one way wee another" (M/R, 218). This statement stands in stark contrast to her father's scrupulous ferreting out of "Popish" tendencies in the Massachusetts churches. He paid a visit to the Watertown church in 1631 to investigate reports that the ministers (George Philips and Richard Brown) had referred to " 'the churches of Rome' " as " 'true churches.' " In fact, so exercised was he about this heresy that he visited Watertown a second time to gain assurance that the statement did not represent the ministers' thinking (Palfrey, 350). If, as this evidence suggests, toleration was an issue on which Thomas Dudley and the Bradstreets differed, the depth of feeling evoked in the elder Dudley about this subject may be explained, in part, by the existence of family discord. Dudley himself was a poet, but only one of his poems has survived. Written on a scrap of paper found in his pocket after his death in 1653, the poem is a farewell to wife and children, but it concludes startlingly with an admonition against "toleration," seen as a generative force in the commonwealth. This "Egg" hatches no harmless duckling, to cite again John Cotton's metaphor:

> Let Men of God in Courts and Churches watch
> O're such as do a Toleration hatch,
> Lest that Ill Egg bring forth a Cockatrice,
> To poison all with Heresie and Vice.
> If Men be left, and otherwise Combine,
> My Epitaph's, *I Dy'd no Libertine.*
> (Mather 1702, 2:17)

Clearly the issue of toleration plagued this magistrate to the day of his death. In her public eulogy of Thomas Dudley, Bradstreet speaks openly about the fact that she was praising her father, knowing full well that others did not agree with her. "Who heard or saw, observ'd or knew him better? / Or who alive then I, a greater debtor?" (M/R, 165) she asks, echoing the theme of indebtedness. Her opening lines suggest that she rejected two possible approaches to what is obviously a difficult task. She refused to write this eulogy simply because of mere "customs," but she also refused, she says, to let "Relation near" tie her hand. Speaking thus openly about the fact that a family member (probably Simon Bradstreet)[17] might want to hold her back on this occasion suggests that the conflict is public knowledge and that she has, at least to some extent, resolved the tension of dual allegiances.

Bradstreet's poetic outpouring between the years 1638 (the date of Hutchinson's second trial and Bradstreet's Sidney elegy) and 1647 (when John and Mercy Dudley Woodbridge left for England with the Bradstreet poems in their possession) can be attributed both to the presence of richly stimulating associations and friendships, ones in which women were accepted as learned beings and to the destabilizing influence of conflicts not only within the larger Commonwealth but within the smaller commonwealth of the Dudley-Bradstreet family. Although the first poems address the subject of family relations only figuratively, they can be seen as composed in response to pressures that Bradstreet later in "Contemplations" singled out as within families, stresses from which, as she said, one "never finds cessation" (M/R, 174).

A further source of tension in these years is suggested by the scant details we have about Anne's sister Sarah Dudley's life during the period 1638 to 1647. The evidence suggests that Anne Bradstreet felt close to her younger sister. In 1638 she bore a second daughter and named her Sarah; that naming suggests fondness, perhaps identification. As Sarah's older sister, Anne Bradstreet was no doubt in the role of her sister Sarah's educator and caretaker in their younger years. In 1638 Sarah Dudley married Benjamin Keayne of Boston—a marriage that proved disastrous. That year Benjamin's father, John Keayne, a wealthy Boston merchant, was convicted and fined for taking excessive profits. He was, Morison writes, an "unpopular man" whom the deputies wished to make an example of" (160). It is possible that the business-minded Simon might not have considered Keayne's profit taking excessive, although there is no record of his having voted for Keayne. Surely to have a man with this reputation as Sarah's father-in-law would not have pleased Thomas Dudley and perhaps not Sarah's three sisters either, all of whom had married upstanding citizens. Benjamin Keayne apparently did not have his father's business acumen, and in 1645 he deserted Sarah and went to England, according to one historian on business for his father (White, 174), and according to another to avoid his American creditors (Jones, 470). Sarah stayed behind, gathered their belongings, and set out for England but was in a ship that capsized and lost all of their goods at sea. Keayne's response was to repudiate her for losing his goods and money (Jones, 470).

When she did arrive in London, Sarah was reported to have " 'growne a great preacher' " (White, 174),[18] as John Winthrop's brother Stephen informed him. It has been assumed that Stephen was using the word "great" with a tinge of irony, but he was writing to John Winthrop, Jr. and his news may have been admiringly communicated and admiringly received; John Winthrop, unlike his father, might not have scorned a woman's preaching. When Sarah returned to Boston, she returned without her husband and immediately to charges reminiscent of those made to Anne Hutchinson a decade earlier: she was admonished for "hir irregular Prophesying in mixt Assemblies and for Refusing ordinarily to heare in ye Churches of Christ" (White, 174; Ulrich, 111). The charges apparently were made on the basis of the first of three letters that Keayne wrote that year to Thomas Dudley, John Wilson, and John Cotton. The letter to Dudley stressed Sarah's "errors" in religious judgment, and the second two letters, to Wilson and Cotton, charges Sarah with having "impoysoned" his body with syphilis. No evidence was presented that Benjamin's infection had come from his wife, but it was clear that, as Benjamin declared, he meant "never again to live with [Sarah] as a Husband" (White, 175).

On the basis of this declaration it was possible for Thomas Dudley to push a divorce proceeding through the General Court. The fact that Dudley was again governor (in the years 1646–49) no doubt made it easier to persuade the court to grant the divorce (White). When in 1647 Sarah was excommunicated by the Boston church for "irregular prophesying," that charge and an additional charge of "odious, lewd & scandalous uncleane behavior with . . . an Excommunicated person" remained on the books because they had not been answered (White, 176). Sarah then married Thomas Pacey. She was helped with the financing of a house in Roxbury by Thomas Dudley, and at his death received a small bequest of money. She died in 1659.

Sarah Dudley was not brought to trial in the way Anne Hutchinson had been. Her accusers provided no particulars of her crime. She was given no chance to respond. Historian Laura Ulrich cautions us about jumping to conclusions about Sarah's guilt. She writes,

The charge of "unclean behavior" would seem to corroborate Benjamin's accusation, though such evidence must be approached with great caution. Attacks upon religious dissenters frequently included charges of sexual irregularity, as though disruption on one social boundary inevitably entailed the disruption of another. It would be helpful to know what Sarah had been preaching in those mixed assemblies. Puritan authority (both in New England and Old) was continuously challenged from its own left flank by men and women who turned spirituality into a weapon for attacking the established order. The first church was still weeding out Anne Hutchinson's supporters when Sarah came [from Ipswich] as a young bride to Boston; ten years later the memory of Hutchinson's disruptive teaching still colored the church's response to female dissent. But without further evidence we can only speculate. Sarah may have been visionary, or rebellious, or simply unlucky. Married to a man threatened by her ardor, she fell victim to jealousy, gossip, and a nasty virus. (112)

What made Sarah Keayne's positions "irregular" is not known. Benjamin Keayne's report that Sarah refused to "heare in ye Churches of Christ" may have meant (as Ulrich suggests) that she did not listen or that she did not attend church regularly or that she did not attend the right church. Any one of these choices would not have made her, necessarily, into a Familist, Socinian, Anabaptist, or other sectarian of the kind so feared by the New England Congregationalists. As Cheryl Walker (citing David Latt's work) reminds us, "during the 1640s and 1650s—when Bradstreet wrote most of her poems—there was an outpouring of especially virulent misogyny in the mother country" (Walker, 3). Thus, on the basis of our present evidence, to see Sarah's behavior as "irrational" and conclude her to have been "really unbalanced" (White, 174) is to factor in neither the unreliability of Keayne as a witness nor the misogynous lens through which the Puritan world, old and new, had come by the mid-1640s to view women who "prophesied."

We could speculate forever about what made the soil right for the planting of Bradstreet's particular genius in Ipswich in the late 1630s. To the two factors proposed earlier—the company of like-minded friends and the disruptions within family and community that threatened the much-prized "harmony" and "unity" of life in this period, a third can be added: the possibility that initially, at least, Anne Bradstreet shared in her sister Sarah's enthusiasm. Bradstreet, in fact, also "prophesied" (i.e., copied and interpreted) in the poetry of *The Tenth Muse*. We can infer from the activities ascribed to Dorothy Dudley in Bradstreet's tribute to her that Dorothy Dudley took part in that activity as well. In fact, she may have been the model for three of her daughters in this regard—Anne, Sarah, and Mercy, who was a poet too.

One can imagine that Bradstreet and her like-minded Ipswich associates in 1638 focused their attention on the question of whether or not a woman could be a wise woman, priest, or prophet. They certainly thought so in two specific instances: the first case was Solomon's, who was said to owe his wisdom to the teaching of his mother, Bathsheba, as one of John Dod's commentaries on Proverbs suggested.[19] The second case is that of Queen Elizabeth, to whose wisdom, as we have seen, Bradstreet accredited her divine powers as a ruler. Cotton Mather's tribute to Anne Bradstreet proposes that we think of her as similarly empowered—by Solomon's wisdom, which is basically attributable to Bathsheba's "instructions" of him. Mather's tribute places Bradstreet in the position of Biblical Wisdom—at the "gates" of the city—and adds that "of [Bradstreet] may Solomon's words be really verified" (Adlard, 18). For Mather, Bradstreet's work was the further working out, or proof, of Solomon's Wisdom inheritance. The continuity through families of this tradition is underscored in these statements.

We catch something of Bradstreet's enthusiastic mood in 1638 in her elegy to Sir Philip Sidney, a mood that stands out vividly in relief when compared to the mood of the significantly revised (and flattened) version of the elegy as it appeared in *Several Poems* nearly 40 years later. Gone from that version is the religious and erotic enthusiasm of the earlier poem. The claims for the poet in 1638 and for her relationship to the famous Sidney are hyperbolic—interestingly so since Sidney's literary reputation by 1638 was in eclipse. In Bradstreet's poem that is far from the case. His powers (and by implications, the novice poet's) are likened to the sun's, but the figure works in a complicated way: the speaker of the poem, in an extended depiction, is again an "ambitious fool" who adopts the persona of Phaeton. Phaeton, in classical mythology, asked for the privilege of driving the chariot of the sun across the sky for a single day but lost control of the horses and crashed into the earth, nearly causing it to catch fire. In Bradstreet's poem Apollo comes to the poet–chariot driver's rescue; he bids the poet "drive" while "he would hold the sun." In other words, the sun stands still in this poem in order to protect Apollo's darling, Sidney, just as the God of the Israelites stopped the sun over Gibeon in order that the Israelites might take revenge on their enemies. Sidney is not just protected by Apollo, he *is* Apollo, or he shares Apollo's divinity. This little scene parodies a prefiguration of the millennium, but if Bradstreet is poking fun at solemn foreshadowings of the ultimate day, she is doing so perhaps not entirely facetiously. She addresses Sidney in this 1638 version of the elegy as "*the quintessence of men*" (a term she also uses for Du Bartas). This exalted figure she later changes to the flat line " 'mong [the] most

renowned of men." In the 1638 poem Sidney is, in other words, a
magical force yet alive in the universe, doing the work of transmutation. For occult philosophers, "the World-Soul radiates its energy
from the sun, using as its instrument a fifth essence [the quintessence]
which flourishes everywhere as the spirit of the world's body" (Shumaker, 124). Sidney, then, as such an instrument would, in effect, be
the means of the world's redemption. Of course, Bradstreet is not
replacing Christ with Sidney, but she is suggesting that poets-mages
of Sidney's kind are empowered to play a role far beyond that usually
afforded to poets. Bradstreet, who has "the self-same blood yet in my
veins" (in this version) and who is driving the poet's chariot across
the sky, is indeed claiming for herself what she calls Sidney's "pattern"
(M/R, 149).

Furthermore, the poet in this early version addresses Sidney as "you"
(an address that changes to the third person in the second version). He
is somehow within the hearing of her voice. She and he are, moreover,
consanguine—not just abstractly related by literary vocation. The
blood that ran (or "*yet*" runs?) in his veins also runs in hers. The phrase
suggests that a literally impossible set of phenomena characterize their
relationship and that what was dead still lives or lives again. The 1638
poem is a heady poem, indeed a magical one, and the elements that
make it so were all excised later.

The 1638 elegy suggests a half-playful, half-enraptured sense of the
poet that no longer marks the poet of the 1678 elegy. Such a character-
ization appears to be one that Bradstreet (or her editor or family) no
longer wished to make. Perhaps the times changed, or perhaps she did,
but in the earlier version Bradstreet puts on the role of "magi-
ciannesse," as Agrippa called wise women. Her manner of playing a
prophetic role differs from Hutchinson's. She is more deliberately
artful—perhaps surreptitious, perhaps, as Cheryl Walker might say,
ambivalent. She again speaks with a flawed poetic voice, with the
implication that she is not yet the mage that Sidney was, but the
generational relationship between the two in this poem suggests that
the younger poet has not ruled out the possibility that she might grow
into the stature that the older poet once possessed.

In its dynamic implications this poem claims for the poet a place in
the sun. Yet it is important to note that, unlike Bradstreet, Sarah
Dudley Keayne and Anne Hutchinson *spoke* their messages of enthusiasm publicly. Bradstreet wrote hers, and although her work saw publication, the very act of writing served to submerge or bury or even hide

the poet's statements, as Wisdom's words were said to be hidden in the matrix of the axiom or proverb.

There is every evidence that Bradstreet saw the world as not yet an auspicious place for women's words, let alone women's rule, but there is also evidence in the 1638 elegy that she saw the world as ready for revolution in this regard. The 1638 elegy is a tribute to the dawning presence of a new consciousness of the kind that Bradstreet's Old English colleagues were envisioning and that her learned Essex county compatriots might well have appreciated. It is exactly this tone of confidence in the dawn's approach that is excised from the 1678 elegy, as is the poet's implied participation in that dawn.

In 1643 during the period of Sarah Dudley Keayne's unfortunate marriage and her sojourn to England, Dorothy Dudley died. Of all the personally destabilizing events of these years, perhaps this one, which Bradstreet does not mention except in the tribute "An EPITAPH," must have been among the most profoundly unsettling. Bradstreet's poem about her mother has, in contrast to the eulogy for Thomas Dudley, nothing of that unease or apologetic uncertainty about it. Indeed, Bradstreet's poetry can be seen as her effort to follow her mother's example, to be a "true Instructor of her Family" (M/R, 167). As both the poetry and the prose suggest, however, "instruction" may have been increasingly difficult to formulate in these disturbed and disturbing years. Bradstreet's autobiographical letter indirectly suggests a difference that is perhaps generational between herself and her mother, at least in the daughter's eyes. Her "Tribute" suggests and idealizes the presence of a mother who kept a steady course, who knew what she was called to do, and who answered that call. Bradstreet's letter to her children, as we have seen reveals doubts about her calling. The letter and the poem "The Foure Monarchies" suggest that Bradstreet, as time passed, was not reassured by proclamations of the New England way. She could no longer connect, as she says in her letter, "such a God as I worship in Trinity, + such a Sav^r as I rely upon" with the God who her "Reason" told her existed. She knew such a God existed not by watching the unfolding of the history of Massachusetts or even the history of her family clan, but "by the wondrovs workes that I see, the vast frame of ye Heaven + ye Earth, the order of all things night and day, Summer & Winter, Spring and Autvmne, the dayly providing for this great hovshold vpon ye Earth, ye p^{r}serving + directing of All to its proper End" (M/R, 217–18). It was thus in nature, finally, that Bradstreet said she found her assurances. Here nature (as household) and the God who presides over it are subtly gendered as feminine. In the Bible God is imaged as a good wife who (to use John Dod's words) "order[s] the household so that no exercise of religion be hindered" (Mollenkott, 60–68). So, too, the first three quaternions, as we have seen, testify, in women's voices, to this sense of God's natural "household." In the poem to her mother, Bradstreet identifies her mother's steadiness with the deeper workings of the cosmos: just as all things in creation are ordered to their proper end, so too, Dorothy Dudley, in the microcosm of family life, "ordered" things "with dexterity." When she died, it fell to the oldest daughter to take up that ordering—additional reason to write poetry that would discover and articulate order in disordered times.

A Reading of Selected Poems

Conflict and Complexity

Bradstreet's uses in her poetry of the personas of sister and wife reflect a vision of the Creation in which the feminine has a role to play in assuring to the World-Body that a vitality endures. *The Tenth Muse* opens with a portrayal, in the quaternions, of sisters whose relationships (articulated in physical, psychological, and intellectual terms) reassure the reader of the existence of an ultimately positive and sustaining reality alive in the cosmos, and it closes with "Of the vanity of all worldly creatures," a poem that echoes Ecclesiastes in asserting the possibility of the possession of true wisdom by the poet who is a woman. The volume thus can be said to shine a positive light on the implicit association made during both the Keayne and Hutchinson trials between women's bodies and women's minds.

Bradstreet affirms the existence of health and wholeness at a time when the elders and magistrates were finding evidence of the aberrant and destructive. Furthermore, during both Anne Hutchinson's and Sarah Dudley Keayne's trials, the elders drew a likeness between the deformity in the accused woman's opinions and the diseased or deformed character of her sexual and reproductive parts. Ulrich's finding that the "attacks upon religious dissenters frequently included charges of sexual irregularity, as though disruption of one social boundary inevitably entailed distruption of another" (112) would apply in the cases of both these women.

Sarah Keayne was accused of infecting her husband with syphilis, and Anne Hutchinson, following her trial, was reported to have given birth to a "monstrous shape" that was "reported to be many false conceptions in a lump" (Emerson, 230). The word "conceptions" speaks volumes. Mary Dwyer, one of Hutchinson's friends, was said to have given birth to a stillborn fetus that men (who did not witness the birth) described in elaborate detail as something like a gargoyle (Hall, 214). All of these women, as literal and spiritual sisters and wives, seem to have posed an especially virulent threat. Throughout her trials, Hutchinson's accusers referred to her as "sister," the term reserved for women members of congregations. The elders' identification with Hutchinson as a sister-member of their own church family must have fueled their anxieties; the feared contamination might take not only spiritual form but intellectual and bodily form as well.

At the very least, we see in the examples of these women that women's roles in families (whether the literal, congregational, or spiritual "family") were characterized by complexity.[20] One of the identities that Bradstreet claimed in the "Meditations when my Soul hath been refreshed" is sister to Christ. There she says that Christ's identity as brother provides the means to her relationship with the Father. On the literal level, in actual families to be a sister was to be in transition. A woman as daughter and sister would live under obedience to her father until she married, and in that birth family, brothers, especially older brothers, were given special responsibilities as intercessors for, protectors of and caretakers of sisters.

Sisterhood understood as a spiritual condition was neither a temporary state of being nor a means to the love of the Father. As we have seen, John Dod reminded husbands that wives were ultimately sisters. The condition of sisterhood, thus, in part, denoted a woman's (often future or eventual) identity, beyond the subordination that marked her roles within the power relations of literal families. Bradstreet reflects this view in the elegy to her grandchild, Simon Bradstreet, whom she directs to heaven in language that refers to his sisters as members of both his literal and spiritual family: "Go pretty babe, to rest with sisters twain / Amongst the blest in endless joyes remain" (M/R, 188).

Basic to this complex portrait of sisterhood is the example of Christ whose life, death, and resurrection were played out in several roles. As son he descended into the world, as brother he assumed a mortal life, as son he died, but then as one with the Father he ascended to heaven. It is thus in Christ's nature to take on many, even contradictory roles, including his presence in the world as Divine Wisdom who is gendered as female and who is sometimes called "sister Wisdom." Christ as the paradigm of mutability stands behind Bradstreet's self-portrayal in "Meditations when my Soul hath been refreshed." She has a model in Christ that enables her to work through what a modern sociologist might call role conflicts. She writes in a tone of energetic acceptance of the stages through which she has grown and expects to grow, even though her dissatisfactions with the limited and limiting life of each stage is also apparent. Furthermore, the shadowy likeness to Christ in this self-portrait helps us to see that the lowest conditions in the hierarchy (servanthood and childhood) are (mysteriously) the conditions that Christ invited his followers to aspire to. Thus while the life of servant and child appear to be like the grub stage from which the moth emerges there is the added implication that the process is not simply one of movement in a single line to blessedness. Rather, the process takes place outside or beyond earthly definitions of progress. That stage from which one has just emerged is both less *and* more blessed than the stage to come.

Distinctive in Bradstreet's presentation of roles in this meditation is her emphasis on the identity of the woman as a thinking person. Thinking, in this portrayal, does not vanish when the self has "come to heaven." In effect, she still thinks with the same mind, just as, after death, Old Age saw his "very eyes." Similarly, her expectation is that she will "vnderstand pᵣfectly what he hath done for [her]" in the same way that elsewhere she expects, in effect, no longer to see "darkly" but "face to face" (to use Paul's words to the Corinthians). In this meditation the idea is projected that the poet's true art and work will be revealed when she comes to "understand." She then prays for the purifying transformation that will take her, as it took Christ, through death and dissolution to a condition she calls simply "bee[ing] wᵗʰ thee wᶜʰ is best of All" (M/R, 223). Being able to write praises (as she "ought") is here presented as a matter of having been enabled by God to tap into the knowledge that He has in store for her. When Bradstreet says she joined the divine body, He as head, she as a member (following Paul's words in 1 Corinthians 12), she is, in part, expressing her realtionship to Christ as a source of wisdom or "mind," to which she, even as a female artist and thinker, has access now and in the future.

At the same time as Bradstreet presents herself as journeying toward eventual sisterhood or wifehood, she does not spiritualize the process; she does not simply expect to wed Christ, the bridegroom of the second coming, but to *know* Christ in an earth that is infused with his presence. Proverbs 8 provides a full picture of Christ's wisdom activities within the creation, including the idea that before God made the earth and even when He prepared the heavens, Christ's wisdom was there. The Geneva Bible commentators observe that thus Christ as Wisdom "toke mans nature, and dwelt among us, and filled us with vnspeakable treasures"[21]—all of this before Christ's birth as Jesus of Nazareth. The very existence of the sister elements and the humours ("these [who] are of all, the life, the nurse, the grave") attests to Christ as Wisdom's ongoing presence in the creation. These already compose the very foundation of the World Body, even though their ultimate harmony is, as Wisdom's is, hidden, obscured, as yet unrealized. The poet's act of representing them, of learning and knowing about them, is thus a religious act. These "sisters" are not, in and of themselves, divine. They are, rather, the presently factious articulations of the Christ who, as Wisdom, is the in-dwelling "vnspeakable treasure" that was nevertheless spoken as the Logos and that henceforth assures the eternal pattern of the creation, now and as it was in the beginning.

The Bradstreet poems considered in this chapter place particular emphasis on the words of Solomon and thus evoke the presence of Wisdom. To insist, as Solomon did, on Wisdom's sisterhood is, Dod suggests, an important "similitude" that serves to cement the closeness between the believer and Christ, as if Christ were a member of the family. In his commentary on Proverbs (Thomas Dudley brought this commentary with him to the New World; Bradstreet must have known it, even as a child), Dod writes of Solomon's purposes in likening Wisdom to a sister:

[Solomon did so in order] to require that there be such inward friendship and familiaritie betwixt us and her as if she were our sister, and neerest kinswoman. It is a pleasing thing to brothers and sisters, if they love as they ought, to live together in one house as *Lazarus, Martha* and *Mary* or if by occasion of marriage they live in divers houses, yet they delight one in another, and feast together, as did Jobs sonnes and daughters. And thus conversant and familiar ought we to be with Wisdome, we become of kindred and alliance with our Saviour Christ.[22]

If it is Bradstreet's purpose that readers of *The Tenth Muse* become "conversant and familiar" with Christ as sister Wisdom, it is fitting that the volume should open with poems spoken by "sisters" whom the poet hopes her readers will come to know and understand. It is equally fitting that she should close that volume with "Of the vanity of all worldly creatures," a poem that speaks Solomon's words and that addresses the sources of what Bradstreet calls "Mind" or "true knowledge."[23] In effect, the Wisdom-filled speaker of this poem poses and answers a Puritan woman's question: "Where shall I climbe, sound, seek, search or find, / That *summum Bonum* which may stay my mind?" The poems of *The Tenth Muse* can be said to center on this question, which is not a narrowly intellectual question but one in which the speaker challenges the reader's assumptions about knowledge, identity, and gender. In *The Tenth Muse* Bradstreet describes hidden sources that are available to a world that needs to rediscover them. The sources do not exist beyond the traditions from which Puritanism sprang. In effect, Bradstreet calls forth from Judeo-Christian tradition a counterposing vision of a multigendered Christ, a Christ in whom "all the treasures of wisdom and knowledge are hidden" (Col. 2:3), a Christ who is immanent as well as transcendent, who is present as the members of one's own family.

"Of the vanity of all worldly creatures"

Borrowed speech from the Old Testament book of Ecclesiastes ("Vanity, all is vanity") runs like a refrain through the poem "Of the vanity of all worldly creatures." Bradstreet would have understood Ecclesiastes as having been written by Solomon, who there, the Geneva commentators tell us, speaks in the role of preacher. Again, Solomon is not simply speaking his own words: he is speaking the words of Wisdom. Dod explains that Solomon's words are actually

Wisdome or *Wisdomes,* the most high and excellent Wisedom *Jesus Christ* the eternal wisdome of God, in whom are hid all the treasures of wisdome and knowledge. Col. 2.3. who taketh upon him here, and in certain other chapters of this booke [Dod is referring particularly to Proverbs here], the person of a Matrone, a Ladie, or Princesse, according to the feminine gender, where of the word that signifieth wisdome is in Hebrew. (Dod 1615, 12)

In effect, then, when Bradstreet borrows Solomon's speech, she is speaking the words of Sister Wisdom.

Dod thus suggests that Christ acts in the world in a variety of personas. This divine strategy is an important clue to the working of a poet who would, as Stanford has suggested, protect herself by adopting personas (60–61). The speaker here is actually composed of multiple presences. The speaker is, in effect, a palimpsest of wisdom-filled voices: not only is Christ present in this voice, but Solomon's mother, Bathsheba, is, as well, since she was said to have taught Solomon his wisdom, as Proverbs 31 makes clear. Bradstreet thus achieves a doubly female precedent. The Goodwife Bathsheba is one layer of the palimpsest, one that would remind Puritan readers of the ultimate and authoritative, female voice of wisdom. Taken altogether, this speaker sees the world from the viewpoint of a Christlike, albeit feminine consciousness that sees "earth's" "consolations," its honors, wealth, knowledge, and the "sensual senses" as "brittle" (M/R, 159).

Each of earth's vanities in the poem belongs to the kind of "preheminence" that we have seen Bradstreet elsewhere assign to men. Sometimes when she speaks of men's advantages, she adds an implied "sobeit," but here her speaker directly undercuts men's worldly achievements. Men rule; they own property; they work for profit; they pass on inheritances, and all of these activities are termed "vanity." Here again Bradstreet characterizes "youth" and "age" as male ("manly"), and here again her attitude toward these stages is negative: "the first is prone to vice, the last to rage."

The turning point in the poem comes when the speaker takes up the question of the vanity of knowledge (in lines 12–20, M/R, 160). The "vain" achievements enumerated in the first half of the poem are not ones that Bradstreet as a woman would have pursued or experienced— with one exception: when she insists that consolation "sure if on earth" . . .must be in "wisdom, learning, arts," we recognize that she has turned to her own vocation, which is then tested and found wanting. She answers her own questions with a version of the voice of Ecclesiastes: "Yet these, the wisest man of men did find, / But vanity, vexation of the mind" (160). The original biblical phrase is "vexation of the spirit," not of the "mind," and it is used in Ecclesiastes to refer to many kinds of human enterprises, including, but not exclusively, intellectual ones. Bradstreet's poem turns, then, at the point where the wisdom-filled speaker no longer sets herself apart from men's achievement; at the point where she acknowledges that her work ("wisdom, learning, art") might also be listed as among the "vanities."

Learning thus becomes a central concern of the poem, a concern reinforced by the word "mind," repeated in the central question, "Where shall I climbe, sound, seek, search or find / That *summum Bonum* which may stay my mind?" Bradstreet's statement that the "wisest man of men" found earthly wisdom to be vanity suggests Solomon as that man, this section of the poem also echoes Agrippa's thinking. Late in life, Agrippa wrote a scathing critique of his own earlier three-volume study of the occult sciences. His work "Of the Vanity of the Arts and Sciences" was also based on Ecclesiastes. He concluded, as Bradstreet did, that Divine Wisdom is the only source of knowledge for artists, philosophers, and natural scientists. His figures for Wisdom are the traditional ones used by Bradstreet: the fountain, the tree of life, and the spring.

Thus it is possible to read the "wisest man of men" as another palimpsest. Multiple exemplars of that phrase come to mind, including Christ himself, who could be described as "the wisest man of men." Wisdom thus characterizes not simply the sisterly voice that speaks the poem or the vantage point from which the initial judgment of men's accomplishment is made. It also at midpoint is said to characterize *the* man among mortal men who adopts or espouses wisdom. Thus earthly things begin to take on a divine cast; in effect earthly life is changed as soon as true wisdom is discovered to be its source. Thus satisfaction, true assurances, exists everywhere where nobody thinks to look for them. That hidden source is described by natural figures, transformed and rendered divine.

There is thus a double answer to the central question, "Where shall I seek?" In one sense the answer is obvious: there is nowhere to "climb, sound, seek" to find assurance; it is not even to be found in knowledge, art, learning. In another sense, the sense that the poem finally celebrates, the answer lies in a set of impossibilities: all of the earthly prizes that were called vanity in the first part of the poem are redeemed of their decay, deceit, mortality, and serve as emblems of the true riches held forth in "the Living Cristall fount." We notice, then, that what was mere "World" in the first half of the poem serves to picture the ultimate blessings promised in the second half. There is a similar shift in the role and perspective of the speaker, who is transformed, as well.

The speaker begins as if speaking from on high, as if, as sisters were said to be, removed from the things of this world. She adopts the point of view of the Solomonic voice, speaking as a member of Wisdom's family, but when she turns to the subject of knowledge and art, she in effect, descends from on high and presents herself as one among other "worldly creatures." As soon as the speaker admits that she no longer knows but has to ask where to search, she begins to grow and change. Using the imagery of the book of Revelation, she proceeds to answer her question by painting a picture of a landscape that is nowhere. Her vocation as artist and wise woman is demonstrated not in religious tenets but in the scene she sketches on the canvas, a scene that evokes the visible to undercut and critique our sense of the unquestioned reality of the visible. The nub, the crux of the speaker's enlightenment, as well as of Bradstreet's artistic method, is found in the words "who drinks thereof, the world doth nought account." The sentence reads both ways. The world thinks nothing of the one who drinks from this fountain, and the one who drinks thinks nothing of the world. The canvas thus manages to erase as it portrays. In this moment, the scene and the participant in it, indeed the world itself, become "nought." It is when the abyss opens up that the speaker is fed with the gracious waters that have a changing effect on her view of the world. She, as Christ did, passes through a dissolution and then emerges with a renewed vision, one that "satiates the soul [and] stayes the mind."

Thus this speaker achieves sisterhood through a process that is fully expressive of the mutability of Wisdom. In a Christlike trajectory she enters the "world," moves through crisis and nothingness, and then is represented as restored to security and power. The poem, in effect, tells of the process of the mind's conversion to *true* Wisdom by taking the mind through death and the experience of nothingness, of "nought." The transmutation and re-presentation of the very achievements that were considered to be vanity in the earlier section of the poem tells us that Wisdom is to be found not only in heaven but in earth as well: in fact she is to be found in the "world." The speaker's experience of true wisdom does not eradicate the world; it transforms rather than expunges the vanities. In effect, the lead of what was "vain" is transformed into gold.

Sister Wisdom is thus a pervasive presence in this poem. In the second half of the poem she is present as both masculine and feminine. She characterizes the "wisest man of men," and in the final action she is present in the resolution of the gender polarities suggested earlier. In the line "Possessed of Christ" the believer "shall [like Christ] remain a King" it appears that the female believer, in becoming king, becomes male. When we understand the scriptural and theological context of Christ-Wisdom as "King," however, we understand that such a "Reign" is a transformed expression of power. Just as men can become wise, even wisest, so women can put on, as Bradstreet says in "Flesh and the Spirit," "Royal robes." Christ's "Kingship" is the ultimate transmutation of the world's power.

When Bradstreet concludes, "This satiates the soul, this stayes the

mind, / The rest's but vanity, and vain we find," her allusion to the
"mind" as having to be "stayed" tells us again that the conversion of the
world will strengthen and reinforce her identity as an intellectual and
artistic woman. She will "wear his Crown unto eternities," just as in
"Meditation" she expects to "bee with him." The separation of human
life into death and life, this world and the next, has been softened,
obscured. So, too, has the reification of gender roles. Wisdom's promises
are not of a spiritual, bodiless hereafter but of power (as in the elegy to
Queen Elizabeth) exerted in *wise* and *just* ways; and the poem puts us in
contact with sources of power and consolation that will answer perpetually to our needs—for male and female alike, now and hereafter.

In this poem and in the later poem, "The Flesh and the Spirit,"
Bradstreet argues for a view that distinguishes the "earth" from the
"world," and the use of the biblical references play an essential part in
that argument. The fact that the imagery of the last half of the poem
comes from the book of Revelation implies that this scene (in addition
to being hidden from view) is hidden in the sense of being not yet
revealed, not yet come to pass. The references to the Solomonic texts
suggest that the world already contains and reflects something of the
divine, which if or when transformed, will make earthly life into a
reality that corresponds to God's original intention for the creation.
Bradstreet uses the biblical echoes in her poetry to affirm the potentiali-
ties of the earthly and at the same time to affirm the imperfection, even
destructiveness, of earth's institutions, habits of thought, and political
and social structures. These are, as she says, "on brittle earth," suggesting that they do not grow and change. Human achievements do not
simply wear thin or "decay"; they ossify. Yet "brittle" suggests break-
able, and the poem seems to advocate breaking as part of the process; it
advocates the breaking forth of the unseen within natural life.

"The Flesh and the Spirit"

Similar themes are expressed in "The Flesh and the Spirit," published
in 1678 in *Several Poems*. The speakers of this poem are cast in the role of
sisters; the poem again takes the form of a dialogue. The subject is,
again, enslavement to things of the world. The voice of "Spirit" has the
last word. Following Paul in Romans 8, she insists that heavenly things
are finer, richer, and more satisfying than any earth has to offer, but
Spirit's is not necessarily the point of view of the poet, who here frames
the dialogue is such a way as to tell us how she views the conflict. Any
interpretation of the poem must incorporate the fact that the poet

positions herself as an observer and reporter of the two sisters' argument. Bradstreet introduces her poem by telling us where "I" stood to witness the scene:

> In secret place where once I stood
> Close by the Banks of *Lacrim* flood
> I heard two sisters reason on
> Things that are past, and things to come.
>
> (M/R, 175)

The word "secret" suggests that this place is "hid from eyes of men, that count it strange," like the scene of "the Living Cristall fount" in "Of the vanity of all worldly creatures." This place is not a fountain, though; it is a river of tears, and only rather faintly (in its suggestion of sorrow) points to Christ's presence—this in contrast to Spirit's bold future vision of "A Chrystall River . . . / Which doth proceed from the Lambs Throne." A haunting tone, perhaps nostalgia, even world weariness, marks these lines in the word "once." What is to unfold, the poet informs us, relates to the realities of the past and future, perhaps to these as sad realities.

The dialogue and the argument do not seem to focus on time or on history. Flesh takes the first turn. She voices an indeed spirited attack on her sister's intellectual and devotional activities. Her questions have the bite of sarcasm as she mirrors back to her sister a portrait of someone whose fantasies and preoccupations have put her out of touch with satisfactions offered here and now. Flesh's advice is, in effect, a bird in the hand is worth two in the bush. She says, "Then let not goe, what thou maist find, / For things unknown, only in mind." In this sense, Flesh argues for seizing the day, for recognizing that what presently *is* is "enough of precious store." Emerson's "Hamatreya" takes flesh's side in this argument. In this sense, the poem is about time, with implications of historical time.

Spirit breaks in with a "Be still," perhaps indirectly telling us that this portrait is making her uncomfortable. Perhaps the portrait has some truth to it. Spirit reacts, as modern people might say, defensively. Flesh's words have struck home:

> Disturb no more my setled heart,
> For I have vow'd (and so will doe)
> Thee as a foe, still to pursue.

> And combate with thee will and must,
> Untill I see thee laid in th' dust.
>   (M/R, 175–76)

Unlike the playful feuds of the four elements and humours, this feud is a "deadly" one. Although these two speakers are "sisters . . . yea twins," they do not share consanguinity of the kind that enabled mother-daughter Old and New England to surmount distance, circumstances, and age to look ahead to the coming Judgment. Yet so close have these twins been that Spirit has not had an easy time resisting Flesh's "charms." Often in the past, as she tells us, she gave in and lived to regret her credulity:

> How oft thy slave, hast thou me made,
> When I believ'd, what thou hast said,
> And never had more cause of woe
> Then when I did what thou bad'st doe.
>   (M/R, 176)

Spirit looks to the future (indeed she "vows" to look ahead), and meanwhile in the present she lives on "meat thou kno'st not off." Again, the sources are hidden or secret: 'The hidden Manna I doe eat, / The word of life it is my meat." Spirit's single present, here-and-now, resource is the immanent Christ and his grace (his "manna"), freely given to the regenerate soul. In addition to that palpably real source, Spirit has her "thoughts." Spirit's mind's eye is able to "pierce the heavens, and see / What is Invisible to thee." The reality of her presently poor clothes is compensated by the future "Royal Robes" [she] shall have on, / More glorious then the glistring Sun." She will assume Christ and be clothed in his attributes in the future; now she has the nourishment provided by his secret and hidden presence as the "meat of life."

This poem, too, is thus suggestive of Christ's presence in a multiplicity of roles, including that of Divine Wisdom. In one sense relationship to Christ can be seen as the heart of the issue (the cause of the "deadly feud") between the two sisters. Spirit addresses Flesh as "thou unregenerate part," as one who has not been joined to Christ. Spirit says that Flesh was fathered by "Old Adam" whereas Spirit's "arise is from above, / Whence my dear father I do love." Spirit's strengths come from her attachment to, her rootedness in, the divine, further evidenced by time spent in meditation, contemplation, and speculation, all of which Flesh denigrates. These are Spirit's activities, as opposed to the "industry" which Flesh recommends. Industry, Flesh points out, "hath its recompence," which we read as an alternative to the kind of repayment that Spirit seeks—namely, Christ's redemption, the full effects of which may be hidden now but will be fully revealed in the future.

These sisters, then, are pitted against each other. They do not seem to play out their parts in that great household on the earth that elementally, is composed of their mutual interactions. Nor are they related together as sisters in the realm of the blest. Spirit may join that sisterhood, but Flesh apparently will not. Nor is their rivalry harmless. Spirit vows to destroy Flesh, just as Flesh's "charms" have proven to be "deadly harms" for Spirit. The evils of the world in this poem do not belong to "masculines"; they belong, each sister feels, to the other.

How, then, do we interpret this little drama, which Bradstreet has staged on the banks of the river of tears? If we follow the poet's cue, that this poem is about things past and things to come, we may say that Flesh stands for a certain point of view on the world, of which the persona of Spirit is particularly critical. Flesh can be seen as a kind of New England attitude, one of whose characteristics is industriousness. She would be among those who stressed the importance of "works" as a test of faith, since works can be seen and measured. Another characterizing feature of this point of view is its common-sense, down-to-earth distrust of speculation. These practical folk look on contemplation and meditation as the inventions of those who are fancy-sick, who are engaged in "catch[ing] at shadowes which are not." Another characteristic of the Flesh position is her faith in the earth's productivity and plenty and a willingness to exploit these. Finally, Flesh uses artful speech—sarcasm, innuendo—in the service of her worldview; she uses language as persuasion, even if it dissembles, if it "speak'st me fair, but hat'st me sore." Taken altogether, these features suggest aspects of belief that, in the wake of the Antinomian crisis, were presently real and that Bradstreet implies may threaten to take over in the future.

A careful reading of the poem, however, shows Bradstreet not to be exclusively on Spirit's side in the argument, even though in her vivid portrayal of God's biblical promises we can read a concern that these promises must continue to burn bright in her readers' consciousnesses. Bradstreet has mounted a richly scriptural, and richly ancient, reminder of the true nature of the heavenly "City" toward which she, as we have seen, yet hopes to move. But Spirit is no tolerationist: she excludes Flesh as not only unredeemed but apparently unredeemable.

Spirit's is strong language: "This City pure is not for thee, / For things unclean there shall not be." Spirit proclaims the vision of the book of Revelation as still standing beyond and above the actualities of the Puritan commonwealth in Massachusetts.

The subtlety and richness of the poem derives from the fact that the sisters appear to be taking stands neither of which fully represented the ideal. The poem reveals the closeness, indeed the *twinship* of the two points of view, despite the two speakers' declarations of their mutual enmity. In fact there is an apparent polarity here that Bradstreet (and other Puritans of a like persuasion) did not espouse. As we have seen, in Bradstreet's work "flesh" is not simply corrupt, nor was it so in the Bible. Being of "one flesh" is the promise of an ideal state; it is a reminder of God's ultimate intention for Adam and Eve—"They shall be of one flesh" (Gen. 2:24). In Isaiah "all flesh shall see it [the day of God's revelation] together" (Isa. 40:6), and even though the spirit of the Lord blows on the grass and withers it, yet that destruction is not, as the Geneva Bible commentators point out, the final condition of "flesh." Job's words stand behind Old Age's final speech in the "Four Ages." Job declares that "though after my skin *wormes* destroy thise bodie, yet shal I se God in my flesh" (Job 19:26). The Geneva Bible commentators explain that "herein Job declareth plainely that he had a ful hope, that bothe the soule and body shulde enjoye the presence of God in the last resurrection" (Geneva, 228). Bradstreet reflects these understandings of the word "flesh" when she declares the essential nature of wife's love for husband as "Flesh of thy flesh, bone of thy bone" (M/R, 181).

In fact the dichotomy being portrayed in this poem is not a static body-spirit dualism. In Paul's vision in Romans 8 the spirit leads, intercedes for, and helps the flesh through the process of renewal. Not only does Bradstreet's use of flesh connote one aspect of ultimate (and hoped for) life, but the "riches" that Spirit is envisioning are, once again, the transformed riches, honors, and pleasures of the world, which Flesh had mentioned in her effort to tempt Spirit. The very opulence of Spirit's "city" accounts for the seductiveness of the strategy at work here. Not only does Spirit's speech top Flesh's for lushness, her scene is made even more alluring by the fact that Flesh cannot see what Spirit is describing. Spirit's city is heavily bejeweled (with Christ's emblems, of course), but the fact that Spirit is the only one who can "see" this sight must be the ultimate tease. Further, Spirit's streets of gold are made even more alluring by the fact of their gold's "transparence." It is beyond any gold that we have seen. The paradox here achieves a remarkable complexity.

This reference to transparent gold the Christian alchemist would read as a reference to Christ; thus the invisible Christ is made visible and tangible by an image that is unseeable.

Spirit thus is being consummately artful in the service of her own worldview. She is not merely "catch[ing] at shadows." Her promises, even more than Flesh's, are highly concrete signifiers of wealth and power. In these respects the two sisters are like antagonists. Although the poet seems to be emphasizing the opposition between them, Flesh and Spirit can be seen as simply two aspects of Christian belief, aspects that all believers felt should be yoked together. It was the precise nature of their relationship that Puritans argued about, but no one said that works or grace alone constituted the whole evidence of sanctification. In the Antinomian controversy, each side tended to argue a "straw man," rendering the other impotent by positing it as espousing all work or all grace. In truth, Flesh and Spirit were parts of one kernel or, to switch the metaphor, two sides of the same coin. Against this background, the feud between them may, I would suggest, account for the poet's melancholy as she listens to the dialogue.

Even though Bradstreet's poem comes out more strongly on the side of Spirit than of Flesh, there is clear evidence in the figures used that Flesh, representing as she does the "unregenerate part" of society or of the individual believer, should not be "laid in th' dust"—that is, be destroyed. Rather she should "die" in the way Christ died. She needs to "die" to the things of this world and be redeemed by the grace that at present Flesh "know'st not off." Flesh may be unseeing and unknowing, but she is not unredeemable. There is more life to come for Flesh if she is not abandoned by her far-seeing sister. Flesh is, thus, a kind of Caliban, toward whom in this poem her sister feels disdain.

Bradstreet's poem presents a complex set of insights in tension. The dichotomy between Flesh and Spirit exists because of the roles the two have assigned themselves and each other. Their roles are evidence of what Bradstreet called "brittle earth" in the other poem. The two sisters appear to be locked into a life-long feud, and the poet's attitude, as observer of the scene, is represented wholly by neither one. The poem is composed of interlocking ironies from first to last. Perhaps one of the final ironies is that Spirit, who has the last say, declares that she is ready to leave the world to Flesh. Spirit opts for heaven, but it is the experience of the creation, of its "substance" and "meat," that are in this poem what heaven is composed of. That last stance on Spirit's part is a self-annihilating gesture. Once the sisters are separated from each other, and the earth left to Flesh only, both sisters will suffer an irreparable loss.

Repeatedly in her other work, Bradstreet says that she (like Job) expects to see God "in the flesh." The poetry and the meditations suggest that Bradstreet saw the world as containing Christ as Wisdom and expressing his presence, albeit in secret, obscure, imperfect ways. The hidden or transparent gold that the Spirit claims for heaven is in fact the principle of which all things in nature are ultimately composed. The two realms, Bradstreet's other poems suggest, are intermeshed. Indeed, elsewhere in the poetry Bradstreet reflects Flesh's sense of the world; the wife who speaks the poem "A Letter to her Husband, absent upon Publick employment" (M/R, 181) praises her husband as her "magazine of earthly store" much as Flesh in this poem praises earth's "precious store." Thus although Bradstreet may here seem to come down on Spirit's side of the argument, she presents Spirit too as less than all-knowing; certainly here Spirit is less than compassionate. Unlike the spirit of Paul's epistle to the Romans, Bradstreet's Spirit appears here to be attempting to leave Flesh behind. She is attempting to flee into another realm, and that endeavor, Bradstreet's framing words may be implying, is tragic; it is toward death in the sense of ultimate separation and not toward death as a prelude to resurrection and reunion.

Turning now to the subject of women's bodies and women's opinions with which this section began, we can see yet another set of implications in this poem for what I called the Bradstreet project of putting another face on women's identity. If we take the "twins" here as figures that are intentionally female—that is, as figures that are not simply counters, abstract vehicles for ideas—we can read them as the two parts of the Puritan woman's self: Flesh is the Martha, the industrious housewife, and Spirit is the Mary, the spiritual seeker, removed from the world. The implicit dynamic transmutation of one into the other and back again, the mutability of their roles is here seen as disrupted, forestalled. If one part of what Dod referred to as Christ's family unit or one part of a woman's life (the daily round of her practical duties) grew to be thought of as separate from the other (the activities of the "saint" or "visionary"), then the self would be divided into two; it would be polarized and no longer seen as parts in a dynamic continuum. The dialogue would degenerate into hostility, into positions that are fixed rather than alive and capable of change. Art would degenerate into figures used in the service of opinion.

The kind of split that is being described in this poem is not only to be seen as one that Bradstreet witnessed in the society of women with whom she associated, although there are strong overtones here of positions taken in the Antinomian controversy. The split also can be understood as one that as Ann Stanford suggests, she experienced internally or perhaps as one that found expression in her own extended family. The mention of contemplations and meditations (both titles of works written in her later years) may hint at an actual sister's accusations of her as a person who was off in her own world. But if we understand the poem as a highly structured representation of inner conflict, staged in such a way as to reveal the full complexity and irony of such conflicts, we begin to understand how the subject necessitated poetic utterance. Bradstreet's poem is no piece of conventional piety. It probes and exposes to view the consequences of a split in identity of the kind that occurs when obligations, consciousness, and sensibility rigidify and when our concepts polarize and our self-definitions turn "brittle."

The Marriage Poems

A further working out of the relationship between flesh and spirit is central to the five poems known as the "marriage poems," in which Bradstreet, speaking as wife, declares her love to and for her husband. These poems' statements of personal feelings distinguish them from the poems we have considered thus far. To most modern readers these poems are Bradstreet's most accessible; indeed, for twentieth-century critics these poems have provided evidence (some would say the only evidence) of a true poetic sensibility in an otherwise Puritan poet—or so the conventional distinction is made.

As we move into a consideration of the five marriage poems, we should bear in mind that we are dealing with poems that were in fact published, albeit posthumously in the 1678 volume, *Several Poems.* The poetic statements here are personal and direct, and in four of the five poems the ostensible audience for the poems is the husband himself. And yet as natural and unmediated as these expressions of feeling appear to be, they nevertheless do not belong (as the autobiographical letter and meditations do) to that group of writings in longhand that were intended for the immediate family. In that more private group of writings in manuscript we also find poems on the subject of the husband's absence. There too the speaker is sometimes specifically identified as wife, but these poems lack the formal elements of the published poems. They are, most frequently, verse prayers addressed to God on

specific occasions—Simon's voyage to England in 1661 for the purpose
of renewing the Massachusetts Bay charter, for example.

Yet even these manuscript poems lack the immediacy and directness
of letters or diaries. Missing from the Bradstreet collection are writings
intended for her eyes only. Bradstreet may well have kept a diary, and
no doubt she wrote letters—perhaps from Ipswich to her mother and
father in Roxbury, perhaps to her sisters Sarah and Mercy in England.
But, if so, no diary and no letters have survived. We must, I think,
conclude that the five marriage poems were considered by her family
after her death as neither so private nor so personal (nor so "un-
Puritan") as to warrant exclusion from *Several Poems*. It is not clear what
role Bradstreet played in the selection of poems for eventual publication
or even for *The Tenth Muse,* published during her lifetime. But what is
clear is that the marriage poems bear the same stylistic features as other
of her poems that were considered to be publishable.

The marriage poems are iambic pentameter poems; they thus share
their form with all the other major poems. Bradstreet did not choose
the jaunty hexameters of the poem to her children as "eight birds hatcht
in one nest." Nor did she choose the ballad stanza she apparently felt
was appropriate to the offering of prayers at a loved one's death or
departure or of thanksgiving for return or release from "affliction." To
be sure, in comparison with, say, the quaternions and the elegies, these
five poems are marked by economy of expression (another feature that
endears them to modern sensibilities), but the poems nevertheless rever-
berate with the same biblical voices heard earlier, particularly with the
Solomonic voice of Proverbs and Canticles. The reference to the solar
system and to alchemical process throughout identify the marriage
poems as again the products of a mind that was deeply immersed in
Renaissance science. These poems too are marked by biblical figures
suggestive of Christ's presence in the life of the married couple, particularly of his presence in the body of the world that the poems celebrate.
Again, although we have not noticed this feature of the marriage poems
to the extent we perhaps should, Bradstreet has adopted a feminine
speaker, the voice of one of her roles, for this set of erotic and at the
same time devotional utterances.

In short Bradstreet's use of the persona of the wife is no less a
"public" strategy than was her earlier use of the voices of daughters,
children, and sisters. In my reading of the poems Bradstreet's speakers
do not fall easily into the widely accepted categories of public and
private, as described in Kenneth Requa's essay "Anne Bradstreet's Po-

etic Voices."[24] Requa's essay was the first to underscore the importance of Bradstreet's voices, and it too finds "conflicts" expressed in her work that she "never fully resolved." The equivalences between domestic and private and between intellectual and public are ones I would like to call into question. Another way of approaching the same point would be to say that modern readers have assumed that wife and mother were roles Bradstreet really played and therefore she was speaking as her real-life self when she spoke as wife. The evidence of the social historians suggests, however, that of all the Puritan woman's roles, that of housewife was the most elaborately conceptualized and allegorized of the cultural constructions that defined her identity. Furthermore, in the influential prototype of Bathsheba both the housewife and the wise woman are joined. The marriage poems present a highly sensitive construction of the role of wife in a redefinition of that role. Although not caught in rebellion against the role or in an attempted escape from it, the poet does develop her statements by means of paradox and tension. Resolution of conflict is indeed part of the intentional (and public) strategy through which the poet takes the reader.

I have just coupled the terms erotic and devotional when I described these poems, in part because I believe that it is the conjunction of these qualities that can seem such an impossibility to modern readers—not, perhaps, when the seventeenth-century poets are male but when the poets are women and "Puritans" and wives. Bradstreet unabashedly portrays her marriage as rich with sexual satisfaction, and this statement need not be interpreted as apostasy. She recalls the experience of lying in her husband's arms (M/R, 180), of being embraced "once a day," of being "treated by [his] loving mouth" (M/R, 182). A deliciously sensuous allegory, again based on imagery taken from Canticles and Proverbs, concludes the poem entitled "Another":

> Together at one Tree, oh let us brouze,
> And like two Turtles roost within one house,
> And like the Mullets in one River glide,
> Let's still remain but one, till death divide.
> (M/R, 183)

Bradstreet signs the poem "The loving Love and Dearest Dear, / At home, abroad, and every where. / A.B."

In all five marriage poems the reunion with the husband is sometimes impatiently, sometimes prayerfully, sought. As deliberately di-

vine as the likeness of the husband is, however, and even though the
husband travels, has responsibility for public affairs, and is not the one
whose life is threatened by childbirth, he is not presented as having the
more important role in the union. The poems make repeated use of the
phrase "if ever two be one," indicating (in its subjunctive verb form)
the literal impossibility of that arithmetic and at the same time suggesting, anticipating, that union, which is a union of equals. Each partner's
powers equals the other's: her love is such that "Rivers cannot quench"
(M/R, 180) and his has a "power to dry the torrent of these streams"
(M/R, 182). They belong to a pair (of deer, doves, fish) like Edenic
animals paired and ready for the ark. In their two-by-two relationship,
they are thus portrayed as eternal; they are in that ultimate and original
state the creator described as "of one flesh" and that Bradstreet as wife
calls "Flesh of thy Flesh" (M/R, 181).

For a poet whose hallmark has been a tendency to apology, these
energetic declarations are remarkable for their forthrightness. In these
poems wife speaks to husband not simply as his spiritual equal but as his
corporal one too. Furthermore the wife celebrates a sexual union that
resonates with the divine in which she, as wife, does not keep silent. She
seems to possess a sanction for these declarations, even though the Massachusetts leadership censured women for speaking out. In these poems the
wife does attend "to household affairs," as Governor Winthrop thought
women should, but the poems do not reflect Winthrop's sense that
women's activities should be limited to what he called "such things as
belong to women." Governor Winthrop rebuked another intellectual
woman (Ann Hopkins) for going "out of her way and calling to meddle in
such things as were proper for men, whose minds are stronger." Bradstreet's work, as we have seen, demonstrates the strength and appropri-
ateness of her intellectual calling, even though she sometimes cushions
the impact of her assertions with apologies and demurers. Furthermore,
Winthrop called Ann Hopkins's husband to task for the very qualities
that the Bradstreet poems celebrate in the husband: for being "very
loving and tender of her." It was, Winthrop said, because the husband
failed to guide and discipline his wife that Ann Hopkins strayed from the
"place God set for her (Winthrop 2:216).[25]

Winthrop's clear sense of that place supports his diagnosis of the cause
of Ann Hopkins's insanity: had she not strayed "out of her way" she
might have "kept her wits, and might have improved them usefully and
honorably in the place God had set for her." Bradstreet had a very
different sense of her place, a sense that, in the marriage poems, is fully

consonant with the view of the cosmos presented in the earlier poems. Sanctions for the view of women's bodies as sexually distinct from, but nonetheless equal to, men's would have come to Bradstreet from the writers whose work supported her ambitious undertakings in the quaternions. In the *Microcosmographia* the physician-anatomist Helkiah Crooke, for example, described women's and men's bodies emphasizing their equality and their equal significance in nature. Bradstreet refers to Crooke's treatise (first published in 1615) as the authority on which she relied for knowledge of the humours and the elements.[26] She would have found the *Microcosmographia* important, too, for its delineation of the relevance of anatomy to poetry and moral philosophy. It seems that Bradstreet made use of "sources" that the "world" of the Massachusetts leadership did "nought account."

Crooke writes that there are "two fruites of Anatomy." The first is the "knowledge of our owne Nature, and then of the invisible God."[27] As we have seen, Bradstreet's work focused on the hidden Christ, both in the workings of nature and in the human body, particularly as God's presence is evidenced in her own and her family's health. (Her poems and meditations repeatedly record the onset of and recovery from sickness.) Crooke then points out the "other benefittes and commodities of Anatomy proper and peculiar to Poets, Painters [and craftsmen] . . . to teach them the better to bring their Arts to perfection." Crooke argues that natural philosophers, too, need a knowledge of anatomy. "For inasmuch as the proper and proportionable subject of his art is a body Naturall, and the body of Man as it were the square and rule of all other bodies, he ought not, nor cannot be truly accounted a Naturall Philosopher, who is ignorant of the historie of man's body" (16). (Crooke means human, including female, anatomy and physiology.) Bradstreet's quaternions certainly reflect this understanding of the relationship of the human body and of its life stages to the body of nature. Crooke's recommendation of the subject of anatomy to the moral philosophers goes on to stress the metaphor of "household" government, reflected in Bradstreet's description of her intentions for the quaternions. Crooke writes that the moral philosopher

shall easily learne by the mutall offices and duties of every part, and by the constitution of the Natural household government appearing in our bodies, how to temper and order the manners and conditions of the minde, how to rule and gouern a Commonwealth or Citie, and how to direct a private house or family.(16)

Of particular relevance to an understanding of how the wife's body is understood in the marriage poems would be Crooke's description of women's bodies in the section on "generation" in *Microcosmographia*. He writes,

Both the sexes of male and female do not differ in the kinde as we cal it or species, that is, essential form and perfection; but only in some accidents, to wit, in temper and in structure and scituation of the parts of Generation. For the female sexe as well as the male is a perfection of mankinde: some there bee that call a woman *Animal occasionatum,* or Accessorium, barbarous words to expresse a barbarous concept, as if they should say, A Creature by the way, or made by mischance; yea some haue growne to that impudencie, that they have denied a woman to haue a soule as man hath. The truth is, that as the soule of a woman is the same diuine nature as a mans, so is her body a necessary being, a first and not a second intention of Nature, her proper and absolute worke not her error or preuarication. The difference is by the Ancients in a few words elegantly set downe when they define a man, to be a creature begetting in another, a woman a creature begetting in her selfe. (258)

To be sure, Crooke later holds to the conventional view that the man has the seed and the woman does not. She has the place, the blood, the "garden," in which the seed it planted and nourished. Bradstreet's reference to children as "those fruits which through thy heat I bore" (M/R, 81) reflects Crooke's understanding of the process of "generation." For Crooke the fact that men were "hotter" than women meant that women were better suited to childbearing. Crooke's thinking on this subject was basically alchemical. He thought of "generation" as the human version of the natural "propogation of kindes," which "is made in the Elements by Transmutation, and in Mettals by Apposition." It is clear that children, even though not the product of the union of two zygotes, are nonetheless inheritors equally from both parents. Crooke writes, "The Generation of man and of the perfect creatures is farre more noble, as whereto three things are alwaies required; a diversity or distinction of sexes, their mutuall embracements and copulations, and a premixtion of a certain matter yssuing from them both which potentially containeth the *Idea* or forme of the particular parts of the body, and the fatal destiny of the same" (258).

These citations from Crooke's influential work highlight the background ideas about human sexuality that Bradstreet brought to the marriage poems, but they also make clear the significance and meaning of the idea of the future in the marriage poems and especially of the threat posed to that future. Even in the poems that do not mention children, the separations of the partners from each other are treated in such a way as to call the consummate, much anticipated reunion into doubt. Crooke's emphasis on sexuality as a means to the reproduction of children is not made in a narrowly prohibitive way. Sexuality is linked to the ongoing process, as he sees it, of transmutation and redemption, with the explicit purpose of showing his readers that the human body is not only the "measure" or the moral example; it is the means whereby a transformed human life is assured. Crooke and Agrippa were among those early Renaissance men of science who, in effect, rewrote the sexual legacy from Adam and Eve.

The most distinctive feature, however, of the marriage poems is not the fact of the poet's delight in a shared bodily and spiritual life with her husband; it is the fact that delight is represented as perpetually interrupted, forestalled, threatened by separation—separations endured by husband and wife against their (in this case, especially the wife's) will. Against such statements as Crooke's of the "ultimate destiny" as well as the naturalness and health of sexual "embracements and copulation," the separations described in the marriage poems take on an augmented significance. Bradstreet's highly allusive language, furthermore, endows separation not simply with personal but with cosmic dimensions of meaning.

The difficult distance between Ipswich and Boston where her husband has gone on "public employment" forces one kind of separation. By implication, this poem suggests a distance too between their socially prescribed roles, since the wife does not go abroad on "public" business. Death causes another kind of separation, as imagined in "Before the Birth of one of her Children" and as anticipated too in "To My Dear and loving Husband." The separation in "Phoebus make haste" (also entitled simply "Another") is of a more global, universal kind (each partner occupies a different "Hemisphere"), and the "husband" is given solarian powers of the kind earlier attributed to Sidney. The poem magnifies the significance of marriage, in its suggestions of the potential workings (on a cosmic scale) of the fifth essence. When the poet calls for this process to restore the married partners, she uses the language used in hermetic lore to describe the redemption of the world body. Phoebus is instructed to "conjure him not to stay."

Separation also threatens the symbolic union implied throughout these poems of Christ as bridegroom and the church as bride. In this group of poems the language of the occult is interwoven with the allegory of the Christian journey to the end of history. The imminence of that "reunion" is a theme in much Puritan preaching and writing, among those of a scientific bent of mind as well as by others. John Cotton set forth his millenarianism in an exposition on Canticles, preached in 1621 (Bradstreet was then a member of Cotton's congregation in old Boston). There Cotton states his own eager expectation of the church's deliverance into the arms of her beloved. Cotton referred to the day of Christ's coming as "our marriage day" (Morgan, 163), and elsewhere predicted that 1656 would be the date. Bradstreet uses the allegory of the union with Christ, the bridegroom, in the last poem she wrote, dated 1669, a devotional poem in which she expects her own death, like the death of history, to be a sexual reunion, but in this more directly devotional statement no mention of the literal husband is made. Instead the language is directed to Christ as bridegroom: "Lord make me ready for that day / then Come deare bridegrome Come away" (M/R, 211).

In each of the marriage poems, then, the love relationship is set in a context of ominousness. And it is this threat that Bradstreet calls oppressive. Bradstreet's use of that word does not in the marriage poems refer to the oppression of women in marriage. Oppression is, rather, one of the effects of separation. Her "mind" is "oppressed" as a consequence of the cultural, physical, global, and astrological forces that control (or appear to control) the lives of the married pair. In winter the "Sun is gone so far in's Zodiak" that the poet's "chilled limbs now nummed lye forlorn." The "Dove" who mourns the "loss" of her mate feels her separation at a point beyond numbness. She says she seems "no wife." Her identity is robbed by the loss of the other. She is powerless to direct her life: "But worst of all, to him can't steer my course, / I here, he there, alas, both kept by force" (M/R, 183).

Exactly what that "force" is we are not told, but it is alive in the universe of these poems (in the stars, in nature, in the political life of the commonwealth), and it attacks the wife's mind and her self. The wife suffers particularly from depression; she lives in the husband's "little world," which, during his absence feels like "a fathom under water." Her "Place" is cold, flooded, northern. His absence, like the sun's absence, dwarfs or thwarts her speech: "Tell him I would say more, but cannot well, / Oppressed minds, abruptest tales do tell" (M/R, 182). Separation thus accounts not only for her depression; it affects her powers of expression. In the husband's presence the poet is enabled to speak; his presence does not curb, curtail, or silence her speech. It is, rather, his absence, or the threat of his absence, that forces an alteration in her style; in separation her expression turns "abrupt."

Thus, there is a direct relationship between the brokenness of the whole that the married union signifies and the style adopted for these poems. The poetic statement here is highly compressed, to the point of terseness. Punning ("As loving Hind that [Hartless] wants her Deer"), paradox ("Commend me to the man more loved then life, / Shew him the sorrows of his widdowed wife"), oxymoron ("Yet love thy dead, who long lay in thine arms") constitute the poetic strategies. The intention seems to be for that which appears one way to be read another, even to be read as its opposite. Nowhere is the "doubleness" we earlier observed as typical of Bradstreet more in evidence than in the marriage poems. Here she adopts "abruptness" as a poetic method, one that has its roots in biblical proverb or parable. John Dod described such language when he described the language of Proverbs, as "short, sweet proverbial sentences, full of weight and wisdom." Dod makes clear that the language of the proverb and the parable are a contrived language whose meanings are hidden and must be unlocked and that the quality of terseness and surprise typical of biblical axioms is directly designed to suit the times in which the Solomonic author lived. The times that this style was said to fit was a time out of joint, a time of longing for and separation from the beloved or from the Messiah, a time that was, of course, predicted to end in reunion.

Before we look in further detail at Dod's commentary on the style of Proverbs, let us examine two Bradstreet sentences from the marriage poems that have the quality of compression or "abruptness" I have just alluded to. The last two lines of these six from "Before the Birth of one her Children" provide us with one example of her style in this group of poems.

> How soon, my Dear, death may my steps attend,
> How soon't may be thy lot to lose thy friend,
> We both are ignorant, yet love bids me
> These farewell lines to recommend to thee,
> That when that knot's unty'd that made us one,
> I may seem thine, who in effect am none.
> (M/R, 179–80)

Here both husband and wife are "ignorant" of time, that is, of "how soon" the dread event that will part them will occur. Despite igno-

does what "love bids" her to : she writes. The effect of her
hat she hopes will take place) is a "seeming" to be joined to
her hu. nd, even though she is "none." Knowledge of just *when* that
joined state will be reached grows less important as poetry promises a
substitute for knowledge of that (linear) time. Indeed, this poem is
written in response to a power (love's bidding) that renders the effects
of time irrelevant. Curiously, it sounds as if mere "seeming," mere
appearance or make-believe, is being pitted against the entire weight of
reality—of death, separation, mortality itself—surely, as she might
say, a "vain" contest.

On the side of this "seeming thine," however, are some paradoxical
formulations that tell us that Christ is present, in fact that he is integral
to the transmutation being described. A serious use of puns marks these
lines, which when unlocked, reveal Christ's presence. Christ is the
"knot" that ties husband and wife and makes them "one." The couple is
"knit together in love" as the congregation at Colossus was. The Colossians were exhorted by Paul, as we have seen, to come to know the
mysteries of Christ, "in whom are hid all the treasures of wisdom and
knowledge" (Col. 2:2–3). In Bradstreet's poem initially a certain kind of
knowledge knot is "unty'd," and that knot can be punned as "nought" or
nothingness, which, as we saw in "The Vanity of all worldly creatures," is
a word used to characterize Christ. Again the mutability of Christ's
presence undergirds the poetic statement. When the speaker describes
herself as "none," which at first we take to mean dead or simply nothing,
we realize that she is also suggesting that then she will share Christ's
signifiers "knot" and "nought." Thus, even though the marriage relationship undergoes an apparent dissolution when one partner dies, it is
eternally secure in Christ as "nought" and even as "knot." What was on
earth a mere "seeming" is in reality an eternal condition, a nothingness in
which Christ "ever" knits together husband and wife.

Another three lines achieve a similar doubleness of meaning in "A
Letter to her Husband absent upon Public employment," but in this
case by a slightly different although no less cryptic manner. There the
speaker, anticipating her husband's return, writes,

> But when thou *Northward* to me shalt return,
> I wish my Sun may never set, but burn
> Within the Cancer of my glowing breast,
> The welcome house of him my dearest guest.
>
> (M/R, 181)

It is clear that here Bradstreet's use of the figure of the sun suggests Christ, as did her references to the husband as "head" and "heart" in the opening lines of the poem. Bradstreet frequently refers to Christ as the Sun of Righteousness, and as we saw in the Sidney elegy, the biblical promise of the sun's eternal shining is used in her poetry to suggest the arrival of the millennium, as described in the book of Revelation. So too in this poem is the reference to "the dearest guest" a reference to Christ as the guest in the house in Revelation, a reference that also suggests Christ's second coming.

At one level, then, the husband is likened to the biblical figure of the sun and thereby to Christ, and to Christ as the "head" of the "one body" of the congregation and as its eventual bridegroom. In this poem, however, Bradstreet gives the sun's powers to the wife as well. When she writes that she wishes "[my Sun] may never set," the pronoun "my" is ambiguous. It can refer to *my husband, the sun,* or to *my own sun*—that is, to the sun that is within. Further, here, the sun burns "Within the Cancer of [the wife's] glowing breast." The year has suddenly changed, and this northern wife now possesses the power of summer. Furthermore, her breast glows, with the fire of love or faith or with the power alchemists said changed things. Here the wife's solarian powers mark the climax of the poem; they are not excised as the poet's Phoebus-like attributes were from the later version of the Sidney elegy. The wife here burns with the sun—that is, with feelings of erotic desire, with a sense of Christ's presence, or with an unnatural experience (in winter) of summer's heat. It is impossible to separate the religious from the secular in this highly compressed set of images. That the sun's powers here belong to the wife is fully attested to by the clear sexuality of the description of her husband as the "dearest guest" who enters and is welcomed into the "house"-"breast" of the wife's body.

Yet there is, I believe, a still further contradiction built into the closing lines of this poem. The figure of the wife's "house" suggests that her body is, too, the birthplace of children, of the parent's posterity; at the same time that house suggests temple, it is a reminder of the partners' mortality. "House" is also, as it is in the Emily Dickinson poem, "Because I could not stop for Death," a figure for the grave. Bradstreet's use of the figure of the house is ever so slight a stroke of the brush, but with it she tells us that, however, supernal this marriage is, it is undeniably earthly. Even before she has exhorted the husband to "ever, ever stay, and go not thence," we know that that overreaching request is impossible to fulfill. She then turns and asks a more reason-

able time of "stay": "Till natures sad decree shall call thee hence."
Time, in other words, enters the poem, and the certainty of death is
reaffirmed. Thus, the husband's return is not a permanent assurance of
the sun's never setting. The reunion of husband and wife is not the
millennium. In fact it sounds certain that (in the same way the seasons
will change) the husband will go out again on "Public employment."
"Natures sad decree" in all areas of life keeps calling him "hence." In
fact the meanings of the little words "thence" and "hence" and "here"
and "there," which are such important ideas in the poem, suggesting
travel back and forth, have by the end of the poem tended to merge.
The husband's movement is away and back; he travels not in a straight
line but in a circle.

In the poem's final couplet ("Flesh of thy flesh, bone of thy bone, / I
here, thou there, yet both but one" (M/R, 181), "here" and "there" no
longer signify mere geographical locations. Nor do they refer to the two
realms that husband and wife were assigned by their culture. Nor do
they refer to summer heat as distinct from winter cold, nor to one
member of the mystical body as head or leader and to the other as
follower. These counters have been conflated, and the demarcations
between opposites have been smudged, if not erased. The categories
that the poem itself introduced are, by the end of the poem, con-
founded with one another. Flesh sounds like spirit; life like death;
north like south; female like male (at least in their "oneness"). One is
reminded of the hymn, "In Christ there is no East or West" or, more
germane to Bradstreet, of the lines written by Anne Bradstreet's son-in-
law Seaborn Cotton, in his Commonplace Book, that "Womans the
centre & lines are men" (Ulrich, 3). Thus, in part, this poem functions
as an invitation to men to "return," to give over the pursuit of public
employments. By vividly anticipating the husband's return, then, Bradstreet has affirmed a kind of ideal but not the ideal of a point at the end
of time to be reached by the journeying tribe in a straight line. Employ-
ing all the conventional imagery of the resurrection, she has recreated a
vision of the world as continously and variously informed by Christ's
death and resurrection as an ongoing process in what Crooke calls the
"Natural household government," especially (in these poems) "appearing in our bodies." Bradstreet seems to have in mind a countervailing
vision of the relationships within marriage, one from which her readers
can learn, as Crooke continued, "how to temper and order the manners
and conditions of the mind, now to rule and gouern a Commonwealth

or Citie, and how to direct a private house of family." These are thus significantly public *and* private poems.

Bradstreet's vision, as we have seen, embodies—it is constructed of—tension. The vision is not worked out with the logic of either the scientist or the theologian. Perhaps Bradstreet's handling of the materials of theology and Renaissance science reflect the fact that she was not university trained and thus not a systematic thinker about the issues she was handling. But it furthermore reflects the fact that she was positioning herself (on such subjects as the resurrection, providential history, the relationship of spirit to body) in a "place" that the world did not "account." She did not side (one can see that in these poems) with either party in the Antinomian controversy. She is not a Hutchinsonian, as is seen in the simple fact that she was so attached to the body and believed the body to be filled with the presence of Christ both now and in the future beyond the grave. Nor did she side with the elders; she presents women's bodies as emblematic of the divine—in fact, so close to the divine that she can suggest here that the return of the husband home is a return of the church to a Christlike wife who then expects him to go out again, in anticipation of another return. Bradstreet's insistent use of mutability also changes the gender roles in the line cited from Canticles in which the lover (understood as Solomon) calls out to his beloved, "Returne, returne, O Shulamite, return: returne that we may behold thee." In Bradstreet's poem it is the wife who cries out to the husband, as if the husband were the errant *ecclesia,* who at the end of time will be joined with the messiah. Laura Ulrich, in her citation of Seaborn Cotton's memorable lines, writes that women's lives and the patterns of household care to which women were socialized actually made for a sense of home as circle. (We glimpse here the nineteenth-century image of home as sanctuary in, for example, *Uncle Tom's Cabin*.) Ulrich emphasized the meaning of this configuration for Puritan historicism. She writes that women "as wives and mothers, . . . have represented the fixed circle of human history, a presumed counterweight to the moving line which traces the founding of commonwealths or the development of ideas" (4).

In itself, Bradstreet's use of the marriage allegory would have signaled to her colonial readers that she was referring to the Puritan expectations of their errand into the Massachusetts wilderness, particularly since her father and her husband played such major leadership roles in that venture. Her use of the Solomonic voice (again her "ventriloquism") served as well to anchor the marriage poems in the biblical tradition that, above all, presented Christ's immanence and raised the issue of change alive in the worlds of nature, history, and families. This strategy allowed her to stay faithful to the ultimate promise of the reunion with Christ and to the postmillenarian vision of a gradually improving life on earth in anticipation of that ultimate "Day" and yet to present her own reconsideration of a more "pathless" path toward that end. In fact, here she presents reunions and restorations that are not ends at all but moments in the arc of a circle and that represent the closing of the circle.

That circle should not be thought of as narrow and confined, however. Again the biblical sources and the biblical commentators help the modern reader to understand what the references to "household" could imply. Proverbs 5:19, the chapter from which the references to the 'hind" and the "dear" are taken, stresses the importance of the husband's faithfulness to the "wife of thy youth." At one level, the biblical source celebrates the sexual relationship in middle age of the married pair, long after the first years of that marriage. John Dod's commentary on this passage emphasized the fact that this proverbial wisdom is addressed to the middle-aged couple. The Geneva Bible gloss adds that the passage encourages the husband and the wife to draw in and conserve the energies of their faith, presumably during a period of drought, winter, or persecution. There the reader is advised not to let the rivers of waters flow but to reserve them for "thy self, thy familie & them that are of the householde of faith." If there is a "public" statement that these late poems make to the citizens of the commonwealth, it may well be directed especially to a circle of like-minded readers who share in the Bradstreet's "household of faith." The cry from Canticles does suggest, as the Geneva commentators put it, "the desire of the people of Jerusalem for the return of their city and for peace" (282), but the poet also may be implying that the audience for this message of hope is not the entire Puritan world but a "household of faith" that is reserved perhaps not exclusively but primarily to the family and its posterity.

Not only does Dod's commentary on Proverbs enable us to take a perspective on Bradstreet's poetic intentions in the marriage poem, it instructs us, as I have indicated, about the method she has chosen. Again, as in the earlier poems, Bradstreet appears to be inviting us to "unlock" her sentences and to discover and take seriously the paradoxes and ambiguities to be found there. John Dod's commentary on Proverbs describes a similar requirement made by the biblical text of its readers. He explains that the proverb, or as he calls it, the "parable," is especially suited to the revelation of Christ as Wisdom. She is, Dod says, "treasure which is hid in some close, strong, and secret place, as in the ground or within a wall" (1615, 20). In an important statement about literary style for the understanding of Bradstreet's deliberate artlessness, Dod writes that vast learning, sophisticated means of inquiry, and elegance of style are not prerequisites for discovering her. Rather, in an alchemical similitude, he counsels that "A plaine iron key will serve for good use, to unlock the door of a golden treasure." Dod takes pride in the fact that his own writing in this commentary is "devoid of all polishment and elegancy" (1615, preface). Such, of course, is the style that Bradstreet insisted was hers too.

Dod argues that just as Wisdom's treasure is hidden and requires a key (a plain iron one will do), so too the literary form in which wisdom is articulated is appropriately difficult to pierce, open, and explicate. By "Parables," he writes, "are sometimes meant darke, and mystical sayings, not easie to be understood, as when they say to Christ, *why speakest thou to them in parables?*" (1615, 1). Dod continues to notice that Christ is a borrower of others' speech—a literary characteristic we have noticed in Bradstreet's work. He writes that parables sometimes refer to "a borrowed speech, a similitude, or comparison, as when it is said, *all these things spake Jesus to the multitude in parables.*" Lastly, Dod defines parables as "sometimes short, and sweet proverbiall sentences, full of weight." Dod then goes on to link "speaking Wisdom" to the making of music. Citing Psalms, he writes, "My mouth shall speake wisdom, and the meditation of my heart is knowledge. I will incline mine eare to a parable, and utter my grave matter upon the harpe" (1615, 2).

Thus Bradstreet's method is an integral part of her message and derives from Solomonic tradition. By "abrupt" speech she may well mean speech that is cryptic and compressed and that affects us, as Dod said parables do, with a sense of shock. Above all, when we probe Bradstreet's texts we find ourselves surprised. We find ourselves discovering that the sentence does not mean what it initially seemed to. Because the image so often works both ways, in effect, the interpretation does not yield a meaning that like the spirit escapes or sloughs off the flesh. It is this difficult "knot"—this interweaving of what the tradition presented as opposites—that Bradstreet sought to present to her readers. This "knot," "nought," "not" is the expression of a "both but one" that is impossible to present in usual speech. Its statement requires a recursion by the poet to the axiomatic, the parabolic. Its interpretation requires that the reader consider the intertextuality with the Solomonic texts and consider the gender of Christ's presence in those texts. Nothing but poetic utterance would serve Bradstreet in this difficult set of perceptions of the relationship of spirit to flesh.

Chapter Four

Mother-Artist: A Typology of the Creative

Life in Andover

From 1633, the year her first son, Samuel, was born, to the years of her grandmothering in Andover, Bradstreet's life affirms, as Cheryl Walker writes, an "association between self-presentation in children . . . and self-presentation in art" (Walker, 11).[1] The concern of this self-presentation is, however, not so much with the experience itself—how pregnancy feels, what life with toddlers is like—as it is with posterity, with, again, how the seed planted in one generation will bear fruit in the next. Bradstreet's many-layered references to mother—as literal parent, as creator of poetry, as a prophet-"scribe" in her last years—sit in the context, as Patricia Caldwell reminds us (using Joel Porte's figure), of "a whole society trying to give birth to itself, to preserve itself, to *utter* itself" (Caldwell, 27).[2] This colonywide expectation, in turn, existed against a backdrop of the vision of the biblical birth of the new heavens and the new earth in Revelation 12:1–2, where "a great portent appeared in heaven, a woman clothed with sun, with the moon under her feet, and on her head a crown of twelve stars; she was with child and she cried out in her pangs of birth, in anguish for delivery." This "woman" who gave birth to the "manchild" then fled into the wilderness, the place described in Revelation as prepared to nourish and protect her until the dawn of the millennium.

When the Bradstreets moved to Andover from Ipswich in 1644 or 1645,[3] they moved to a yet more remote region, and the move (set in motion as early as 1638) can be seen as an attempt to find a more auspicious place than Ipswich for planting a family. A sense of Andover's auspiciousness would derive from its economic advantages: Simon's ownership of a thriving sawmill and large agricultural holdings on the outskirts of town. The Andover settlers looked back to England for the pattern by which to organize the town. Characterized by a hierarchical structure of both wealth and rank, Andover "reflected traditional patterns of agricultural life in the open-field of England."[4] Simon Bradstreet was "unquestionably the town's wealthiest and most influential settler."[5] Andover was a remarkably homogeneous and stable community in which families maintained their continuity into the twentieth century.

As a group, the first settlers were young families, and the transition from hardship to comfort was rapid. In Andover the Bradstreets had three more children,—Mercy in 1946, Dudley in 1648, and their last child, John, in 1652. The initial population experienced "exceptional healthiness," according to Philip Greven (Greven 1970, 26). Even children—the group with the highest mortality rate—had, as Greven says, an "astonishingly high" record of survival. These findings suggest that Bradstreet's life in Andover may not have been so harsh as her twentieth-century readers sometimes have assumed.

Perhaps we should say not *harsh* in physical, external, material respects. Bradstreet's frequent mention (particularly in her later years) of illness and recovery may suggest, as White believes, that her health deteriorated after the birth of her last child (White, 298).[6] Actually, as we have seen, she says she feared that she had been *less* blessed with affliction than others had—that she had not been "tried" enough. She continued throughout her life to describe "deliverance" in relationship to "sicknesses" and "weaknesses." The process of her "refining," as she called it, even when it does not describe a birth does resemble one. Thus, we should be alert to the possibility that the cessation of childbirth may have prompted Bradstreet to record times of "affliction," in which, as in childbirth, she came close to death, loss, or terror. Certainly Bradstreet interpreted childbirth as a time of trial of the kind she considered essential to her spiritual development. She wrote that she wished for her children the same experience with affliction as she had had, and this wish is said to lie at the heart of the will to record and the ability to create. She explained that "to ye End y^t if you meet wth the like yov haue recourse to ye same God who hath heard + deliuered me, and will doe ye like for yov if you trvst in him; And when he shall deliuer yov out of distresse forget not to giue him thankes, but to walk more closely with him then before, This is the desire of y^r Loving mother. A.B." (M/R, 227). Noticeably absent, then, from Bradstreet's poetry and prose written in Andover is a celebration of the good health, wealth, and status that Simon and Anne Bradstreet evidently had achieved. One would guess from the poem about the burning of her house that Bradstreet grieved over the loss of a few treasured posses-sions. One would not guess that in 1650 this house was the "showplace of all the countryside" (Fuess, 41).

Nor did the fact that Andover was (and remained) an isolated outpost mean that the Bradstreets were not part of a group that had transatlan-tic ties. In 1645 John Woodbridge was ordained and chosen minister of Andover. The Bradstreets must have been glad to be in the congrega-tion of that generous man whom Cotton Mather described as "by *Nature* wonderfully Composed, patient, and Pleasant" (1702, 3:219). Not only was his wife Mercy (Dudley) a poet, but his younger brother, Benjamin, was too. Benjamin had come to New England as recently as 1640 to complete his studies at Harvard (in 1642). He must have been a frequent visitor in the Woodbridge house in Andover where he no doubt befriended Anne Bradstreet. He wrote "Upon the Author, by a known friend," one of the commendatory verses for *The Tenth Muse.* In the 1640's Simon Bradstreet supported the Scotsman Robert Child's protest of the suffrage restrictions in New England, and these were also the years of the Civil War in England, when New Englanders tried to sort out their responses to that complicated event.

These years ended with the departure for England of all the Wood-bridges and Nathaniel Ward, the long-time political ally of Simon Bradstreet, who was clearly a supporter of Anne Bradstreet's writing profession. Benjamin Woodbridge and Nathaniel Ward did not return to New England. In 1647 in England, Ward published his famous work *The Simple Cobbler of Agawam;* he took a small parish in Essex just miles from where the Bradstreets had lived; he died in 1652. John and Mercy Woodbridge made an extended visit to England, returning in 1663. These people were not simply family and close friends—indispensable to life in a small community; they were also a significant audience for poetry. They composed an important part of the intellec-tual group that nurturned Bradstreet's talents.

It was on their 1647 voyage that the Woodbridges took Bradstreet's poems—probably not yet in manuscript form as *The Tenth Muse*—to England. Although it is possible to be skeptical of Woodbridge's claim that Bradstreet did not know that he had her poems with him and intended to show them to publishers, there can be little doubt that she lost control of her drafts at that point and that changes were made that she did not know about until some years later when she saw the book in finished form (M/R, xx). Undoubtedly the book's chances of publica-tion were helped by the fact that Nathaniel Ward's *The Simple Cobbler of*

Agawam was having an enormous success in England. It was Ward's publisher, Stephen Bowtell, who published *The Tenth Muse* in 1650 (White, 251–72).

Thus the Bradstreets' first years in Andover ended with separations from dear friends and family and, in a simile Bradstreet used about her book, with birth separation from *The Tenth Muse*—no longer a gestating infant. The 1650s appear to have been a watershed. A year after the Bradstreets' last child was born, Thomas Dudley died,[7] and in this decade the older children began to leave home. Simon was at school in Ipswich; in 1653 Samuel graduated from Harvard. In 1654 the first marriage took place: Dorothy Bradstreet married Seaborn Cotton, son of John Cotton.

In all these respects the decade was a climacteric, in which the daughters Dorothy and Sarah (to be married in 1656) took on the roles of wife-mother and the sons, Simon and Samuel, took on the roles of recorder and continuator of their mother's work. When Samuel graduated from Harvard, he wrote an almanac poem for that year, using his mother's themes and figures. The poem celebrates the marriage of *Tellus mater* with the sun, Apollo. Not only does "Hymen joyn" the "hands" of the cosmic pair, but Apollo assures her that "Babyes deft will thence arise anon." Both the epigraph ("Everything that lies concealed will be manifest in due time") and the image clusters are quintessential Bradstreet (Daly, 40)[8]

The almanac is an interesting form for a descendant of Anne Bradstreet to turn to because it could suggest the reflection in daily life, in all its bodily particularity, of the larger forces that govern the world— God's providence in nature and history. Almanacs, as David Watters emphasizes, were used in Puritan households for the guidance of daily activities, including not only the planting of crops but also the recording and predicting of women's sexual cycles, of milestones in infants' development, of deaths, diseases, and so on. With blank pages interleaved, the almanacs could be used by families to record such occurrences, yearly, over long periods, even over generations.[9] As a genre, the almanac falls, thus, somewhere between the personal journal and the family or the natural history, embellished with literary compilations of proverbs and poems. Almanacs were thus repositories of wisdom and could serve, as Robert Daly has shown, a prophetic purpose, as well. Almanac poetry, in Daly's words, was thus a "particular kind of public writing."[10]

Samuel Bradstreet, apparently his mother's intellectual heir, left for

England in 1657 to study medicine. His departure and his return (in 1661) were both occasions for Bradstreet poems (M/R, 230–31). In 1657 Bradstreet, for some reason, focused a little series of poems and prose pieces on her sinkings of spirit, her illnesses, and her recoveries. These imperfectly rhymed ballads and prose paragraphs (which have come down to us in Simon's transcription) are the closest we have to a spiritual diary. Of these, the dated poems and prose suggest the kind of writing one might find interleaved in an almanac. These are affliction tales, and some are told with power and directness. Bradstreet writes in 1656, "Now I can wait, looking every day when my Sav^r shall call for me." She prays, "Lord gravnt y^t while I live I may doe y^t service I am able in this frail Body" (M/R, 226), as if she were in old age. Actually she was only 44 years old and only four years beyond the birth of her last child. Perhaps she did feel depressed during this period. It does sound as if her "winters," "stormes," and "clowdes," which this poem records as "now all fled," refer to more than the literal weather (M/R, 227). These dated poems may represent a spiritual exercise of the kind we saw in the 1632 poem, where she wrote, "My race is run, my thread is spun / lo here is fatal Death." The occasion for that poem *was* a recovery from serious illness, but in 1632 Bradstreet—was writing too as if at the end of her life. We can speculate that, with her sense of the clear demarcations of the periods of one's life, Bradstreet may, in both 1632 and 1656–57, be *preparing* for a new phase. In this little 1650s affliction series she appears to be working herself into the role of one who is alone awaiting Christ's coming. Noticeably absent from these pieces is the artful voice of a half-ironic speaker. The poet here does not affect the persona of child, sister, or wife. The ambitiousness of the earlier poems is gone. It is as if the poet has somehow moved off the world's stage and into the wings where she can wait and watch—of course, sending instruction and counsel to her children from this curious perspective, in which she is both involved and distanced.

We can, in fact, take Samuel Bradstreet's epigraph ("Everything that lies concealed will be manifest in time") as a keynote for Bradstreet's descriptions of her later years. As we will see in the next section of this chapter, she repeatedly positions her speakers at a birth moment—at the boundary between what is yet concealed and what will be manifest. She treats the manifest and the concealed as if they were two dispensations, and she refers to them as two kinds of mothering: in the first kind of mothering, as we have seen, she brings actual children into the world ("wth great paines, weaknes, cares + feares"), and in the second (an exact parallel to the first), she "travails in birth again of yov, till Christ be formed in yov" (M/R, 216). This is the travail of the artist, and in the decade of the 1650s Bradstreet presents herself as entering that second phase. We might expect this more spiritual and distinctly more prophetic phase to move beyond immediate concerns, but in Bradstreet's case the opposite seems to occur: in the creations of the poet's body—her children and her poetry—is found the evidence of God's dealings with her and, by implication, with her posterity and the world.

Although we should not exclude the relevance of the 1650s as a postmenopausal period, we should not limit our readings of Bradstreet's work to that biological reality. The 1650s were also a time of distress in Massachusetts, with consequences for Bradstreet's sense of the future. Her sister, Sarah Keayne, had remarried and disappeared from public view (disappeared from the public record, that is). She died in 1659. Certainly gone too was the heady pre–Civil War excitement in England that Sarah seems to have been a part of. The approach of Christ's kingdom on earth, touted in the long Parliament of 1641 in England, in Bradstreet's dialogue of 1642, and predicted by John Cotton for 1656, appears to have slowed down, perhaps to have been interrupted. Another popular date for the millennium, 1666 (Keith, 141), was some years away and, incidentally, would be associated with a last period of major poetic productivity on Bradstreet's part. As I have argued, Bradstreet casts the earlier marriage poems (probably written in the 1640s) in terms that suggest a dawning of the millennium, at least in the "little" life of the Bradstreets' married relationship (C/S, 201). That strategy appears to have been abandoned by the 1650s. The shift in her presentation of her marriage does not suggest a change in her feelings for her husband. (The later poems that pray for his health and safety attest to her devotion to him.) But Bradstreet no longer joined the literal and the spiritual marriage references. She continued to use the figure of Christ as bridegroom to the end of her life, and she continued to express her attachment to her husband, but these are no longer fused and figured as one in the later poems. In fact she writes,

> Tho: husband dear bee from me gone
> Whom I doe loue so well
> I have a more beloued one
> Whose comforts far excell.
>
> (M/R, 234)

We can tentatively point to public events, in Massachusetts and in England, that may have confirmed the suspicion that Christ's second coming had been delayed. In 1652, for one, the first instance of witchcraft in nearby Ipswich was reported. In that case, a man, John Broadstreet (no relation to the Bradstreets) came to trial. Then, in 1656 a woman, Eunice Cole, did. Her case was dealt with far more severely than Broadstreet's. The same kind of "proof" was used against Goody Cole as against Anne Hutchinson almost 20 years earlier, and the report is equally lurid. As the constable of Salisbury was stripping Cole in order to whip her (in his words), "looking upon her breasts under one of her breasts, . . . I saw a blew thing . . . Hanging downwards about three quarters of an inch long not very thick." This growth was then "pulled or scratched off" and said to be proof of her "familiarity with the Devil" (Waters, 288). Cole was emprisoned in Ipswich and later in Boston for her "crimes." For Bradstreet, a poet whose body provided the evidence of God's dealings with her and with her posterity, who gendered the immanent divine presence in nature as female, and who looked forward to the millennium as a birth event, this attack on women's anatomy and this allegation, again, of deformity must have proved unnerving. Bradstreet would not have taken this apparent proof as true proof of the devil's intervention, but the doubt it raises—basically, that white magic might be mistaken for black magic—was an old and familiar one to her and to the scientists from whom she learned her view of nature. Agrippa had contended with this issue in his preface to *Of Occult Philosophy,* where he explained that to be a "wise" man

doth not amongst learned men signifie [+ be] a sorcerer, or one that is superstitious or divellish; but a wise man, a priest, a prophet; and that the Sybils were Magicianesses, & therefore prophecyed most cleerly of Christ; and that Magicians, as wise men, by the wonderful secrets of the world, knew Christ the author of the world to be born, and came first of all to worship him; and that the name of Magicke was received by Phylosophers commended by Divines, and not unacceptible to the Gospel (Hirst, 49)

An additional attack on the reputation of magic (that is, on the belief in the hidden riches of nature or the philosopher's stone, which when uncovered would restore the creation) would have come from across the Atlantic. In England in 1650 the diaries of John Dee were finally published and his reputation suffered a severe and lasting blow. Dee, as we have seen, had been a formative influence on Sidney and his circle and on John Winthrop, Jr. (in fact Winthrop adopted Dee's emblem, the *Monas,* for his own bookplate). The published confirmation of Dee as a "deluded charlatan" (Yates, 1984, 233), a sorcerer, would have made it particularly difficult for an artist like Bradstreet to reflect or echo Dee's vision of the world in this witch-baiting international climate. The scandal caused by the publication of the Dee diaries is one reason for arguing that Bradstreet's poem "Phoebus make haste" is an early Ipswich poem since it echoes not only Dee's enthusiasm, but the language and figures of a Dee cosmology. In Dee's disgrace, we also find the possible reason for the later changes in Bradstreet's Sidney elegy—changes that alter, even erase, the astrological, alchemical, and millennial references in that poem. The fact that Samuel's almanac poem reflects those figures suggests that he picked up and wove with threads that could surface again within the family tradition.

By the time of these troubling events, Andover was being served by Woodbridge's successor, the tolerationist minister, Francis Dane, who was a critic of the witchcraft trials. There is evidence that the Bradstreet family were opponents of the witchcraft hysteria. Later, in Salem, as White writes, Simon Bradstreet was to prove "couragious in his refusal to co-operate with the hysterical fanaticism of the witchcraft trials" (White, 307). Andover continued to experience witchcraft episodes. In the 1690s Dudley Bradstreet, a judge who followed in his father's footsteps as selectman, magistrate, and militiaman, refused to sign warrants for the arrest of suspected witches in Andover. He was denounced, and his wife was named a suspect. Apparently they left town until the hysteria died down (Fuess, 87). In this respect, too, then, a Bradstreet child (Dudley) appears to have honored his father and mother, both his father's tolerationism and his mother's adherence to a view of magic as "the most perfect and chief Science, that sacred and sublimer kind of Philosophy . . . ; magic as 'nothing else but the survey of the whole course of nature.' "[11]

In 1661 and 1662 public events had a clear impact on the Bradstreets' life, one that was recorded in, again, a series of poetic and prose journal-like entries. Among these are poem prayers on the occasion of Simon's trip to England in 1661. The General Court sent him and his old friend John Norton to renegotiate the Massachusetts Bay Charter. In "Vpon my dear & loving husband his goeing into England. Jan. 16. 1661," Bradstreet prays to God to "keep & P^rserve / My husband, my dear friend," and to "Remember Lord thy folk whom thou / To Wildernesse ha'st brovght." The poem emphasizes the faithfulness of both husband and wife to the accomplishment of God's "Work," but it appears to raise doubts about whether God is still mindful of His part in the bargain. The poet pleads, "Let not thine own Inheritance / Bee sold away for Novght" (M/R, 233). In the concern expressed here over New England's "inheritance" Bradstreet speaks in the conventional helpmeet role of Puritan wife. But she also phrases her concern in a way that reflects a constant Bradstreet theme: her damaged expectations of the wilderness "folk" on whom God (as in Psalm 44, which this poem echoes) may have turned His back. The poem gives voice to Bradstreet's doubts about the future, doubts certainly strong enough to have brought her history of the monarchies to an impasse.

New England at this time was threatened by divisions within and by the changed circumstances in old England where the emissaries felt they might not find a friend in the new king Charles II. It is for this reason that Bradstreet prays for "favour in their eyes to whom / He [Simon] shall make his Addresse." Norton and Simon Bradstreet did return with a renewed charter, but they did so in exchange for an agreement to religious toleration by the colony. The Massachusetts public was not happy with this outcome, and their ingratitude was evident. The historian Thomas Hutchinson characterizes the two men's response to their hostile reception home in this way: "Mr. Bradstreet was a man of more phlegm, and not so sensibly touched; but Mr. Norton was so affected that he grew melancholy. He died suddenly, soon after his return" (White, 321; Ellis, lix–lxi).

The poems written on the occasion of this trip are straightforward in their statements and controlled in tone. These poems do not require an audience of *Hermes Christiani* to interpret them. Gone is the exaggerated discourse, the verbal doubleness. The shortness of the poetic line, the terseness, the awkward simplicity of the rhyme help to convey the impression that the artist as mage has been replaced by the artist as a pious anchorite. When Bradstreet writes (during her husband's absence) "And thy Abode tho'st made wth me / Wth Thee my soul can talk," we hear a different "wife" from the one whose "house" is a "glowing breast" and the "welcome house of him my dearest guest" (M/R, 181). Here she appears to have a separate place, a shadow existence, in addition to the role of wife grieving a "dear husband his Absence." She writes that "In secret places, Thee I find / Where I doe kneel or walk," but "thee" here refers to God and not to her husband. "Secret," "silent," "alone" are adjectives that characterize the speakers of the major poems

written in the decade of the 1660s. The mother speaker of "The Author
to her Book," for example, writes, "If for thy [her verses'] Father askt,
say thou hadst none" (M/R, 178). With the solitariness of this speaker
belongs the poet voice of "The Flesh and the Spirit" (probably written
in this period), who, as we have seen, overhears the "sisters" arguing—
but from a distance. The attitude of the poet in these later works,
including the grandmother of the elegies, is marked by a certain wistful-
ness, a sense of removal, a contemplativeness—a "taut, laconic moodi-
ness," to use Caldwell's phrase (27).

In the 1660s Bradstreet turned her hand to major creative projects,
including her finest poem, "Contemplations," tentatively dated 1664–
65. She also began the series of prose axioms, "Meditations Diuine and
morall" to which she gave the date 20 March 1664, the date of the
spring equinox.[12] Perhaps the return of Mercy and John Woodbridge
meant that again the poet had an audience for her work, an audience
that might even have prodded her to write. Perhaps the threat to the
Massachusetts Bay charter shook the foundations of Bradstreet's hopes
for the future. Perhaps as witchcraft accusations mounted, it was time
to reconsider the design of nature and history and to "seek" again the
"*summum Bonum*" that would "stay the mind." Perhaps the appearance
in 1662 of the extraordinarily popular *Day of Doom* by Michael Wigglesworth (describing a vision of the end of the world that Bradstreet
did not share) proved catalytic. Whatever the reason, the old energy,
not just for expression but for making nothing less than a universal
synthesis, returned.

It is from the Bradstreets' son, Simon's, journal that we hear about
the fire that destroyed the parents' house in Andover in 1666 (White,
347)—about which an important late poem was written by Anne and
later copied by Simon. Simon's journal belongs to a special genre; it is
"A Brief Record of remarkable Providences and Accidents gen[11] and
p^rticular" and it spans the years 1664–83. In it are recorded such
occurrences as house fires, comets, storms, murders, the deaths and
ordinations of illustrious men—all in chronological order, but in a
grouping that to the modern reader seems otherwise altogether haphaz-
ard. This journal is notable for its omissions, too; Simon does not, for
example, record the deaths of four of his brother Samuel's five children
or of Samuel's second wife, all in the 1660s, his mother's death in
1672, or his father's remarriage in 1676. These personally affecting
events clearly did not have the same kind of significance that the
burning of the house had for Simon, and perhaps for others—the

significance, that is, of a special portent, the record of which might be used to ascertain the design of God's intentions for his people during these years of millennial expectations.

Bradstreet's poem has similar implications. It treats the fire as a judgment on the "house"; it addresses that special moment that, as I have argued elsewhere, is "both the end of its earthly life and the beginning of its spiritual one" (C/S, 201). Bradstreet's biblical sources again serve to place her speaker in an almost eerie "place" that is not quite *here* but not quite *beyond* either. She is located in "silent night" and the entire stage is set with "not's"—"No pleasant tale," no "things recovnted," "No Candles" (M/R, 237). The double meaning of the poem's key sentence ("Let no man know is my Desire") tells us that she both wished for and dreaded that "fire." This poem mourns the loss of family possessions, but somewhat understatedly. The wife grieves over the fact that "My pleasant things in ashes lye / And them behold no more shall I" (M/R, 237), but this speaker is more than wife or mother. She is a liminary presence. She stands on the edge of time, like the prophets who were said to have one foot in the world and one foot in the life beyond. Here the poet speaks as one who is in transition from one 'house' to another. This fire is thus an agent of destruction and of transmutation. It is a "remarkable Providence or Accident," as Simon recorded it, illustrative of some design in history that is as yet beyond the poet's ken. In a voice that is the mother's but also the prophet's, the poet prays "the world no longer let me Love." She prays that this *time* will end—the time designated for her acting in the world with love.

All of the events of the 1660s—Simon Bradstreet's return from his mission in England, Samuel's return from medical studies there, the house fire, and the deaths of Samuel's family members (elegized in short poems published in *Several Poems*) are characterized as portentous.[13] None more so, I believe, than the poems that focus on Samuel and on his bereavements. Samuel, Bradstreet tells us on more than one occasion, was a special child: "The Son of prayers, of vowes, of teares / The child I stay'd for many yeares" (M/R, 228). In fact, Bradstreet's poem celebrating his return from England is more elaborately enthusiastic than her poem honoring her husband's return. In this poem, dated 1661, it is the son who sounds like Christ: "He's come for whom I waited long." Samuel's voyage back from "Dangers manifold," on the sea and in England, is described as a deliverance, a birth passage "To the Land of his Nativity." The voyage is portrayed as a second birth parallel to his first, by means of which the son, already special, is, in effect, sanctified. He is brought as the Israelites were, "On Eagles wings": he is that wisdom-filled presence whom the mother and the world awaits, the sign of God's "Mercyes," which the world can now "behold."

Thus the fact that Samuel's wife and offspring did not survive conveys an ominousness that other deaths, even of dear family members, do not. Samuel is clearly the child who shared the mother's interests as poet and physician, and the relationship echoes the sense of an inheritance of the kind Bradstreet said she shared with her father. The fact that Samuel soon left New England for Jamaica may have dealt a fatal blow to his mother's hopes for his repayment of the intellectual and spiritual and artistic "debt" owed. This collapse of expectations is expressed in the 1669 elegy for Mercy Bradstreet, Samuel's wife, who died while he was on his way to Jamaica. Using the word "Relation" to indicate Mercy's special status as wife, Bradstreet writes that the "tree" has been felled—tree not in the narrow sense of family tree, since Samuel and seven other children still lived, but tree in the sense of the promise of a spiritual and intellectual continuum, with the biblical overtones that Cotton's "Farewell sermon" gave the "trees" of New England's plantation in 1630. The poet surely felt these deaths as personal losses, but her elegy for Mercy describes the loss of an even larger hope for Samuel and his household. (One recalls the Emily Dickinson poem, "A Great Hope fell.") Bradstreet is addressing Samuel, not Mercy, when she writes,

> Ah, woe is me, to write thy Funeral Song.
> Who might in reason yet have lived long.
> I saw the branches lopt the Tree now fall.
> I stood so nigh, it crusht me down withal;
> My bruised heart lies sobbing at the Root,
> That thou dear Son has lost both Tree and fruit:
> Thou then on Seas sailing to forreign Coast;
> Was ignorant what riches thou hadst lost.
>
>   (M/R, 188)

The elegy seems to suggest a subtle rebuke. While this irrevocable damage was being suffered, Simon was sailing away, "ignorant" of what "riches"—that important word—he had lost. His wife and his children are the family treasure or "store," which will yield, as the investment from her father did, in the future. The very "tree" itself falls in this poem: The continuity is broken. In its destructiveness, the scene exceeds the original fall in the garden of Eden. Simple disobedience (unless Samuel's removal can be considered a sin) is not the cause of this fall. The word "bruised" also echoes Genesis, where enmity "bruises" the woman's head and the man's heel, but here the poet's very "heart" is bruised. She is (in that powerful word from Job) "crusht." She "lies sobbing at the Root," as the mother who cannot restore the root of her posterity to life. Here again a force is at work like the force causing the separation in the universe of the marriage poems. The point here is the obliteration of continuity itself. The loss is like the one she feared New England might suffer: the selling of God's "inheritance for Novght" (M/R, 233). Bradstreet is thus not simply eulogizing Mercy: she is singing "Thy"—that is, Samuel's—"Funeral song." She "sounds this wailing tone" for a violent negative transmutation in her relationship to the intellectual, poetic, and spiritual scion, who was to have been her representative at the day of Christ's appearing. The elegy's poetic energy dissipates after the statements of the first 12 lines, as the poet moves into a highly conventional expression of sympathy, ending with the wholly lacklustre conclusion beginning, "Cheer up (dear Son) thy bleeding heart" (M/R, 189).

It is clear what stirs the poet's grief here (to some extent the same is true of the other elegies). In the language of strong emotion (sobs, wails) she reacts to the loss of the continuance of the family, including its traditions of mind and belief. With her magical sense of the capacity of life to reproduce cherished forms, she is in despair over the prospect of this process's having been ruptured by Mercy's death.

Continuance is also the theme of the last picture we have of Bradstreet before she died. Apparently at the end of her life Anne Bradstreet suffered a debilitating disease, which Simon called a "consumption" by which she was "wasted to skin & bone." In his diary account Simon writes that "she was much troubled with rheum" and that one of the women who was caring for her said that "shee never saw such an arm in her life," presumably so frail and thin. Bradstreet, again revealing her vision of the ongoing life of the body, is reported to have replied, "I [or aye] but y^t arm shall bee a Glorious Arm" in the future—that is, after death (White, 358–59). Presumably Bradstreet was buried in Andover (now North Andover), but no burial stone has been found. Four years later, as was customary, Simon Bradstreet was remarried. In 1678 he was elected deputy governor and then (from 1679 to 1686 and 1689 to 1692) he served two terms as governor of Massachusetts. In his last years he lived in Salem.

Six years after Bradstreet's death, the poems of *The Tenth Muse* were reprinted, edited, and added to in a collection printed by John Foster, this time in Boston. Critic Jeannine Hensley's suggestion that John Rogers served as editor of *Several Poems* is now generally accepted (White, 365).[14] John Rogers was the physician son of Nathaniel Rogers, the Ipswich scholar who followed Nathaniel Ward as minister there. Presumably with the permission of other family members, Bradstreet's poetry from the 1650s and 1660s was included in this volume—as we have seen, some of it Bradstreet's finest work. Sadly, these poems are perhaps the least reliably authentic of the Bradstreet texts to have come down to us. Editors McElrath and Robb write that they are "skeptical" of the 1678 texts and of the numerous changes and variants. "In a poem such as 'Contemplations,' " they add, "we have the consequences of what was in effect a collaborative production by Bradstreet, editor John Rogers, publisher John Foster, and perhaps others having access to Bradstreet's literary remains (M/R, XXXIV). No doubt, especially given the very great respect John Rogers expressed for Bradstreet's work (M/R, 531–33), he would not have made wholesale changes, but we should be cautious of overinterpreting every verbal nuance in these poems. Almost a century later, in 1758, a second edition of *Several Poems* appeared, suggesting enough interest in this pre-Revolutionary period to warrant republication.

It was not until 1867 in John Harvard Ellis's *The Works of Anne Bradstreet, in Prose and Verse* that the poetry and prose that had been preserved by the family in manuscript form were finally published. Some of these were in Bradstreet's own hand, and some in her son Simon's, presumably copied from originals of his mother's that no longer exist. These texts in manuscript together with *The Tenth Muse* and *Several Poems* now constitute the "complete" works, reprinted in the McElrath and Robb definitive edition of 1981.

A Reading of Selected Poems

As we have seen, Bradstreet adopted the persona of mother to represent three interrelated but distinct sets of activities: that of the creative artist who gives birth to poems, as in "The Author to her Book" (M/R, 177–78); that of mother and grandmother of literal children, as in the autobiographical letter, in the "Meditations Divine and morall" and in the short poems I have just discussed; and that of a prophetic mother who combines, yet transcends, the first two. In the poem "In reference to her Children, 23. June, 1659," the poet combines all three sets of activities. This combination and interdependence are, in turn, once again exemplified in the figure of Bathsheba, Solomon's mother, who spoke wisdom, bore children, and left in Proverbs a legacy to Solomon and his posterity.

Again it was Cotton Mather who likened his great aunt, Anne Bradstreet, to Solomon's mother, Bathsheba. In Mather's *Ornaments for the Daughters of Zion,* he used the example of Bathsheba as prophetic writer to demonstrate that women can be "scribes" of that *"Spirit, who moved Holy men, to write the sure word of Prophecy."*[15] Mather found Bathsheba's powers rooted in her typological relationship to two other mothers, Eve and Mary; although one had the "disgrace of the first transgression" assigned to her and the other the "glory" of bringing Christ into the world, both women were said to have suffered affliction. Each of these mothers was thought to have had a literal, historical existence, but each also belonged to a typological cluster in the Bible that gave their stories a providential purpose and significance beyond their individual histories—or so Mather and scholars since Patristic times believed. Typology was a means of interpreting the bible as prophecy and of discovering (imposing?) patterns that were said to suggest God's design for the history of the world. Typologists saw the figures of Solomon and Moses, for example, not simply as forerunners of Christ but as prophetic representations of him. In the same way a typological connection was made between Eve and Mary, who were said to foreshadow the birth of the manchild to the woman in the wilderness, and the establishment of the New Jerusalem, the "mother of us all." As Mather points out, Bathsheba belonged to this figural cluster. It is in this context that Mather, in an elaborate encomium, refers to Bradstreet as a "scribe" in the likeness of Bathsheba, thus once again defining Bradstreet as a spokeswoman for biblical wisdom.

Evidence of Bathsheba's prophetic identity Mather finds in the fact that she like Eve and Mary had "many wounds upon her" (1692, 6). She was seduced by David who killed her husband in order to have his way with her and marry her. God then destroyed their first son as a punishment. After a life of suffering, Bathsheba saw her son Solomon ascend the throne. As mother, she was thus both within the realm where power was exercised and marginal to it. Her chief power was the wisdom that she imparted to Solomon. Bathsheba was the model biblical instructress; she provided the paradigm for Bradstreet's tribute to

Dorothy Dudley and for Bradstreet's self-characterization as one who
"Taught what was good, and what was ill, / What would save life, and
what would kill" (M/R, 186). Bathsheba's prophetic likeness can be
said to inform the mother speaker of "In reference to her Children,"
particularly as she "lives in her children's lives after her death." She
writes,

> Thus gone, amongst you I may live,
> And dead, yet speak, and counsel give;
> Farewel my birds, farewel adieu,
> I happy am, if well with you.
>   A.B.

As it did in Bathsheba's case, the mother's "counsel" in Bradstreet's
work took the form of proverbial sayings, titled "Meditations Diuine
and morall," which have come down to us in Bradstreet's own hand and
are addressed to her son Simon, who, as she implied, had grand ambi-
tions as a writer—to outdo "nightingales" (M/R, 185). These "meditations," in other words, are to be part of the generational "store" to be
used (as Bradstreet used Solomon's words in her work) in future literary
creations. Of course, the wisdom embodied in these proverbs is to be
used by succeeding generations in the management of their daily lives.
Again, literary, spiritual, and practical everyday activities are not presented as belonging to separate spheres.

The Bradstreet meditations and her autobiographical letter constitute, as she said, a "small legacy" and in fact belong to that genre
known as the "mother's legacy."[16] Seventeenth-century mothers, particularly as they faced childbirth, compiled notebooks of advice for
their children, who faced the possible loss of their mothers during this
life-threatening event. The dedication of Bradstreet's letter "To my
dear children" again expresses the thought that she, though dead, may
yet speak, as if alive—"That being gone, here yov may find / What was
yr liueing mothers mind"[17] (M/R, 215). Although these pieces of
Bradstreet's legacy to and about her children were written when she was
in her fifties, not during her childbirthing years, they portray the
mother as essentially a presence between two realms—as she puts it,
ready to "take [her] flight" from the "top bough" of the tree (again she
uses that figure) where she nests. She is poised to fly "into a country
beyond sight, / Where old ones, instantly grow young, / . . . [and]
spring lasts to eternity" (M/R, 186). In fact, she already has a vision of

that "country beyond sight." She spends her time "In shady woods," where she "sits" and "sings," bringing to mind "things that [are] past." She is again in a "place" that is similar in its perspective and in its feelings to that of the speaker who introduces "The Flesh and the Spirit."

"Contemplations"

In the poem "In reference to her Children" motherhood was divided into two parallel, related but changed stages or periods. As we have seen, the children's actual births constitute the first stage, or dispensation, of the mother's life and their redemption the second. Bradstreet portrays the mother's death, then, as a translation to yet a third stage, which she is certain bears the features of the first two but which has not yet been revealed. Bradstreet's figure of the mother and the artist is thus, in its basic outline, a typological one in which certain features persist: the pattern of affliction and deliverance, and the presence of a nourishing maternity who ensures and prefigures the spiritual and physical future of her "children". In the bible these patterns persist into the unrevealed last time and are described in terms of motherhood. In Isaiah 66, for example the ultimate reunion of God and His people is seen as a birth of a manchild to the mother Jerusalem. At tht time peace will be extended "like a river, and the glory of the Gentiles like a flowing stream." In Isaiah that river is figured as a nurturing presence where the people of Israel shall "suck" and "be borne upon her sides, and be dandled upon her knees."

For the writer of scripture, for the scholars who interpreted scripture, as well as for the poet who designed her work typologically, writing was essential. For the figures to mean what they do and to persist as expressive personas in a spirit-filled continuum, the threads of both the previous and the future life must be woven into the verbal tapestry. Eve's life as fallen parent is shadowed forth in Mary's suffering and birth, and both are shadowed forth in the life of Bathsheba, who exists between the two and reflects them both. The poet speaker of these later Bradstreet poems, including "Contemplations," reflects back in time and forward beyond time, and this process seems essentially enabling of the rebirth that is the poet's explicit and implicit purpose to accomplish in her art.

In "Contemplations" the speaker (not explicitly gendered at first) begins at a "place" that she, through the course of the poem, outgrows or moves beyond. Like so many Bradstreet poems, "Contemplations" takes the reader through stages of awareness. Although different readers have described these stages differently, there is some agreement that the speaker grows and changes.[18] The speaker begins at a point of naive or wooden admiration for nature, where nature is pictured as "delectable" to the senses, particularly to the sight. Next, by an exercise in simple logic, she deduces the "goodness, wisdom, glory and light" of God, based on the evidence of His creation. Then the example of a 100-year-old "Stately Oak," with overtones of the human family tree, further impresses her with the enormity of God's time, "Eternity." When she arrives (her eye continues to travel upward) at the "glistering Sun" she ponders this deific power for four stanzas, at the end of which she falls silent. This first major turning point in the poem begins abruptly with, "Silent alone, where none or saw, or heard, / In pathless paths I lead my wandring feet" (M/R, 169). She has crossed over into another realm, as she did in "Of the vanity of all worldly creatures." She turns silent and she loses her powers and her "way."

The examples of the "merry grasshopper" and the "black clad Cricket" who seem "to glory in their [deceptively] little Art" make a slight but significant transition to the next major section of the poem in which the poet reviews "Ages past." She thus indulges in retrospection, that pump-priming activity so characteristic of the poetic speaker of this period in Bradstreet's verse. Immersed now in history, she tries to find her footing by taking the measure of her life. Compared to "the fathers ages" she finds modern people "living so little while we are alive." From this historical review she turns to nature, where the parallel fails her in another way. Human life, she finds, is not comparable to the seasons because human death is not part of a cycle. Unlike things in nature, "Man grows old, lies down, remains where once he's laid."

By stanza 19 the speaker has discovered that human life is "curs'd" by both nature and "custome." This originally enraptured speaker has marked off her life against the record of history and the patterned motions of nature and has concluded that everything in human life is finally consigned "to oblivion." In the next turning point, stanza 20, the poet's admiration for the evidently "bigger" and "stronger" bodies of natural things dissipates when she turns to the idea of the original birth and purpose of the creation—that "man was made for immortality." The wonder embodied in that predication lacks immediate logical or sensual confirmation or proof. A kind of nothingness opens up that takes the poem into the next major section—into the realm of the unseeable. The figures used to express "endless immortality" are the conventional ones for the life of the spirit: the ocean and the air; the poet moves from the "shady woods" to a "goodly Rivers side" and from there to ocean and air. By likenesses drawn to fish and birds, she manages to create an experience of the unearthly, the impossible. For two stanzas the speaker participates in the life of that "sweet airy legion" who have a place beyond—in the realm humans were ultimately "made for."

Thus when the poem returns in stanza 29 to what sounds like a definitive statement about "man" as "at best a creature frail and vain," it does so this time against the background of that glimpse of the unearthly, and the effect has impact. Because the preceding section (stanzas 21–28) has introduced us to the true picture of "heav'ns bower," it prepares us for the full effect of the important accusation, "Fond fool, he takes this earth ev'n for heav'ns bower." That sentence exactly portrays the state of mind with which the speaker began her contemplations. The narrator's initial attitude was in fact that of the blithe "mariner" (in this stanza) who is ignorant or careless of the forces that govern life.

The poem has come full circle but with a difference: "sad affliction comes & makes him see / Here's neither honour, wealth, or safety." This earthling, having been touched by the thought that earth might become "heav'ns bower," is thus being readied for acceptance of the redeeming work of affliction. Indeed, the contemplation, we realize, has all along been an extended process of affliction, beginning with the crisis of doubt in stanza 7, through silence and self-loathing in stanza 8, through an epic review of fallen human history, to a dramatic preview of the existence of the "merry bird" outside of or beyond history and nature. (The adjective "merry" was used for the "little" songster, the grasshopper; the presence of the cricket and the grasshopper at that crucial point in the poem prefigures the nightingale in stanza 27.) All of these experiences "grind" the soul—even the free-flying images of the spirit, which intensify the depth of the sense of human loss and degradation by establishing the contrast and by prompting in the speaker a longing for such a deliverance. The new birth of this speaker would not take place without the memory or the prospect of her "immortal" origins.

The last stanza summarizes the speaker's realizations. The curious fact is that the poem ends with a picture of the oblivion that is drawn over kings and kingdoms. The poem, in other words, starts with scenes from nature and ends with considerations about history, but history with a special twist: the last stanza predicts a future time when monuments and "names" will no longer be known. All "Records" will be forgotten. "But he whose name is grav'd in the white stone / Shall last and shine when all of these are gone." The particular focus of the last stanza is words and wisdom—records, names, wit, knowledge. These are, again, seen as vanity, except for the name of Christ, "grav'd in the white stone," a reference to the book of Revelation. This caballistic reference also suggests that the promise that earth will be a heaven is written into the body of creation, and that the raptures the speaker thought she experienced do await her at some future point.

Thus the reference to Revelation (which echoes Bradstreet's retelling of Daniel's prophecy in "The Foure Monarchies") refers not simply to the promised end of salvation history but as well to the eventual alchemical marriage (promised in nature) of mercury and sulphur.[19] The "white stone" is also the philosopher's stone, the chemical philosopher's analogue of Christ, the cornerstone of the universe, whose power will try all sinners as base metals are tried and turned to gold. We realize at the end of the poem that we have been taken not only through an individual conversion experience but through a process by which we see how both history and nature are to be redeemed. This realization sends us back to reconsider how this ambitious intention has been worked out.

Fortunately we have an important essay by Anne Hildebrand to help us in our review of the means by which "Contemplations" redeems history and nature. Hildebrand demonstrates that there are "similarities in theme, material, and method in "Contemplations' and the quaternions which indicate that Anne Bradstreet is dealing with a central problem, with two different approaches"[20]—and, I would add, at two different periods in her mature life. Hildebrand shows the extent to which Bradstreet's concept of nature (based in classical and medieval traditions) "derives from the exhaustive study of the scheme of the four elements she had compiled earlier" (C/S, 144). Hildebrand observes that "Contemplations" reflects the recognition "early in [Bradstreet's] career that divine unity appears through both the value and the vanity of the world" (C/S, 139). The reworking in "Contemplations" of these early materials also suggests an implicit and an explicit feminism in "Contemplations" that is consistent with the feminism expressed in other Bradstreet works.

Significant diffferences exist between the two poems. For all their verbal delight, the quaternions are rather static pieces, in comparison with the evident dynamism of "Contemplations." Differences can be found, too, in the rhetorical strategies and the poetic forms, but perhaps the most significant difference lies in the identity of the poetic speaker and in the figurative portrayals of nature and history. In "Contemplations" the speaker is no longer an argumentative sibling, an apologetic novice-child, or a passionate wife. Her tone is less intrusive as an element to be contended with; it is less visible. At the first (and I think most important) crisis point, the speaker describes herself as "silent" and "alone." We might expand that to mean meditative, reflective. The voice is most noticeable (as a voice) when it cries out in passionate envy of the lives of the "happy flood" and the "merry Bird" who represent the life to be lived in immortality. The identity of this speaker is discovered in her growth and change; she is defined, I believe, by her subtly marked transmutations, transmutations affected by the shifts of scene.

   The dynamism of "Contemplations"—its movement through stages to an ultimate resolution—depends for its effectiveness on the poet's establishing two starting points from which the interwoven threads of nature and history are teased out. Both of these starting points are figured as feminine, and both have a dark or damaged character. The first is the startling image in stanza 5, where Bradstreet (again) treats the sun as "Bridegroom," as a "strong man [who] joyes to run a race." As in the marriage poems and in "Meditations," the sun is undeniably the force in the universe of nature that brings all things to life and back to life, but here the image of his clearly masculine strength takes a disconcerting turn. It is shaded with violence in the last line where his "heat" "dives" into "the darksome womb of fruitful nature." The "darksome womb" of nature does suggest fertility, but with the added implication of shadows and cheerlessness. The action of the sun here connotes rape, damage, and threat of separation. At this point in the poem the narrator (still enraptured) begins at once to abstract herself from the immediate scene. The poet's safely distanced description of the sun's "course" and "path" in stanza 6 then turns to doubt in stanza 7. She questions his role in the universe. Separation has occurred: he is so "high" that nothing of "earthly mould" can approach him. The speaker's initial naive confidence in the relationship between nature and divinity, earth and heaven, has been dissolved. It has been annihilated by the suggestion of violence at the sexual core of that relationship.

   The other starting point is the reference to the equally dark beginning of human history in Bradstreet's disturbing portrait of "our

Grandame [Eve]" who sits "in retired place." There is a historical
mixing in the portrait here; Eve was, of course, mother to Cain and
Abel, not grandmother. This "Eve," as *our* grandmother, has the shadowy quality that other mother figures in Bradstreet's late poetry have—
sitting off to the side, present and absent. Bradstreet, I believe, has not
mentioned Eve in her poetry before, and this portrait begins with
violence—with the "bloody" child in her lap—and it ends in a quality
of forlorn self-blame over her loss of "bliss" and the view of her posterity's "unknown hap and fate forlorn."

These two afflicted procreative figures are then joined in the poem by
a creative female figure, Philomel. This third major figure of the poem
is a spiritual likeness of the first two. The speaker's meeting with
Philomel provides her with, in effect, a glimpse of the antitype of the
two originators of nature and history. This meeting transforms the
original rapture of the speaker into something different but yet akin to
it:

> The sweet-tongu'd Philomel percht ore my head,
> And chanted forth a most melodious strain
> Which rapt me so with wonder and delight,
> I judg'd my hearing better than my sight,
> And wisht me wings with her a while to take my flight.
>
> (M/R, 173)

The speaker's first vision of nature was one to the eyes; that vision
will now be replaced by a vision in sound, one that, as faith is said to,
speaks to the heart through the ear. The seen, the manifest, has been
replaced by the unseen. The "place" where the speaker's meeting with
this bird takes place is like the maternal riverside foretold in Isaiah 66.
This place is "Thetis house," the house of the dead, a "place" beyond
time and history where type and antitype "embrace and greet"—where
all types will be fulfilled. The maternal figurations of the dawn of
human history and the fall of nature are reduplicated in the maternal
imagery of this ultimate realm. In this last dispensation (which is as yet
to be revealed) the artist sings. The song is the fulfillment of the little,
the fallen art of the grasshopper and the cricket. With them, the
speaker of the poem had earlier identified herself as one who *tries* to sing
but fails. Thus the figure of Philomel, the nightingale, not only *em-
braces* and fullfills nature and history; she is the fulfillment of the
identity of the artist-speaker who emerges at this point as both a

woman and a poet. When the speaker meets Philomel, she meets the prophetic fulfillment of the promise of her own muse. She, then, in a stance that suggests the prophet, returns from the realm of the blessed, as if from the top of the mountain or from an ecstatic vision of the oneness of creation, ready to tackle the world—the history and nature of which she is a part.

Cheryl Walker has suggested that in the figure of Philomel, Bradstreet has combined both "the power of art and the power of motherhood" (Walker, 16). I would like to suggest, further, that the typology of the nightingale suggests again the typological cluster to which Eve, Mary, and the "scribe" Bathsheba belong. Although Philomel in "Contemplations" is said to live beyond the world (she "fears no snares",[21] she, like these other mothers, shares with them a similarly dark and damaged sexual history. She too has undergone "affliction." Philomel had been raped by her sister's husband and her tongue cut out so that she could not report the need. She later wove her story into a robe that she gave to her sister Procne, who deciphered it. Thus mutability and suffering have marked the life of the "merry bird" who, like other maternal figures in Bradstreet's work, bears a figural resemblance to Bathsheba, whose powers of prophecy were directly related to her sufferings. The prototypical figure of the poet that emerges from Bradstreet's later poetry and that is confirmed in the cluster of figures developed in "Contemplations" is of a "mother" who has prophetic powers that are the result of her sufferings and who gives voice to hidden or cryptic utterances that must be deciphered by a reader who is attuned to them. We have seen this portrait of the artist described both by Cotton Mather and by John Dod in his interpretations of Proverbs.

If we consider the poem "Contemplations" to be, then, a prefiguration of prophecy of the nightingale's song, that likeness tells us that dark deeds have occurred that have not been said openly—which the speaker represses in the initial stanzas. The poem thus begins, as it ends, with a reference to oblivion. If the task of the poet-prophet is to reveal the truth in events, she will do so, as Bathsheba and Eve and Mary did, by giving birth in pain. The poem looks forward to a time when the speaker will be able to put before her readers' eyes not the bloody body of Cain but the new birth that the name in the white stone promises. To experience this poem is to be refined, be translated, and to experience that "birth again" that the author said she travailed to bring about in her children and here, in this public poem, in all her readers. The promise of the name in the white stone is not the promise of a land of Nod, a never-never land. It is the promise of a deliverance. The name in the white stone can thus be seen to be the antitypical fulfillment of the poem itself; it is the fulfillment of which the poem is a prophecy.

Read typologically, then, "Contemplations" reveals an interdependence between the figures of Eve, Philomel, Bathsheba, and Divine Wisdom who is alive in nature and in the words of the prophetic speaker or "scribe" who undergoes change. The poem's implied circularity, its focus on nature (not simply on history), and its use of key creative and procreative female figures signal that in Bradstreet's cosmos there were forces at work that were not governed simply by salvation history but by the ever-circling patterns in nature that Bradstreet and others thought of as gendered female.

Thus the theology of this poem has an admixture that is not readily found in Reformation and Postreformation Protestantism. A significant strain in the poetic representations comes closer, in fact to the sapiential theologies of the Middle Ages. Bradstreet, thus, in her theology, as in her science, appears to hark back to earlier times. Historian Barbara Newman reports the popularity of the Wisdom tradition in the Middle Ages,[22] and Newman's work on St. Hildegard of Bingen's "theology of the feminine" serves to highlight significant aspects of Bradstreet's theology—ones that, I believe, have been present in her work from the beginning. Hildegard, like Bradstreet, emphasized "the mystery of the Incarnation, envisioned as the center and final cause of creation—presented by God 'from the foundation of the world' " in Christ as Wisdom" (Newman, 45). Because this mystery was given birth "by a woman [Mary], it is evoked in visions that . . . highlight the feminine dimension of the divine reality" (45). In Hildegard's theology, as I think we have seen in Bradstreet's work, "this complex of ideas and images by no means precludes a more linear understanding of salvation history, cast in the form of a narrative beginning with creation and the fall culminating with the death and resurrection of Christ, and concluding with the Last Judgment." Hildegard's theology is thus inclusive and doubly gendered. So, too, Bradstreet, as we have seen, adopted an androcentric model for her "Four Monarchies," turning her history over to the personages of kings, princes, and prophets. (Parenthetically, we should notice that it is masculine history that she gave up on.) When Hildegard was "following this narrative pattern, discussing the great and unrepeatable events in history, [she] normally used masculine designations for God—Father and Son, King and Redeemer and Judge" (45). (To this list Bradstreet would add bridegroom.) Bradstreet, too, when she prayed to the God who was in covenant with New England, prayed to a father God, but as in Hildegard's work, "the feminine designations, on the other hand, evoke God's timeless or perpetually repeated interactions with the cosmos." Thus, Hildegard used "feminine symbols to convey the principle of divine self-manifestation; the mutual indwelling of God in the world and the world in God" (45). Such was the contribution of a sapiential or Wisdom theology to the first three quaternions, where the "mutual indwelling of God in the world and the world in God" is the dialectic which that universe (and the similar universe of "Contemplations") depends. Similarly that dialectic accounts for Bradstreet's perception, as Anne Hildebrand wrote, that "divine unity appears through both the value and the vanity of the world." It is that dialectic that provides the "consolation" of all "Worldly creatures" and that provides the assurance that "revolution" will bring Queen Elizabeth (who now "lies in silence") back into the world. That dialectic is threatened by the separations in the marriage poems and is presented as broken in the relationship between the "Flesh" and the "Spirit."

This parallel with St. Hildegard serves to point out how deeply traditional and yet how deeply feminist Bradstreet's texts and verbal contexts were. These contexts were, it now seems clear, selected because (as she wrote at the end of her life) they "most concerned [her] Condition, and as [she] grew to haue more vnderstanding, so yᵉ more solace [she] took in them" (M/R, 215). I thus tend to find in the Bradstreet canon continuity rather than disjunction. The evident shifts in tone, in personas, and in the ostensible subject matter are aspects of an organic development, one that is remarkably consistent in its themes, its preoccupations, and even its compulsions. Bradstreet emerges for me, finally, an artist. By that I mean someone who has one many-faceted subject that, even over a lifetime, was not exhausted, not fully worked out.

This sense of a revolutionary dialectic at work in the creation was, it now seems clear, not Bradstreet's individual discovery. We glimpse in "Contemplations" the extent to which Bradstreet not only chose her materials from a wide range of sources but was, in a sense, chosen by them. One of the problems for modern readers is that we are just beginning to come to know something about the discourse (particularly the female discourse) that provided Bradstreet with examples of the woman artist's vocation. For those of us interested in working on the relationship between the seventeenth-century woman artist and her sources, the caveats raised by Michael Clark both enrich and complicate the project. Clark has counseled us to "avoid a naive reduction of the texts to direct expressions of their author's feelings and ideas." He describes the point of view that I have attempted to honour in this study. "Texts," he writes, "are discursive strategies that constitute the individual as author or speaker and so determine his or her place in the cultural order that supports that discourse, whether that culture be understood spiritually as the community of the elect, ecclesiastically as the visible church, or secularly as the manners and customs that govern everyday life of a village."[23] To that list I would add the personal, spiritual, and cultural context on which, as we have seen, so much of Bradstreet's work is focused: the "family." Thus, as author or speaker, Bradstreet is "an effect of language" (Clark, 124) as well as a user and shaper of language. What "she says" about family, about herself as daughter, sister, wife, or mother, becomes inextricably original and imitative, private and public, hers and her culture's. I have tried to take Michael Clark's advice seriously in my attempt to discover Bradstreet's life and work. While attempting to suggest verbal contexts, which were native to Bradstreet's experience, I have attempted to "discover . . . the subject and its text in its own terms . . . and not to continue to treat [these] colonial texts merely as expressions or representations ordered by reference to something else" (129).

I also understand imitation to be part of the artistic process— inevitable to a degree and not necessarily antithetical to it. In doing so I have followed the direction taken by Eileen Margerum and Ivy Schweitzer, who both point out the conventional and the imitative quality of Bradstreet's verbal gestures. Bradstreet's self-mockery, her references to ineptness, are evidence of centuries-old conventions, Margerum shows us, to which the poet had been schooled. Paradoxically, it is in her characteristic apologies for want of skill, Margerum argues, that we sometimes find Bradstreet at her most skillful. Margerum points out that in Bradstreet's "shaping" of the formula to "suit her needs" lies the clear signs of the poet's "self-assurance rather than self-doubt."[24]

Both Wendy Martin and Ann Stanford have pointed out the self-protecting strategy imbedded in Bradstreet's confessions of ineptness, and Ivy Schweitzer goes a step further, calling these confessions consciously imitative. She finds in Bradstreet's "mimicry" a "disruption and modification of the conventions they imitate" (Schweitzer, 293). Throughout this study I have argued that Bradstreet used materials that came to her from tradition and training but that in her "mimicry" Bradstreet shifted the ground away from classical tradition to the biblical and scientific (to the Solomonic inheritance). The conventions cited by Margerum and Schweitzer belonged to classical rhetoric and surely were part of Bradstreet's education as a child of Renaissance parents eager to ensure her learnedness. As we have seen so persuasively argued in Joan Kelly-Gadol's essay, "Did Women Have a Renaissance?," however, it is exactly in the nature of humanistic education that we find the explanation of why the Renaissance woman "cannot compare with her medieval predecessors in shaping a culture responsive to her own interest." Set beside Newman's commentary about Hildegard, Kelly-Gadol's insights help to clarify why Bradstreet at her most feminist seems to echo medieval discourse. In medieval times, according to Kelly-Gadol, the education of women took place in the court of a great lady. In the Renaissance, however, "her brother's tutors shaped her outlook, male educators who, as humanists, suppressed romance and chivalry to further classical culture, with all its patriarchal and misogynist bias."[25] Kelly-Gadol thus concludes with a resounding no in answer to her essay's initial question, citing the example of Renaissance noblewomen and "their sisters in the patrician bourgeoisie" (among whom we would find Anne Bradstreet). The movement forward in time, Kelly-Gadol suggests, was backward in terms of women's power and independence. "Renaissance ideas on love and manners," she concludes, were "more classical than medieval, and almost exclusively a male product." These expressed what Kelly-Gadol calls a "new subordination of women to the interests of husbands and male-dominated kin groups" (164).

Fortunately, as we have seen, classical conventions were not the only or even the principal conventions that Bradstreet wrote into the scripts of the personas who speak her poems. Bradstreet's biblical sources, and with these the countervailing force of the "tenth" or "heavenly" muse (in contrast to the nine muses of classical antiquity), inform the gender identity of her speakers. Typically, as we have seen, in Bradstreet's work, the female masks shift and change shape: at one moment they speak an apology; at the next they claim prophetic power. I believe that what Cheryl Walker identifies as Bradstreet's personal vacillation or ambivalence is present in the traditions she borrowed and in the poetry as its deepest design. Mutability is the most consistent and important characteristic of her art.

In Bradstreet's title, *The Tenth Muse Lately Sprung Up in America,* we can see the suggestion of her intention for that 1650 volume: she was to be the speaker or midwife of an inheritance that would come to birth in America. She (or her editors) did not "put herself into the text," the "world" and "history" as the *first* American poet. Rather, she was the one "lately sprung up," as if her genius had a prior existence, another life, place, or time. The muse of this title is like a seed in the ground or an underground spring or a typological figuration that surfaces when conditions and times are right. In such a self-presentation Bradstreet seems, in Margaret Homan's words about Emily Dickinson, to have followed "the best course," which was "to exploit language's inherent fictiveness, rather than fight against it."[26] If I were to guess, I would guess that Bradstreet lived comfortably with the discourse to which she had been educated and to which she felt herself an heir. When she speaks of the season Spring, she calls her "A natural Artificer complete" (M/R, 48). Bradstreet's admiration can also be read as identification with this maker who falls to her fictive work naturally, who is well furnished for that work, and who is compelled toward the prospect of its completeness.

Notes and References

Chapter One

1. *The Complete Works of Anne Bradstreet,* ed. Joseph R. McElrath, Jr., and Allan R. Robb (Boston: Twayne, 1981), 530; hereafter cited in text as M/R. The major critical responses to Anne Bradstreet's work over three centuries are reprinted with an extensive review of virtually all Bradstreet criticism in *Critical Essays on Ann Bradstreet,* ed. Pattie Cowell and Ann Stanford (Boston: G. K. Hall, 1983); hereafter cited in text as C/S.

2. Charles Eliot Norton, "The Poems of Mrs. Anne Bradstreet," in *The Poems of Mrs. Anne Bradstreet (1612–1672) Together with Her Prose Remains,* ed. Frank E. Hopkins (New York: Duedecimos, 1897), x.

3. *The Works of Anne Bradstreet in Prose and Verse,* ed. John Harvard Ellis (Charlestown, Mass.: Abraham E. Cutter, 1867) xlii; hereafter cited in text as Ellis.

4. Samuel Eliot Morison, *Builders of the Bay Colony,* rev. ed. (Boston: Houghton Mifflin, 1964), 335; hereafter cited in text as Morison.

5. John Berryman, *Homage to Mistress Bradstreet* (New York: Farrar, Straus, 1956).

6. Cheryl Walker, *The Nightingale's Burden: Women Poets and American Culture before 1900* (Bloomington: Indiana University Press, 1982), 2; hereafter cited in text as Walker.

7. Pattie Cowell, *Women Poets in Pre-Revolutionary America, 1650–1775, An Anthology* (New York: Whitston, 1981), 2; hereafter cited in text as Cowell.

8. Ann Stanford, *Anne Bradstreet, the Wordly Puritan: An Introduction to Her Poetry* (New York: Burt Franklin, 1974), contains, in addition, a review of "scholarship and criticism since 1930"; hereafter cited in text as Stanford 1974. Her "Anne Bradstreet: An Annotated Checklist," *Early American Literature* 3 (Winter 1968–69): 217–28, is also useful, although much new material has appeared since these works were completed.

9. Lyle Koehler's *A Search for Power: The "Weaker Sex" in Seventeenth-Century New England* (Urbana: University of Illinois Press, 1980) contains a wealth of new information; hereafter cited in text, as Koehler.

10. Robert Daly, *God's Altar: The World and the Flesh in Puritan Poetry* (Berkeley: University of California Press, 1978); hereafter cited in text as Daly 1978.

11. Josephine K. Piercy, *Anne Bradstreet* (New York: Twayne, 1965), 115; hereafter cited in text as Piercy.

158

ANNE BRADSTREET REVISITED

12. Philip Greven, *The Protestant Temperament: Patterns of Child-Bearing Religious Experience, and the Self in Early America* (New York: Alfred A. Knopf, 1978), 67. See especially "Our Loathsome Corruption and Pollution: Attitudes toward the Body," 65–73; hereafter cited in text as Geven 1980.

13. David D. Hall, "A World of Wonders: The Mentality of the Supernatural in Seventeenth-Century New England," in *Seventeenth-Century New England,* ed. David D. Hall, a Conference held by the Colonial Society of Massachusetts, 18–19 June 1982 (Boston: Colonial Society of Massachusetts, 1984), 270.

14. I have relied heavily on Laurel Thatcher Ulrich, *Good Wives: Image and Reality in the Lives of Women in Northern New England, 1650–1750* (New York: Oxford University Press, 1983); hereafter cited in text as Ulrich.

15. David Underdown, *Revel, Riot, and Rebellion: Popular Politics and Culture in England 1603–1660* (Oxford: Clarendon Press, 1985), 41; hereafter cited in text as Underdown.

16. Regina Schwartz used this expression in a paper on Milton's *De Doctrina Christiana* given at the Modern Language Association Convention, New Orleans, 27–30 December 1988.

17. Hélène Cixous, "The Laugh of the Medusa," *Signs* (Summer 1976). Reprinted in *New French Feminisms, an Anthology,* ed. Elaine Marks and Isabelle de Courtivron (New York: Schocken Books, 1981), 245; hereafter cited in text as Cixous.

18. Rosamond Rosenmeier, " 'Divine Translation': A Contribution to the Study of Anne Bradstreet's Method in the Marriage Poems," *Early American Literature* 12 (1977): 121–34. Reprinted in C/S 190–204; hereafter cited in text as C/S.

19. I am particularly indebted to Professor Carole Fontaine whose lectures at the Andover Newton Theological School have helped me to understand biblical wisdom. Virginia Ramey Mollenkott's *The Divine Feminine: The Biblical Imagery of God as Female* (New York: Crossroad, 1985) gives a general introduction to the subject; hereafter cited in text as Mollenkott. I have relied, particularly, on Claudia V. Camp, *Wisdom and the Femine in the Book of Proverbs* (Decatur: Almond Press of the Columbia Theological Seminary, 1985); hereafter cited in text as Camp.

20. George Adlard, *The Sutton-Dudleys of England, and the Dudleys of Massachusetts in New England* (New York, 1862), 18; hereafter cited in text as Adlard.

21. George Keith writes that "around the middle of the [seventeenth] century most serious scientists were moving over from an animistic universe to a mechanical one. . . . Natural science owed much to the stimulus of hermetic thinking but its emancipation from that tradition was accomplished in the later seventeenth century." *Religion and the Decline of Magic* (New York: Charles Scribner's Sons, 1971), 225–26; hereafter cited in text as Keith.

22. Frances A. Yates, *Ideas and Ideals in the North European Renaissance: Collected Essays,* vol. 3 (London: Routledge & Kegan Paul, 1984), 248; hereafter cited in text as Yates 1984.

23. Ronald Sterne Wilkinson, "The Alchemical Library of John Winthrop, Jr., (1606–1676) and His Descendants in Colonial America," *Ambix 2* (1963): 33–51; hereafter cited in text, as Wilkinson.

24. Désirée Hirst, *Hidden Riches: Traditional Symbolism from the Renaissance to Blake* (New York: Barnes & Noble, 1964), 80; hereafter cited in text as Hirst.

25. Kenneth B. Murdock, *Literature and Theology in Colonial New England* (Cambridge, Mass.: Harvard University Press, 1949), 151; hereafter cited in text as Murdock.

26. Wendy Martin, "Anne Bradstreet's Poetry: A study of Subversive Piety," *Shakespeare's Sisters: Feminist Essays on Women Poets,* ed. Sandra Gilbert and Susan Gubar (Bloomington: Indiana University Press, 1979), 31; hereafter cited in text as Martin 1979.

27. Cotton Mather, *Magnalia Christi Americana,* bks. 1, 2, and 3, ed. Kenneth B. Murdock (1702; Cambridge, Mass.: Belknap Press of Harvard University Press, 1977), 17; hereafter cited in text as Mather 1702, 1, 2, or 3.

28. Bathsua Makin, *An Essay to Revive the Antient Education of Gentlewomen* (1673; Los Angeles: University of California, William Andrews Clark Memorial Library, Pub. No. 202, 1980), 20; hereafter cited in text as Makin.

29. David Latt writes that "in the course of the [seventeenth] century, literally dozens of misogynist works were published in England; in fact, works on women, defending and attacking them, became a minor genre in the period." "Praising Virtuous Ladies: The Literary Image and Historical Reality of Women in Seventeenth-Century England," in *What Manner of Woman,* ed. Marlene Springer (New York: New York University Press, 1977), 60.

30. Underdown also observes that "late Elizabethan and Jacobean writers were unusually preoccupied with themes of female independence and resolve" (38.)

31. Jennifer R. Waller makes this point in " 'My Hand a Needle Better Fits': Anne Bradstreet and Women Poets in the Renaissance," *Dalhousie Review* 54 (Autumn): 436–50.

32. Elizabeth Freund, *The Return of the Reader: Reader-Response Criticism* (New York: Methuen, 1987), 273.

Chapter Two

1. Sarah Mendelson *The Mental World of Stuart Women: Three Studies* (Amherst: University of Massachusetts Press, 1987), 2.

2. John Dod and Robert Cleuer, *A Godly Forme of Hovshold Gouernment: For the Ordering of Private Families, according to the direction of God's Word* (London: Thomas Mann, 1612), 168; hereafter cited in text as Dod 1612.

3. Carl Bridenbaugh, *Vexed and Troubled Englishmen, 1590–1642* (New York: Oxford University Press, 1968), 47; hereafter cited in text as Bridenbaugh.

4. Augustine Jones, *Thomas Dudley, Second Governor of Massachusetts* (Boston: Houghton Mifflin, 1900), 50; hereafter cited in text as Jones.

5. White, 383–90, lists the books found in Thomas Dudley's library at the time of his death (Elizabeth Wade White, *Anne Bradstreet: The Tenth Muse* [New York: Oxford University Press, 1971]; hereafter cited in text as White).

6. Christopher Hill, *Reformation to Revolution, Pelican Economic History of Britain,* 1530–1780 vol. 2 (Baltimore: Penguin Books, 1969), 109; hereafter cited in text as Hill.

7. Jonathan Goldberg, "Fatherly Authority: The Politics of Stuart Family Images," in *Rewriting the Renaissance: The Discourses of Sexual Difference in Early Modern Europe,* ed. Margaret W. Ferguson, Maureen Quilligan, and Nancy J. Vickers (Chicago: University of Chicago Press, 1986), 3–32; Laurence Stone, *The Family, Sex and Marriage: In England 1500–1800* (New York: Harper Colophon Books, 1979), 110, hereafter cited in text as Stone.

8. This attitude is not surprising, given the high mortality rate for women and children. In England 45 percent of aristocratic women died before age 50, and one-fourth of these from complications of childbirth. R. V. Schnucker, "The English Puritans and Pregnancy, Delivery and Breast Feeding," *History of Childhood Quarterly* 1 (Spring 1974): 643; hereafter cited in text as Schnucker. At Anne Dudley's time of birth only 30 percent of the children of peers could expect to live to age 15, and by far the largest percentage of those who died did so in infancy. Levin Schücking, *The Puritan Family* (New York: Schocken Books, 1964), 67; hereafter cited in text as Schücking.

9. Adrienne Rich suggests that by the seventeenth century male midwives were beginning to take over the profession. See her chapter, "Hands of Flesh, Hands of Iron," in *Of Woman Born: Motherhood as Experience and Institution* (New York: W. W. Norton, 1986), 128–55.

10. The countess of Lincoln wrote a famous letter to her daughter in which she advocated nursing for these reasons. The letter's introduction was written by tutor-physician Thomas Lodge. Elizabeth Clinton, *The Countess of Lincolne's Nurserie* (Oxford: J. Lichfield & James Short, 1623).

11. John Brinsley, *Ludus Literarius; or, The Grammar Schoole* (London: For Thomas Mann, 1612), 9; hereafter cited in text as Brinsley.

12. Lucy Hutchinson, *Memoirs of the Life of Colonel Hutchinson,* vol. 1, 4th ed. (London: Longman, Hurst, Rees, Orme, and Brown, 1822), 25–27. White (60) states that Anne Dudley's "education probably began in 1617, when she was four years old."

13. Harrison T. Meserole, ed., *Seventeenth-Century American Poetry* (New York: W. W. Norton, 1968), 3.

14. Lawrence Thompson, *Women in Stuart England and America: A Com-*

parative Study (London: Routledge & Kegan Paul, 1974), 203; hereafter cited in text as Thompson.

15. John Harvard Ellis concurs about the level of Bradstreet's education. He writes that she "mentions many of the principal Greek and Latin authors. . .; but there is no reason to suppose that she read their works, either in the originals or in translations" (xliii).

16. Ann Stanford's finding that Du Bartas was first published in English in 1621 is incorrect, but she too observes that Bradstreet read that edition (9).

17. Susan Snyder, ed., *The Divine Weeks and Works of Guillaume de Saluste Sieur du Bartas*, trans. Joshua Sylvester, vol. 1 (Oxford: Clarendon Press, 1979), 5; hereafter cited in text as Snyder.

18. Terence C. Cave, *Devotional Poetry in France, c. 1570–1613* (Cambridge: Cambridge University Press, 1969), 308.

19. Joshua Sylvester, *The Complete Works,* ed. Alexander D. Grosart, vol. 2 (Edinburgh, 1880), 1; hereafter cited in text as Sylvester.

20. Ann Kibbey, remarks made in response to papers presented at Prospects: A Conference on Early American Literature, Chapel Hill, University of North Carolina, 31 March 1989.

21. Richard Deacon, *John Dee: Scientist, Geographer, Astrologer, and Secret Agent to Elizabeth I* (London: Frederick Muller, 1968), 70, 184.

22. Frances A. Yates, *The Occult Philosophy in the Elizabethan Age* (London: Routledge & Kegan Paul, 1979), 80; hereafter cited in text as Yates 1979.

23. Rufus Jones, *Mysticism and Democracy in the English Commonwealth* (Cambridge, Mass.: Harvard University Press, 1932), 120; hereafter cited in text as Jones.

24. Wayne Shumaker, *The Occult Sciences in the Renaissance: A Study in Intellectual Patterns* (Berkeley: University of California Press, 1972), 205; hereafter cited in text as Shumaker.

25. Roger Thompson, *Sex in Middlesex: Popular Mores in a Massachusetts County, 1649–1699* (Amherst: University of Massachusetts Press, 1986), 105, 195.

26. John Cotton, "The Pouring Out of the Spirit," in *The Way of Life* (London, 1641), 117; hereafter cited in text as Cotton 1641.

27. Peter Lazlett, *The World We Have Lost: England before the Industrial Age* (New York: Charles Scribner's Sons, 1971), 85; hereafter cited in text as Lazlett.

28. Samuel Clarke, *A general Martyrologie, containing a collection of all the greatest persecutions which have befallen the church of Christ from the creation to our present times* (London: Printed at A. M. for Thomas Underhill and John Rothwell, 1651).

29. Wendy Martin, *An American Triptych: Anne Bradstreet, Emily Dickinson, Adrienne Rich* (Chapel Hill: University of North Carolina Press, 1984), 39; hereafter cited in text as Martin 1984.

30. In H.D.'s *Trilogy* (1973) and in her densely annotated translation of Euripedes' *Ion* (1937) these themes are fully developed.

31. Ivy Schweitzer, "Anne Bradstreet and the Renaissance," *Early American Literature,* 23 (1988), 293; hereafter cited in text as Schweitzer.

32. Galmini Salgado, *The Elizabethan Underworld* (London: J. M. Dent, 1977), 111; hereafter cited in text as Salgado.

33. Moses Coit Tyler, *The History of American Literature during the Colonial Period, 1607–1765* (1878; Ithaca, N.Y.: Cornell University Press, 1949), 253.

34. Jane Donahue Eberwein argues against a one-dimensional reading of "The Prologue" and suggests that the reader who is "alert or ironic" will discover the "poet's cleverness in charming while outwitting her antagonist." " 'No Rhet'ric We Expect': Argumentation in Bradstreet's 'The Prologue,' " *Early American Literature,* 16 (1981): 19–26. Reprinted in C/S, 218–25.

35. Alicia Ostriker makes the interesting suggestion that Bradstreet may have begun the quaternions while still in England and thus in childhood. *Stealing the Language: The Emergence of Women's Poetry in America* (Boston: Beacon Press, 1986), 19.

36. Cornelius Agrippa, "A treatise of the nobilitie and excellence of womankynde," trans. David Clapam (London, 1542), 369.

37. Cheryl Walker (6–7) observes that Bradstreet's speaker here is "self-aggrandizing one moment and self-effacing the next." and she regrets that the poet "cannot simply come forward with her anger and her hopes. She must make the required bow toward the patriarchy." I am suggesting that the poem makes a statement that includes or implies anger but that goes beyond it.

Chapter Three

1. Everett Emerson, ed., *Letters from New England: The Massachusetts Bay Colony, 1629–1638* (Cambridge, Mass.: Harvard University Press, 1976), 69; hereafter cited in text as Emerson.

2. John Cotton, "God's Promise to His Plantations," *Old South Leaflets,* vol. 3, no. 53 (1894), 1–16; hereafter cited in text as Cotton 1894.

3. David P. Wharton has reconstructed the life aboard the *Arbella* in his essay, "Anne Bradstreet and the *Arbella,*" C/S, 262–69.

4. Johnson's *Wonder-Working Providence, 1628–51,* in *Original Narratives of Early American History,* vol. 14, ed. J. Franklin Jameson (New York: C. Scribner's Son, 1910), 64; hereafter cited in text as Johnson.

5. See also John Winthrop, *The History of New England, 1630–1649,* vol. 1, ed. James Savage (Boston: Little, Brown, 1853), 132; hereafter cited in text as Winthrop 1 or 2.

6. Richard S. Dunn, *Puritans and Yankees: The Winthrop Dynasty of New England, 1630–1717* (New York: W. W. Norton, 1962), 63; hereafter cited in text as Dunn.

7. David Grayson Allen, *In English Ways: The Movement of Societies and the Transferal of English Local Law and Custom to Massachusetts Bay in the Seventeenth Century* (New York: W. W. Norton, 1982), 119; hereafter cited in text as Allen.

8. Thomas F. Waters, *Ipswich in the Massachusetts Bay Colony,* vol. 1 (Ipswich, Mass.: Ipswich Historical Society, 1905), 512–13; hereafter cited in text as Waters.

9. John Gorham Palfrey, *History of New England,* vol. 1 (Boston: Little Brown, 1859), 51; hereafter cited in text as Palfrey.

10. David D. Hall, ed., *The Antinomian Controversy, 1636–1638* (Middletown, Conn.: Wesleyan University Press, 1968), 327; hereafter cited in text as Hall.

11. Frances A. Yates, *The Rosicrucian Enlightenment* (London: Routledge & Kegan Paul, 1982), 284; hereafter cited in text as Yates 1982.

12. Thomas Tymme, *The Practise of Chymicale, and Hermetical Physicke* (1605), quoted in Stanton J. Linden, "Alchemy and Eschatology in Seventeenth-Century Poetry," *Ambix* 31 (3) (1984): 115.

13. Karl Keller, *The Example of Edward Taylor* (Amherst: University of Massachusetts Press, 1975), 224. Bradstreet and Hutchinson are compared in Ann King, "Anne Hutchinson and Anne Bradstreet: Literature and Experience, Faith and Works in Massachusetts Bay Colony," *International Journal of Women's Studies* 1, no. 5 (1978): 445–67.

14. This point is made by Jesper Rosenmeier; " 'They Shall No Longer Grieve': The Song of Songs and Edward Johnson's *Wonder-Working Providence,*" forthcoming in *Early American Literature.*

15. See Morison, 235–37. The bad relations between Essex County and Boston culminated in 1643, when Simon Bradstreet, Ward, Rogers, and Norton—all supporters of Anne Bradstreet's poetic profession—opposed Winthrop and Dudley's support for one French naval man's military attempt to seize the lordship of Nova Scotia from another.

16. Robert Fitzgibbon Young, *Comenius in England* (London: Oxford University Press, 1932), 8, 93.

17. The reference here and in "Contemplations" to "dearest, near'st Relation" (M/R, 174) is a euphemism for spouse. Esther Edwards Burr uses the phrase as part of an extended commentary on the "tryals" and "Duties" of marriage. *The Journals of Esther Edwards Burr, 1754–1757* (New Haven: Yale University Press, 1984), 266. I am grateful to Jesper Rosenmeier for this citation.

18. White, Underdown (239) point out that in the 1640s London separatist congregations permitted women the right to vote, debate, prophesy, and "even preach."

19. John Dod, *Bathshebaes Instructions to her Sonne LEMUEL: Containing a fruitful and plaine Explosition of the last chapter of PROVERBS* (London, 1614).

20. Ulrich emphasizes the multiplicity of the Goodwife's roles. Historian Roger Thompson (86) (as others have) finds "a tension inherent in puritanism, between church 'sister' and man's wife," which he feels "held the potential for greater female independence and individualism."

21. *The Geneva Bibble: A Facsimile of the 1560 Edition* (Madison: University of Wisconsin Press, 1969); hereafter cited in text as Geneva.

22. [John Dod] and Robert Cleaver, *A Briefe Explanation of the Whole Booke of the Prouerbs of Solomon* (London: Felix Kyngston for Thomas Man, and Richard Jackson, 1615), 113; hereafter cited in text as Dod 1615.

23. White (253) suggests that the arrangement of the poems of *The Tenth Muse* is marked by "chronological and textual confusion" amd assumes that Bradstreet had no hand in supervising their publication. The question of Bradstreet's role in her books' publication is thoughtfully probed by McElrath and Robb (M/R, xxxi–xxxiv). They too conclude that others (Woodbridge, "perhaps Ward, and other friends" and the printer) "undoubtedly 'improved' " her manuscript. I am suggesting that someone (perhaps not Bradstreet) chose to open and close *The Tenth Muse* with these feminist, Solomonic poems.

24. "Anne Bradstreet's Poetic Voices," *Early American Literature* 9 (1974): 3–18. Reprinted in C/S, 150–65.

25. See also Edmund S. Morgan, *The Puritan Family: Religion and Domestic Relations in Seventeenth-Century New England* (New York: Harper & Row, 1966) 44; hereafter cited in text, as Morgan.

26. For a discussion of this indebtedness, see Helen McMahon, "Anne Bradstreet, Jean Bertault, and Dr. Crooke," *Early American Literature* 3 (Fall 1968): 118–22.

27. Helkiah Crooke, *Microcosmographia, or a Description . . . of the Body of Man. . . .* London: William Taggard, 1675), hereafter cited in text as Crooke.

Chapter Four

1. For a definitive exploration of the relationship between creativity and procreativity see Susan Friedman's "Creativity and the Childbirth Metaphor: Gender Difference in Literary Discourse," *Speaking of Gender,* ed. Elaine Showalter (New York: Routledge, 1989), 73–101.

2. Caldwell (16–19) develops the connection between Bradstreet's motherhood and creative selfhood, using as her examples the Apochryphal Anne, mother of Mary, and the Old Testament Hannah, mother of the "miraculously granted offspring, Samuel."

3. The date of the move is not known. White (224) suggests that the Bradstreets initially may have gone back and forth between Ipswich and Andover before finally settling in Andover.

4. Philip J. Greven, Jr., *Four Generations: Population, Land, and Family*

in Colonial Andover, Massachusetts (Ithaca, N.Y.: Cornell University Press, 1970), 42; hereafter cited in text as Greven 1970.

5. Claude M. Fuess, *Andover: Symbol of New England: The Evolution of a Town* (Andover: Andover Historical Society and North Andover Historical Society, 1959), 54; hereafter cited in text as Fuess.

6. Stanford does not agree. She argues that "Bradstreet's notebook does not report a lifetime of poor health; on the contrary, her entries could be the reaction of one who has enjoyed considerable good health and is impatient under confinement" (Stanford 1974, 82).

7. Dudley remarried four months after Dorothy Dudley's death and fathered three more children, the first of whom, Deborah, was born in 1644. It is tempting to speculate whether in 1646 when the Bradstreets' fourth daughter, Mercy, was on the way, Bradstreet had in mind the experience of her own stepmother when she refers to "step Dames injury" in the poem "Before the Birth of one of her Children" (M/R, 180).

8. This poem is reprinted in *The Puritans: A Sourcebook of their Writings,* ed. Perry Miller and Thomas H. Johnson, vol. 2 (New York: Harper & Row, 1963), 632.

9. David Watters, *Readings for Prospects: A Conference on Early American Literature,* Chapel Hill, North Carolina, 30 March–1 April 1989 (Chapel Hill: University of North Carolina at Chapel Hill, 1989), 35–36.

10. Robert Daly, "The Danforths: Puritan Poets in the Woods of Arcadia," in *Puritan Poets and Poetics,* 150–52).

11. Allen G. Debus, *The Chemical Philosophy: Paracelsian Science and Medicine in the Sixteenth and Seventeenth Centuries,* vol. 1 (New York: Science History Publications, 1977), 34.

12. White (40) notes that Bradstreet dated several of the later writings "March 20," and suggests that this might have been Bradstreet's birthday. I think it more likely that Bradstreet, with her scientific interests, was marking the date of the season's translation or transmutation.

13. Critics have argued over the feeling tone of Bradstreet's acquiescence to her maker in these elegies, especially about the resolution to "Farwel dear babe." See Randall R. Mawer, " 'Farewel Dear Babe': Bradstreet's Elegy for Elizabeth," *Early American Literature* 15 (1980): 29–41. Reprinted in C/S; the argument is summarized at 210–15. The problem with attempting to discuss these elegies as statements of feeling is that they all convey so much more than grief, rebellion, or piety.

14. *The Works of Anne Bradstreet,* ed. Jeannine Hensley (Cambridge, Mass.: Belknap Press of Harvard University Press, 1967), xxix. See also "The Editor of Anne Bradstreet's *Several Poems,*" *American Literature* 35 (1964): 503–04.

15. Cotton Mather, *Ornaments for the Daughters of Zion, or the Character and Happiness of a Vertuous Woman* (Cambridge, Mass.: Green, 1692), 6; hereafter cited in text as Mather 1692.

16. *Kissing the Rod: An Anthology of Seventeenth-Century Women's Verse,* ed. Germaine Greer, Susan Hastings, Jeslyn Medoff, and Melinda Sansome (New York: Farrar, Straus & Giroux, 1988), 11; hereafter cited in text as Greer et al. See also Mary G. Mason, "The Other Voice: Autobiographies of Women Writers," in *Autobiography: Essays Theoretical and Critical,* ed. James Olney (Princeton: Princeton University Press, 207–35.

17. Elizabeth Gerymeston left her son the "Portrait of a Mother's Mind" in a legacy called *Miscelanea, Meditations, Memoratives,* published in 1604. It is tempting to think that Bradstreet may have known this highly successful work (Greer et al., 11).

18. See especially Stanford's discussion of "Contemplations" as a formal meditation (Stanford 1974, 81–106) and William J. Irwin's "Allegory and Typology 'Imbrace and Greet': Anne Bradstreet's "Contemplations,' " *Early American Literature* 10 (1975): 30–46. Reprinted in C/S, 174–89. Irwin traces the stages as stages in a conversion experience. His interpretation, although also based on typology, is different from mine.

19. I am indebted to John Brooks of the Tufts University History Department for this insight.

20. Anne Hildebrand, "Anne Bradstreet's Quaternions and 'Contemplations,' " *Early American Literature* 8 (1973): 117–25. Reprinted in C/S, 137; hereafter cited in text, as C/S.

21. Readers sometimes overlook the time scheme of the poem in this section. The past lives in one time; the nightingale in another. In Ecclesiastes 9:12, Solomon warns that "a man knoweth not his time: as the fishes that are taken in an evil net, and as the birds that are caught in the snares, so are men snared in an evil time, when it calleth suddenly upon them." The poet is snared. Philomel no longer is.

22. Barbara Newman, *Sister Wisdom: St. Hildegard's Theology of the Feminine* (Berkely: University of California Press, 1987), 42; hereafter cited in text as Newman.

23. Michael Clark, "The Subject of the Text in Early American Literature," *Early American Literature* 20 (Fall 1985): 121; hereafter cited in text as Clark.

24. Eileen Margerum, "Anne Bradstreet's Public Poetry and the Tradition of Humility," *Early American Literature* 17 (1982): 153.

25. Joan Kelly-Gadol, "Did Women Have a Renaissance?," in *Becoming Visible: Women in European History,* ed. Renate Bridenthal and Claudia Koonz (Boston: Houghton Mifflin, 1977), 140.

26. Margaret Homans, *Women Writers and Poetic Identity: Dorothy Wordsworth, Emily Brontë, and Emily Dickinson* (Princeton: Princeton University Press, 1980), 217.

Selected Bibliography

PRIMARY WORKS

The Tenth Muse Lately sprung up in America. Or Severall Poems, compiled with great variety of Wit and Learning, full of delight. Wherein especially is contained a compleat discourse and description of The Four Elements, Constitutions, Ages of Man, Seasons of the Year. Together with an Exact Epitomie of the Four Monarchies, viz. The Assyrian, Persian, Grecian, Roman. Also a Dialogue between Old England and New, concerning the late troubles. With divers other pleasant and serious Poems. By a Gentlewoman in those parts. Printed at London for Stephen Bowtell at the signe of the Bible in Popes Head-Alley, 1650.

Several Poems Compiled with great variety of Wit and Learning, full of Delight; Wherein especially is contained a compleat Discourse, and Description of The Four Elements, Constitutions, Ages of Man, Seasons of the Year. Together with an exact Epitome of the three first Monarchyes Viz. The Assyrian, Persian, Grecian. And beginning of the Romane Common-wealth to the end of their last King; With diverse other Pleasant & serious Poems. By a Gentlewoman in New-England. The second Edition, Corrected by the Author, and enlarged by an Addition of several other Poems found amongst her Papers after her Death. Boston, Printed by John Foster, 1678.

Several Poems Compiled with great Variety of Wit and Learning, full of Delight; Wherein especially is contained, a compleat Discourse and Description of The Four Elements, Constitutions, Ages of Man, Seasons of the Year. Together with an exact Epitome of the three first Monarchies, viz, the Assyrian, Persian Grecian, and Roman Common-Wealth, from its beginning to the End of their last King. With divers other pleasant and serious Poems. By a Gentlewoman in New-England. The Third Edition, corrected by the Author, and enlarged by an Addition of several other Poems found amongst her Papers after her Death. Re-printed from the second Edition in the Year M. DCC. LVIII.

The Works of Anne Bradstreet, in Prose and Verse. Edited by John Harvard Ellis. Charlestown, Mass.: A. E. Cutter, 1867. Ellis's is the first scholarly edition of Bradstreet's works, including for the first time the prose and poetry originally preserved in manuscript at the Stevens Memorial Library at North Andover, Massachusetts. The introduction remains a good source of information about the poet and her background.

The Poems of Mrs. Anne Bradstreet (1612–1672). Together with her Prose Remains with an Introduction by Charles Eliot Norton. New York: Duedecimos, 1898. Not a reliable text. Norton's literary interpretation and evaluation of Bradstreet are of dubious merit.

Reprint of Ellis edition. Gloucester, Mass.: Peter Smith, 1932.

Reprint. Gloucester, Mass.: Peter Smith, 1962. " 'A Dialogue . . .' and other poems." Old South Leaflets, No. 159.

McElrath, Joseph R., Jr., and Allan P. Robb, *The Complete Works of Anne Bradstreet*. Boston: Twayne, 1981. Anyone seeking to understand the history and circumstances of the publication of the Bradstreet texts and the problem of variants among texts will want to consult this volume.

The Works of Anne Bradstreet, ed. Jeannine Hensley. Cambridge, Mass. Belknap Press of Harvard University Press, 1967. This carefully edited modern edition contains the prose and poems from the Andover manuscript and the poetry of *Several Poems*. It is recommended for its most helpful introduction and its empathetic forward (with a 1979 postscript) by Adrienne Rich.

The Tenth Muse (1650) AND, FROM THE MANUSCRIPTS, Meditations Divine and Morall TOGETHER WITH Letters and Occasional pieces. Facsimile Reproductions with an introduction by Josephine K. Piercy. Gainesville, Fl.: Scholars' Facsimiles & Reprints, 1965. This volume contains a facsimile reproduction of manuscripts in Anne Bradstreet's hand and in her son Simon's that were originally located at the Stevens Library at North Andover and are now on deposit at the Houghton Library, Harvard University.

SECONDARY WORKS

Biography

Anderson, James. "Anne Dudley, Wife of Simon Bradstreet." In *Memorable Women*, vol. 1. London: Blackie & Son, 1862. A first attempt at synthesizing information (in part drawn from the poetry) about family life, religious background, and the historical period.

Berryman, John. *Homage to Mistress Bradstreet*. New York: Farrar, Straus & Co., 1956. A poetic dialogue that evokes an imagined relationship between Bradstreet and the modern poet and retells parts of her biography.

Campbell, Helen [Stuart]. *Anne Bradstreet and Her Time*. Boston: D. Lothrop, 1891. A romanticized re-creation of Bradstreet's life that embellishes the few facts provided in the poetry and prose.

Martin, Wendy. "Part One: Anne Bradstreet." In *An American Triptych: Anne Bradstreet, Emily Dickinson, Adrienne Rich*. Chapel Hill: University of North Carolina Press, 1984. This feminist portrait places Bradstreet first in a continuum among women poets that is described as acquiescence to patriarchal values giving way to independent self-reliance.

Mather, Cotton. *Magnalia Christi Americana or, The Ecclesiastical History of New*

England, from Its First Planting in the Year 1620, unto the Year of our LORD. 1698. New York: Arno Press, 1972 [1702]. Mather memorializes many of the Dudley and Bradstreet family members and friends with brief life histories. He is our chief seventeenth-century source of information about Anne Bradstreet.

Piercy, Josephine K. *Anne Bradstreet.* New York: Twayne, 1965. This study focuses primarily on Bradstreet's spiritual and artistic growth and emphasizes Bradstreet as a preromantic poet in the English tradition.

Stanford, Ann. *Anne Bradstreet: The Worldly Puritan.* New York: Burt Franklin, 1975. An interpretive study and biography, this work contains aids such as a list of books with which Bradstreet was acquainted and a suggested chronology of her works.

White, Elizabeth Wade. *Anne Bradstreet: The Tenth Muse,* New York: Oxford University Press, 1971. This invaluable biography is essential for anyone seeking to know Bradstreet's life history, which White sets against the history of old and New England. The interpretation of the poetry is not as firmly grounded as is the biography itself.

Criticism

Cowell, Pattie, and Ann Stanford, eds. *Critical Essays on Anne Bradstreet.* Boston: G. K. Hall, 1983. In addition to reprinting 16 essays, this volume presents five new essays, and the introduction provides a summary of virtually all work done on Bradstreet to date with a complete list of references to journal articles—an invaluable aid to both the mature scholar and the beginning student.

Daly, Robert. *God's Altar: The World and the Flesh in Puritan Poetry,* 82–127. Berkeley: University of California Press, 1978. A groundbreaking interpretation of the coexistence in Bradstreet's work of an appreciation of the sensible and natural world and a longing to be "weaned away" from it.

Greer, Germaine, Susan Hastings, Jeslyn Medoff, and Melinda Sansone, eds. *Kissing the Rod: An Anthology of Seventeenth-Century Women's Verse.* New York: Farrar, Straus & Giroux, 1988. Bradstreet is presented among English women poets who were, roughly, her contemporaries. The introduction by Germaine Greer sheds new light on Bradstreet's cultural and intellectual contexts.

Hambrick-Stowe, Charles E. *The Practice of Piety: Puritan Devotional Disciplines in Seventeenth-Century New England.* Chapel Hill: University of North Carolina Press, 1982. Bradstreet's work provides case material for this important study of Puritan devotional practice.

Jantz, Harold S. *The First Century of New England Verse,* 36–38. New York: Russell & Russell, 1962. Bradstreet is acknowledged to be a "genuine poet, even though not a great one" and her work is presented alongside other poets of her time and place.

Morison, Samuel Eliot. *Builders of the Bay Colony.* Boston: Houghton Mifflin,
    1930. An evaluative portrayal of Bradstreet, of interest too for its treat-
    ment of Simon Bradstreet and her friends and associates in Essex County.
Tyler, Moses Coit, *A History of American Literature during the Colonial Period,* Vol.
    1. New York: G. P. Putnam's Sons, 1879. Tyler gives the first serious
    consideration to Bradstreet's work. His negative appraisal of the work is
    tempered by his admiration for her efforts amid harsh circumstances.
Walker, Cheryl. *The Nightingale's Burden: Women Poets and American Culture
    before 1900.* Bloomington: Indiana University Press, 1982. Walker de-
    votes herself to the "phenomenon of women's poetry as a sign of women's
    culture" and provides an important analysis of women poets whose "tradi-
    tion" has been undervalued and misunderstood.
Watts, Emily Stipes. *The Poetry of American Women from 1632 to 1945.* Austin:
    University of Texas Press, 1977. A pioneering work that traces a continu-
    ity among women poets in America, beginning with a discussion of
    women poets' themes as these appear in Bradstreet's work.
Whicher, George F., ed. *Alas, All's Vanity; or, A Leaf from the First American
    Edition of Several Poems by Anne Bradstreet printed at Boston, anno 1678.*
    New York: Spiral Press for Collectors' Bookshop, 1942. A sensitive specu-
    lation and appreciation that recognizes the poet's feminism. The essay by
    George Frisbie Whicher identifies the poems still considered to be Brad-
    street's most successful.
White, Peter, ed. *Puritan Poets and Poetics: Seventeenth-Century American Poetry in
    Theory and Practice.* University Park: Pennsylvania State University Press,
    1985. See Rosamond Rosenmeier, " 'The Wounds upon Bathsheba':
    Anne Bradstreet's Prophetic Art," 129–46. This essay introduces Brad-
    street and anticipates the argument made in the present study.

Bibliographies

Dolle, Raymond F. *Anne Bradstreet: A Reference Guide,* Boston: G. K. Hall,
    1990. Arranged chronologically, this guide gives careful, nonevaluative
    abstracts of virtually everything written about Anne Bradstreet and her
    work. Indispensable to the scholar and useful for the beginning student
    too.
Scheik, William J., and Jo Ella Doggett. *Seventeenth-Century American Poety: A
    Reference Guide,* Boston: G. K. Hall, 1977. Updated in 1980. An anno-
    tated list of criticism of Bradstreet's poetry primarily.

Index

Affliction, 3, 32–36, 52–53, 77, 130,
    133–34, 147–51
Agrippa, Cornelius, 11, 28–29, 59–60,
    90, 96, 104, 119, 135
Alchemy. *See* Science
American Literature: Continuity, 2–3
Andover (Cochichewick), xiii, 82,
    129–32
Antinomian controversy, 30, 82, 83,
    109, 111, 113, 125. *See also* Hutch-
    inson, Anne
Arbella, Lady, 9, 71, 74
Arbella (ship), 9, 71, 73–74
Askew, Anne, 9
"[As loving Hind that (Hartless) wants
    her Deer]," 115–16
"Author to her Book, The," 27, 138

Bacon, Sir Francis, 7, 89
Bathsheba, 143, 145, 151, 152; wisdom
    of, 95, 103, 115
"Before the Birth of one of her Chil-
    dren," 119, 122, 127
Berryman, John, 1
Boston (Mass.), 74; the church at, 31,
    75, 82, 93
BRADSTREET, Anne: adolescence and
    marriage of, 31–40; as artist, xiii,
    3, 5, 8–10, 12–13, 87, 96, 100,
    104, 105, 113, 117, 121, 125,
    127–28, 129, 133–34, 145, 151,
    153, 154, 156; audience for her
    work, 60, 61, 81, 88, 94, 113,
    126, 131, 137, 138; birth and in-
    fancy, 19–21; children, xii, 77,
    130, 132; conversion, 35–37; criti-
    cal reputation, xi, 1, 2–3; death,
    138, 141; education, 21–30; fam-
    ily tensions, 40, 87, 90–92; femi-
    nism of, xi, 6, 11, 44, 47, 148;
    interest in politics, 4, 36–37; li-

brary of, 79; literary contemporar-
    ies, xi, 2, 9–10, 12; medievalism
    of, xii, 148, 152–53; relationship
    to Anne Hutchinson, 83–86; reli-
    gious beliefs, xii, 2, 125, 152; Bi-
    ble, uses of, xii–xiii, 5–7, 43, 55,
    63, 64–68, 98, 100, 101–103,
    104, 106, 110, 112, 114, 115,
    121–23, 126, 129, 137, 139, 141,
    145, 148, 150, 151
Bradstreet, Dudley, 136
Bradstreet, Mercy, 140–41
Bradstreet, Samuel, 132–133, 138,
    139–140
Bradstreet, Simon, 37–40, 74–75, 78,
    80–82, 83, 90, 91–92, 114, 129–
    30, 136–39, 141
Bradstreet, Simon (son), 138–39, 141,
    144
Brinsley, John, 21

Caldwell, Patricia, 129, 138
Cambridge (Newtowne), 74
Charles I, 37
Charles II, 137
Charlestown, 74
Child, Dr. Robert, 89–90
Child's remonstrance, 89–90
Christ: as bridegroom, 120, 134, 149,
    152; as the "White Stone", 53, 66,
    148, 151–152; as Wisdom, 45–
    46, 86, 99–101, 108, 112, 127,
    152; the Second Coming of, 50,
    55, 85, 86, 121, 123, 142. *See also*
    history: providential
Cixous, Helene, 5
Clark, Michael, 154, 156
Cole, Eunice, 135
Comenius, John Amos, 10, 18, 89
"Contemplations," 3, 83, 138, 145–52
Cotton, John, 6, 31, 32, 35–36, 38,

71–72, 82, 85, 91, 93, 120, 134, 140
Cotton, Seaborn, 124, 132
Cowell, Pattie, 2
Crooke, Helkiah, 117–19, 124

Daly, Robert, 3, 132
Dane, Francis, 136
Davenport, John, 85
"David's Lamentation for *Saul* and *Jonathan*," 86
Debus, John, 7
Dee, John, 8, 28–30, 85, 88, 135–36; his library, 28
Dennison, Daniel, 81, 83
Dennison, Patience Dudley (Mrs. Daniel), 78
"Dialogue between Old *England* and New, A," 41, 47–51, 63
Dickinson, Emily, 123, 140, 156
Dod, John, 6, 15–16, 19–21, 38, 45, 82, 95, 101, 112, 121, 126–28, 151
D(oolittle), H(ilda), 46
Du Bartas (Guillaume de Salluste Sieur Du Bartas), 25–27, 55–56, 63–64
Dudley, Dorothy Yorke, 6, 14–19, 20–23, 80, 94, 97–98
Dudley, John, duke of Northumberland, 28
Dudley, Robert, earl of Leicester, 10, 28, 29
Dudley, Samuel, 76, 81, 83
Dudley, Thomas, 6, 7, 13–19, 23, 25–28, 30–31, 36, 37, 38, 39, 71, 74, 75, 78, 82, 83, 87–88, 90–92, 93, 132; library of, 17, 79, 101
Dwyer, Mary, 99

"Elegie upon . . . Sir *Philip Sidney*, An," 8, 29–30, 86, 95–97
Eliot, John, 89
Elizabeth I, 29, 46, 51
Ellis, John Harvard, 1, 63, 142
Emerson, Ralph Waldo, 107
Emmanuel College, 15, 37

English Civil War, 48, 134
"EPITAPH On my dear and ever honoured Mother, An," 21–23, 98
Essex County, 88
Essex (England): countess of Warwick, 38, 77
Eve, 143, 145, 150–52

Feminism, 90; theology, 6, 47, 152–53
Firmin, Giles, 88
"Flesh and the Spirit, The," 106–113, 138, 153

Gelpi, Albert, 2
Greven, Philip, 130
Grey, Lady Jane, 10

Hall, David, 4
Hartlib, Samuel, 88, 89
Harvard College, 89
Hensley, Jeannine, 142
Hildebrand, Anne, 148, 153
Hildegard of Bingen, 152–53
Hirst, Desirée, 7
History: providential, 29, 49, 62, 63, 65, 68, 84, 88, 89, 97, 106, 108, 120, 125, 126, 129, 134–35, 137, 138, 139, 145, 152–53. *See also* Christ: the Second Coming of
Homans, Margaret, 156
Hooker, Thomas, 77–78
Hopkins, Anne, 116
Hutchinson, Anne, 5, 9, 22, 36, 82, 83–87, 93–94, 96, 135
Hutchinson, Lucy, 22

Imitation, 5, 9, 12, 154
"In honour of . . . Queen ELIZABETH," 8, 44–47, 58–59, 60, 86, 153
"In reference to her Children," 3, 144–45
"[In silent night when rest I took]," 130–31, 138–39
Ipswich (Agawam), xii, 75, 80–81, 94–95

James I, 11, 18, 36, 37,
Johnson, Edward, 74, 75, 76, 78, 86, 88

Keayne, Benjamin, 92–94
Keayne, John, 92
Keayne, Sarah Dudley (Mrs. Benjamin), 22, 92–95, 96–99, 134
Keith, George, 134
Kelly-Gadol, Joan, 155
Kibbey, Ann, 27
Koehler, Lyle, 90

"Letter to her Husband, absent upon Publick employment, A," 110, 113, 116, 119, 120–21, 122–25, 126, 134
Lincolnshire, 16, 74, 89; science center, 25; Sempringham, xii, 23, 37–38
Lodge, Thomas, 25–26

Mc Elrath, Joseph R., Jr., 32, 142
Makin, Bathsua, 10–12, 89
Margerum, Eileen, 154
Marriage, 15, 22, 38–40
Martin, Wendy, 2, 9, 44, 154
Mary, 143, 145, 151
Mather, Cotton, 7, 10, 14, 16, 39, 78, 79, 81, 86, 88, 95, 131, 143, 151
"Meditations Diuine and morall," 4, 20, 33–34, 79–80, 138, 144
"Meditations when my Soul hath been refreshed," 12, 69–70, 100
Morgan, Edmund S., 120
Morison, Samuel Eliot, 1, 92
"Mother's legacy," 144
Murdock, Kenneth, 9

Newman, Barbara, 152–53, 155
Norton, Charles Eliot, 1
Norton, John, 88, 136, 137

"Of the vanity of all worldly creatures," 12, 102–106
"On my dear Grand-child Simon Bradstreet," 99
Ostriker, Alicia, 2

Pearce, Roy Harvey, 2
Pembroke, countess of, 10
Persona or role, xii, xiii, xiv; complexity of, 99; redefinitions of, 115; "role conflict," 100
Philomel, 150, 152
"[Phoebus make haste, the day's too long]," 119, 136
Piercy, Josephine, xi, 4
Porte, Joel, 129
Preston, John, 36–38, 39
Puritanism: problems of definition, xii, 3

Quaternions, the, 4, 7, 117, 148–49, 153; "The Four Ages of Man," 32–33, 51–55, 68, 85–86; "The Foure Elements," 68–70, 87, 88; "Of the foure humours," 4, 68–69, 87, 88; "The Foure Monarchies," 41, 61–70; "The four Seasons of the Yeare," 156; "The Prologue," 41, 55–61

Raleigh, Sir Walter, 30, 63
Reader response, 13
Requa, Kenneth, 114–15
Robb, Allan P., 32, 142
Rogers, John, 88, 142
Rogers, Nathaniel, 88, 142
Rowlandson, Mary, 4, 80
Roxbury, 82, 88

Salem, 74
Schwartz, Regina, 5–6
Schweitzer, Ivy, 47, 154
Science, 26, 88; alchemy, 7, 34, 52–55, 66, 69–70, 85, 88, 111, 148; anatomy, 117–19; astrology, 120, 123; occult, 7, 79, 96, 119, 135, 136; Renaissance, 7–8, 87, 114, 125
"Sept. 30, 1657," 34
Several Poems, 7, 41, 114, 142
Shakespeare, 59, 111
Shepard, Thomas, 77
Sidney, Sir Philip, 7, 27, 95–97, 136

Solomon: Wisdom of, 6–7, 8, 95, 126, 128, 143
Spenser, Edmund, 30
Stanford, Ann, 3, 9, 113, 154
Sylvester, Joshua, 25

Tenth Muse, The, 10, 41, 91, 98, 114, 131–32, 142, 155
"To her Father with some verses," 41–43
"To her most Honoured Father," 54–55
Toleration, 82, 89–91, 136
"To my Dear and loving Husband," 119
"To my dear children," 5, 8, 24, 31, 32, 43–44, 72–74, 77, 82, 83, 91, 97–98, 130, 144, 153
"To the Memory of my dear and ever honoured Father," 91–92
"To the Memory of my dear Daughter in Law, Mrs. Mercy Bradstreet," 140–41
Transmutation, 4, 12, 53, 60, 96, 105, 118, 149
Tyler, Moses Coit, 54
Typology, 143, 145, 152, 156

Ulrich, Laura, 21, 80, 93–94, 98, 125
"Upon a Fit of Sickness, Anno 1632," 76–77
"Upon my dear & loving husband his goeing into England. Jan. 16. 1661," 136–37
Urania, 10, 26–27, 155
Urania (poem by Lady Mary Wroth), 10

Waggoner, Hyatt, 2
Walker, Cheryl, 2, 3, 94, 96, 129, 151, 155

Ward, Nathaniel, 26, 60, 79, 88, 131, 142
Watertown, 75, 91
Watters, David, 132
Watts, Emily Stipes, 2
Wheelwright, John, 83
Whicher, George, 1
White, Elizabeth Wade, 3, 25, 37, 40, 92–93, 130
Wigglesworth, Michael, 138
Williams, Dr. John, 89
Winthrop, John, 71, 72, 74, 75, 83, 116
Winthrop, John, Jr., 78–79, 81, 83, 88, 93, 136; library of, 8, 79
Wisdom, 45–46, 51, 143; as Athena, 27, 46; as Minerva, 11, 26; as sister, 101, 102–103, 105; hidden in the axiom, 97, 121, 127; in biblical tradition, 6; theology, 153. *See also* Bathsheba; Christ: as Wisdom; Solomon
Witchcraft, 4, 135, 136, 138
Women: body-mind association, 98–99, 112, 117, 125, 134, 135; education of, 1, 18, 21–23, 89; history of the lives of, xii, 3, 4, 5, 97; misogyny, 11, 18, 94; sources of power for, 51, 90; "women's work," 59, 79–80, 116; writers and writing, xii, 4, 153
Woodbridge, Benjamin, 131
Woodbridge, John, 10, 79, 80, 81, 131, 138
Woodbridge, Mercy Dudley (Mrs. John), 9, 94, 131, 138
Wroth, Lady Mary Sidney, 10, 26

Yates, Frances A., 7, 28, 88

The Author

Rosamond Rosenmeier was born and raised in Southern California and educated in New York City and Massachusetts. She received her B.A. in English composition at Mt. Holyoke College in 1950, her M.A. in comparative literature at Radcliffe College in 1960, and her Ph.D. in the program in the history of American civilization at Harvard in 1971. In addition to two essays on Anne Bradstreet, she has written about the Pennsylvania German religious backgrounds of the modern poets H.D. (Hilda Doolittle) and Wallace Stevens. Her essay "Getting Wisdom: The 'Rabbi's' Devotion to *Weisheit* and Its Implications for Feminists" appeared in the *Wallace Stevens Journal* 12(2) (Fall 1988) in a special issue on Stevens and women. She is also a poet. Her first volume of poems, *Lines Out,* was published in 1989.

She is professor emerita at the University of Massachusetts in Boston, where she has taught writing and American literature. She is currently on the editorial board of *Early American Literature.*

Married and the mother of five children, she lives in Watertown, Massachusetts.

The Editor

Pattie Cowell received her Ph.D. from the University of Massachusetts, Amherst in 1977. Since that time her research has been directed by combined interests in early American literature and women's studies. She has published *Women Poets in Pre-Revolutionary America* (1981) and several related articles and notes on individual colonial women writers. Additionally she has co-edited (with Ann Stanford) *Critical Essays on Anne Bradstreet* (1983) and prepared a facsimile edition of Cotton Mather's *Ornaments for the Daughters of Zion* (1978). She is currently at work on a second edition of *Women Poets in Pre-Revolutionary America* and on a study of the influence of the colonial magazine trade on the development of early American poetry. She is coordinator of graduate programs in English at Colorado State University.

MA